Mayan Mania

A Caribbean Cruise Mystery

SANDY CARES

MAYAN MANIA: A Caribbean Cruise Mystery
Sandy Cares

Published by Treasure Isles Press

First Edition, August 2021

Author Services by Pedernales Publishing, LLC.
www.pedernalespublishing.com

Cover by Jana Rade

Library of Congress Control Number: 2021914201

ISBN: 978-1-7364124-5-9 Paperback Edition
ISBN: 978-1-7364124-4-2 Hardcover Edition
ISBN: 978-1-7364124-3-5 Digital Edition

Printed in the United States of America

xx-v8

"I have found out there ain't no surer way to find out whether you like people or hate them than to travel with them."

— Jack Kerouac

Coming or Going?

Welcome Aboard!
Day One: February 15, Monday
Miami, Florida, USA
Scattered Showers: High: 81ºF/27ºC. Low: 68ºF/20ºC.

NO ANSWER.

It was my fourth try. The taxi was already entering the Port of Miami. Where was Wink, and why wasn't he answering my calls?

Honestly, if I'd known what I knew now, I would have turned right back around again and gone to the airport and home. But no! I'd fallen for Wink and was following my heart. Oh, who can blame me after the fiasco of the cruise just ended, and that awful breakup with Seth on the first morning of the cruise? How long ago was that now? Could it really be two weeks? It seemed like ancient history.

Wink was head of all the security for the entire Classica Cruise Line, working all the ships in the fleet to solve onboard crimes and teach security measures to the crew. When a musician came up missing while I was a guest on the last cruise, I offered to stand in for her because I could play the cello. In the end, I found the missing cellist and figured out how she disappeared. That's how I came to know Wink and things heated up from there. You might say we had an "*almost* shipboard romance" because it never quite reached that point, but I suspected he was interested. Then I'd discovered that note he'd left in my carry-on, only to realize it was his carry-on and that he'd switched it with mine just so I'd get the note. It said, "To be continued?" What more did I need to know it was meant for me? It had his contact information right there. So, when the head of human resources on the ship called me as I was checking in at the Delta counter, she invited me to come right back to the ship to replace Angela as social hostess. I saw firsthand how Angela had pouting down to an art form. I don't know why she had it in for me. She detested me to the point of attempted murder. But she was probably already in custody, and it would serve her right!

I was ecstatic with Pauline's invitation for me to return. I mean, I loved the idea of working on another cruise. Who wouldn't? But even more, I looked forward to seeing Wink again. I hung up with Pauline and came straight back to the cruise pier ready to report to duty.

Now I wasn't so sure I'd done the right thing.

I thought it odd that Wink wasn't answering, since we'd only just seen each other scarcely two hours earlier. That morning as we both left the MS *Minerva*, he told me he was heading to the MS *Athena*, the sister ship right across the pier. It was also the ship where Pauline was sending me.

My anxiety was temporarily distracted by the hubbub of activity at this bustling entrepot, the biggest cruise ship port on the planet! I counted ten enormous ships floating serenely on the blue waters of Biscayne Bay and thought of the tens of thousands of people flooding Miami as they headed to or away from the port. Every ship was a self-contained city; it was hard to believe that they could pull in before light and be loaded with everything it takes to run a town of several thousand people by that same afternoon when they'd be ready to sail. At the far end of the port, container ships were converging from far-flung corners of the world, depositing and loading every imaginable consumer commodity. A busy train ran back and forth all day, depositing and collecting containers from the port for the next leg of their journey to their final destinations. Here I was embarking on the adventure of a brand-new cruise from this incredibly important port...and with a staff function, no less. There was an inexplicable thrill about being even a very small cog in a very big wheel.

The taxi driver dropped me off and unloaded my suitcase from the trunk. I wheeled it along with my carry-on. Well, it was Wink's carry-on, as I've already explained. The thought of him brought me right back to the annoying reality that he had not answered my calls in the twenty minutes it took for the taxi to convey me from the airport to the cruise port. Now the task at hand was to check myself in without any boarding documents and no one around to vouch for me.

A baggage handler approached me, likely drawn by my distracted expression. He welcomed me and asked to see my boarding documents. I explained that I'd just disembarked the MS *Minerva* across the pier that morning, and when I arrived at the airport, the human resources director had called and invited me to return to the port and report for duty with the MS *Athena*. It sounded logical to me because it was exactly the truth. But it brought me no traction with the baggage handler. He just smiled and said, "Yes, ma'am, I'm sure that's a very nice way to get another cruise," as he walked away shaking his head.

Suddenly, the reality of what was happening shot through me with a sharp stab of doubt. Seriously, how was it that I'd been invited to join a cruise ship to assume a crew position with absolutely no screening, no training, no professional credentials and no prior experience? Not to mention, no boarding documents. To make matters worse, that darned Wink was either ignoring my calls or maybe hadn't even given me his real phone number. I felt like I was in a strange *Twilight Zone*. Everything that made so much sense an hour earlier was suddenly defying logic. I rolled both bags, mine and Wink's, into the registration area of the terminal, hoisting them onto the security belt one at a time. An increasingly hot cloud of doubt, embarrassment, suspicion and anger enveloped me as I walked through the security arch without setting off the alarm.

How was I to convince the registration agent that Pauline had called me as I was checking in for my flight back home to Grand Rapids and invited me right back to assume a temporary job? How was I to explain that I was supposed to replace the former social hostess, Angela, who was heading for jail at that very moment? How was I to explain that Pauline told me at first to return to the MS *Minerva* and then switched and said to report to the sister ship instead, the MS *Athena* that was docked across the pier? It was even starting to confuse me. Yet, here I was. I only had to trust that Pauline left some notation about me for the registration team.

After nearly a half hour in the long line that snaked forward steadily but slowly, I finally stood in front of one of the uniformed registration agents along a very long counter. Her straight, black hair was shining to reflection and cut impeccably into a youthful bob. Her teeth gleamed through silvery braces. "May I see your passport and boarding documents, please?" she asked with a genuine smile. Her name badge told me she was from the Philippines.

I reached to pull the passport out of my purse and then tried to explain why I didn't have any boarding documents. The memory of boarding the prior cruise as a proper guest only twelve days earlier was still fresh on my mind, only that time I'd come prepared with all my paperwork in place. I stumbled over my own words explaining, "I was asked by Pauline, on the MS *Minerva*, to come over to the MS *Athena* and take on the duties of the social hostess for this cruise while they look for a permanent replacement. I'm afraid I don't have anything more that's official about why I am here..." I felt myself let the rest of the sentence break off. I didn't know what I was saying.

She tilted her head slightly in that "Now what?" pose of polite but veiled amusement. I could tell she was stifling a giggle. I wondered how many times cruise ship registration agents had to fend off imposters trying to hitch a free cruise on a luxury vessel and thought there must be hundreds of ways for people to try to stow away. I was certain she thought that was what I was trying to do. I could feel my ears turning red.

"Oh!" she said, nodding in feigned agreement. "I understand. Then you need to register with the crew in the registration hall next door," she said, pointing at an enormous open double door to her left and still smiling sweetly. She was having fun with this. She probably couldn't wait to get to the crew bar to laugh about it with her colleagues.

"Well, you see," I stammered again, "I'm not really a qualified crew person. I think they are just trying me out for the job. Social hostess," I said, clearing my throat. "I saw how it's done while I was on the MS *Minerva* during the cruise that just ended." A nervous laugh escaped me that I immediately regretted. The more I talked, the deeper I was getting myself into it. The young agent from the Philippines took my passport and asked me to excuse her a moment so she could consult with her supervisor. I saw her name was Maria.

I felt people behind me growing impatient. One man said to his wife, loudly enough for me to hear, "Maybe you can offer to fry eggs and I can give miniature golf lessons so we can get a free cruise too." They laughed heartily, and others nearby joined in. I felt like I was shrinking by an inch with every passing minute. I just wanted to get through this ordeal and either board the ship or turn around and go home. Wink was nowhere around to help me get on the blasted ship, and no one was willing to call the other ship and talk with Pauline on my behalf. Besides, getting anyone to call from one ship to another took more than an Act of Congress, so I knew any request to call Pauline on the MS *Minerva* would fall on deaf ears. I felt more conspicuous and less credible with every passing second.

Another agent appeared at the counter. He was tall and slender. His blond hair was parted right down the center. The sleeves on his uniform were a little too short for his long arms. He asked me to step aside to allow him to process the paying guests standing in line behind me. He said it in a strong accent, putting an emphasis on the word "paying." They passed me with audible scoffs and deprecating tsks.

I didn't know how this was happening to me and was beginning to wonder if this whole thing had been a setup. I immediately flung an arrow of suspicion at that precocious little trickster, Ivy, who'd almost taken me down with her convoluted but brilliant Machiavellian plot on the other cruise. The kicker was, she got the whole idea from one of my own detective books! I was even doubting if the voice inviting me back to the ship was really that of Pauline. Could that little monster have concocted yet one more evil plot to prove that though I won the battle, she'd won the war? I envisioned Ivy riding around on her beach bike doing a victory wheelie somewhere in Delaware at that very moment! I was about ready to pick up my bags and head straight out of the terminal when my friendly agent, the ever-smiling Maria from the Philippines, suddenly reappeared and motioned for me to approach her again at the counter.

"We have some information, Miss Milliner, and we are trying to reach the cruise director to give us the clearance that would allow you to board the ship. The problem is that right now the cruise director is not aboard, and we are waiting for him to return. You may take a seat in the terminal and check back with us in another hour," she said, trying to sound helpful, though I felt it was the royal brush off. I asked her to check the manifest for Wink's room and to call him, assuring her that he would know what was going on and could vouch for me.

"Wink?" she sputtered, laughing almost outright. "Who is that? What is Wink's last name and position?" She sounded as though Wink were my pet squirrel. I remembered Wink was his nickname and suddenly couldn't even remember his real name. My brain went totally blank. I went to the general seating area to collect myself, searching through my purse for his business card. I remembered it was there earlier, but now nothing. I looked around me as more and more people, neatly dressed, freshly groomed and sensibly organized with their boarding documents, passports and designer carry-ons, were lining up patiently, chattering pleasantly and looking forward to boarding the ship and starting their cruise holiday.

What was I doing here?

Taking a deep breath, I picked up the phone and decided to give Wink one last try. Only he had the clout to get me through registration without boarding documents. My plan was to turn around and head straight back to the airport if he didn't answer. After all, I couldn't imagine enjoying a cruise without him anyway, even though I was there to work.

Picking up my phone, I realized there were two voice messages waiting for me. I hadn't heard the phone ring because of all the ambient noise in the terminal. The first message was from Wink. I listened to his voice, my heart pounding like the tom-toms at a Seminole Calumet ceremony. Wink said he was at the airport looking for me! He'd been redeployed right after he arrived at the MS *Athena* that morning and was now flying off to join the MS *Aphrodite,* heading for the Panama Canal. Something of a sensitive security issue had emerged, and he was needed there. He closed by asking me to drop off his carry-on suitcase at any US post office and to tape the label he'd left inside one of the pockets right on the front, which would route it to him eventually. Apparently, he was not even aware that Pauline had invited me to return to the ship to replace Angela. At the exact moment I was listening to his message, he was probably looking for me at the airport. But only because he wanted his carry-on back!

The other message was from Pauline. She said she hoped her message came to me before the taxi driver brought me to the MS *Athena* because, as it turned out, they needed me right back on the MS *Minerva* after all! She apologized for yet another switchback, adding that I would not be allowed to board the MS *Athena*.

Well, at least we cleared that one up, I thought.

She told me she would explain everything when I arrived back on the MS *Minerva* and wished me luck.

2

The Bare Truth

ABOUT AN HOUR LATER, I was back on board the MS *Minerva*. I knocked on the human resource director's door. No answer. I asked at the reception counter next door, but no one had seen Pauline. I peeked in the cruise director's office to see if Pearl was in. She wasn't there either. Instead, there was a man sitting at her desk. He was busily typing something into the computer.

"Hello," I said. "I'm Marianne. Has Pearl been through? I imagine it's a busy day for her."

"That's why I am here," the man said. "I'm her assistant." I took that to mean he was the assistant cruise director. He looked a little old for the job, but what did I know? "Maybe I can answer your questions," he offered. His collared shirt was open at the neck, and his necktie was loosened and hanging off-center down his front. His wire glasses sat loosely between his ears and could have used some cleaning. I could see the fingerprint smudges from where I stood in the doorway.

"I was just stopping by to see Pauline and Pearl

and let them know I am reporting for duty. I'm here to take over the social hostess position for this cruise."

"Really?" the man asked, suddenly focusing on me with more interest. He was not wearing a name badge and did not introduce himself. He went on saying, "That's funny, because we already have a social hostess for this cruise. In fact, you missed her by five minutes. Maybe you're on the wrong ship." I was confused. Then he said, "Oh, what the hell. This cruise is already headed to hell-in-a-handbag. They'll probably need two of you. Who the hell cares? Tell you what; go to your room and see if your room card lets you in. If it does, at least you'll know you belong here. If I were you, I'd get in my room and keep a low profile and not ask for any duties. It will only add trouble to your life. Otherwise, you could have a really nice free cruise and no one would ever know the difference."

I went upstairs to try the room card. It got me right in. Best to unpack and claim my territory while I have the time, I thought.

Before unpacking, I tried calling Wink. He still wasn't answering, so I had to leave a message that I was on the MS *Minerva* and that I'd explain it all when he called me back. I gave him my cell number and the telephone number in the room in case.

I organized my belongings in the various drawers, cubbies and closets. This time, I was in a room opposite the corridor from the room I'd occupied on the prior cruise, so I had to get used to everything being a mirror image. I decided I liked this configuration better. This time unpacking didn't take long at all, and I even left some things in the suitcase that I'd barely used on the last cruise. When I went to push the suitcase under the bed, something was blocking it from reaching all the way to the wall. I got down on my hands and knees to have a look. Whoever had used this room before me had stashed what looked like a year's supply of chocolate laxatives under the bed, stacked up against the wall. I almost threw them out, but they were hard to reach, so I decided to leave them there for the time being. I slid my suitcase into the back of the closet instead. I left Wink's small carry-on in the corner by the bathroom.

I was lost in my thoughts as I hung my scarves neatly on the metal rod inside my closet door when Pearl's warm and familiar voice came through the loudspeaker into my room to announce the mandatory safety drill. I grabbed my life jacket and left.

The two perfectly reasonable looking middle-aged adults I first encountered in the corridor gave me pause. In fact, I stifled a gasp as I took in the couple walking hand in hand past me with absolutely nothing on—not a stitch. The only thing that could remotely pass for a garment was the life jacket each was wearing. And that didn't cover enough!

My first thought was that they must have locked themselves out of their room, and I started to approach to offer assistance when I spotted another couple coming down the stairs. They too looked perfectly reasonable and unremarkable, except for the fact that they weren't wearing anything either!

A thousand questions raced through my head as I joined the ever-increasing throng of beefy, saggy, hairy and blubbery middle-agers jiggling and flopping *au naturel* down the corridors and bottlenecking in the theater doors. They were smiling and chattering the entire way, never letting up the happy banter.

Then I remembered the man in Pearl's office saying something about the cruise already going to hell-in-a-handbag. Could he have meant all the luggage was lost? Were all these people playing along by wearing nothing at all?

I was wondering how the ship could have lost all that luggage and hoped it would be resolved soon. For all the effort it had taken to lug my own suitcase around all day long, I was relieved now, happy to have my clothing. I couldn't imagine having nothing at all to wear on a cruise ship in front of a thousand strangers, like all these other people whose luggage had apparently been lost.

Whatever was going on here, nothing could have prepared me for the sight waiting for me where everyone was convening for the safety drill inside the theater. Not a stitch of clothes on anyone in sight except for the crew! These people were certainly good sports, I thought. They were taking it in stride and making it a fun adventure for themselves. I had to marvel at the miraculous powers of *attitude*!

At the end of the safety drill, Pearl announced the business part of the cruise was over and the fun was about to begin. She invited everyone to enjoy the rest of the cruise, saying the Sail-Away Party was starting any minute on the pool deck with complimentary champagne and two-for-one cocktails. Then she said, "We're taking off and taking it all off!" An explosion of laughter, whoops and applause rang through the crowd. I marveled at how clever Pearl was to turn a disaster like lost luggage into a festive occasion.

As I looked around me, I couldn't find a single person wearing anything at all. But I knew they had to have come on board with clothing. So why was everyone naked? My amateur detective instincts were screaming at me that something was going on here, and I had to find out what it was. I ran against the tide of exposed flanks to get to Pauline's office. This time, her door was open.

She smiled and welcomed me in, motioning to the empty chair in front of her desk. She apologized briefly for the morning's confusion and the wild goose chase I'd been on. Then she got right down to business, handing me a stack of folders. Each was carefully labeled. On top of the stack was a shiny new name badge. It read Mary Ann, not Marianne. She said it was the closest they had and would have to do on such short notice. Before I could even ask her about all the nude people wandering around, she started right in.

"There has been a regrettable mistake in booking, and right now," she explained, "there are two thousand nudists on board, believing their group chartered the entire ship for themselves. Unfortunately, this fact was an oversight that the booking department missed, and several dozen non-nudists were accidentally booked on this same cruise. Those guests are in for one big surprise, if they haven't already figured it out." She shook her head and was not smiling.

Then she mentioned my function might actually change during the cruise because it was a charter cruise, and as the charter host had not requested the ship to provide a social hostess at all, there was no real definition of my function in this setting.

I asked what she meant by a charter cruise. She explained that on occasion an individual or organization leases an entire ship with all its amenities for the express purpose of providing a private cruise contoured to a theme or specific to an organization. She said in such cases, the cruise hosts typically arrange for their own entertainers, musicians, lecturers and other support personnel so the cruise theme offers a customized experience. She asked if I had any questions.

I only had one. "Can I keep my clothes on?"

Pauline chuckled. "No one is forced to be naked. And the term they prefer is 'clothing optional' because it comes down to a personal choice."

On my way back to my room, I saw things I had not noticed before and began to understand how the nude theme was already resonating around the ship. Replicas of famous nude statues like Michelangelo's *David, Venus de Milo* and *Lady Godiva* were situated in prominent areas. Paintings and prints depicting ancient, classical, oriental and contemporary nudes were displayed conspicuously in the public spaces. A poster advertised the cocktail of the day, the Naked Lady.

Now I knew why.

3

Such a Deal

TEN MINUTES BEFORE 6 P.M., I was wearing my name
badge and seated in the Paris Lounge with a little sign
advertising the Solo Travelers Welcome Aboard event.
Bowls of nuts and potato chips had been provided by
the waitstaff. As soon as people arrived, I would invite
them to have a seat and order their complimentary
drinks. The lounge was filling up fast, but not in
my corner. In fact, I was the only one, besides the
waitstaff, wearing clothing. All I could do was wait and
see if anyone came to join me. Ten minutes into it, I
was still alone. The house band, dressed in colorful
island shirts, was playing popular show tunes. The
smiling waitstaff bustled back and forth carrying
trays brimming with umbrella drinks and enticing
salty snacks in silver bowls. Ship officers in crisp navy
blazers with gold stripes on their sleeves stood sentry
at various posts as guests were seated comfortably

on the plush upholstered chairs and divans spread around the room. I noticed that for this event all the chairs and couches had been fitted with slipcovers in lavish designer prints that complemented the room's rich décor. I had to agree with that decision, whoever made it.

Most people sat in the cushy upholstered chairs; others stood and mingled at the tall tables, and then there were those who sidled up to the barstools to stake them out with their bare behinds. They were the hard-core ones who knew no one would bother them to take over their stools for the night. The crowd started warming up as several couples drifted to the dance floor, grooving with the band as it segued from show tunes to Latin rhythms. I noticed they were all couples. I watched and waited, wondering if there were any solo travelers in this nude community brave enough to attend a solo happy hour. I knew I would not have been.

As the minutes wore on, a smartly dressed couple stopped at the entrance and peeked in. They stood out from the crowd because they were wearing clothes. He was wearing pressed khaki trousers and a colorful tropical Tommy Bahamas shirt, and she had on a flirty but sophisticated sheath dress with a subtle pattern of pink flamingos set against an airy seafoam field. They looked around, hesitated and seemed on the verge of turning back and leaving when they noticed me. I must have stood out to them as much as they had to me because I was actually wearing clothes too, my trusty black dress with a red floral scarf. I motioned with a friendly wave, and they came over and took seats.

"I'm Marianne," I said. "I'll be your social hostess this cruise. Please settle in. Would you care to order a drink? It's on me."

"Hello, Marianne," the man answered, offering his hand. "We're the Ringlers, Max and Cathy. I have to say, we are pretty floored by all this." He looked around. "When a dirt-cheap offer came to us, we really thought it was a mistake. Now we know it was our mistake to have booked it."

"Imagine!" his wife added. "They had a few extra rooms and probably decided to bilk the unsuspecting public to fill them all. If we'd known the place was going to become a scene out of *Jesus Christ Superstar*, we never would have booked this cruise."

"Well," I said, trying to put a positive spin on things, "there are a few other non-charter couples on-board, and at least we can identify each other easily."

"Oh! That's right! This group is for solo travelers. Are we breaking a rule being here as a couple?" Max asked.

"Not at all," I laughed. "Charter cruises go by a whole different set of rules, anyway," I said, faking like I knew what I was talking about. "Let's just enjoy getting to know each other and maybe some others will stop by."

Just as the words came out of my mouth, another clothed couple joined us, coming from behind me.

They sat down and shielded their eyes with a dramatic gesture to make the point that they weren't altogether approving of what they saw.

"Mind if we join you?" the man asked as he held a seat for his wife. "I don't know where I can look without seeing something I could live without," he said, half grimacing. "I'm Ted, and this is my wife, Annie. Clarkson," he added. "We're usually sailing around this time of year, but on these big ships we tend to get lost in the crowd— just how we like it. Not gonna happen this time."

"Please join us, Ted and Annie. Meet Max and Cathy. I guess we've all found each other because at least we have one thing in common," I said.

"Yes," Annie chimed in, "respect for others. I just don't get it. How can perfectly reasonable and educated adults trot around like that with everything exposed? Especially in front of strangers?"

"It's precisely because there are so many people, I imagine," Cathy replied. "They'll probably never see them again."

"Either that, or they already know each other from prior cruises and conventions," Max said. "It's probably a pretty close community."

"Close in more ways than one," Ted contributed. "Did you ever see so much flesh as during the safety drill?"

Everyone laughed as the waiter approached with more bowls of snacks.

"Please, order a cocktail," I said. "It's on me."

"Damn well should be on the house," Max said as he ordered a Bacardi and Coke. "I think they call this a Cuba libre in Cuba," he said. "But on this cruise, we're probably more liable to learn where you can skinny dip in Havana instead of any important history about the place." He then turned to Cathy and confirmed that she wanted a strawberry daiquiri before submitting her order to the waiter.

"You're probably right," Ted chimed in. He ordered two cabernets. "This is the kind of thing we would pay to avoid. I'm sorry to say we got a deal to be here. We just walked across the pool deck, and that is one ship amenity we have decided definitely to avoid on this cruise."

"A no-brainer," Annie contributed, wrinkling her nose. "Can you imagine being in the Jacuzzi? Ugh!" She rolled her eyes.

I tactfully redirected the conversation to a more positive subject. "At least it will have no bearing on our itinerary, and it looks like a very interesting one," I said. "I've never been to the western Caribbean, and I'm looking forward to the excursions that explore the Mayan ruins." I immediately regretted saying what was tantamount to an admission of ignorance of a common cruise itinerary. It was not lost on these couples.

"You work on a cruise ship, and you've never been to Cozumel or Costa Maya or Roatan?" Annie sputtered a laugh, scrutinizing me. "Those are three of the most beaten-path ports of call in this hemisphere! We don't even bother leaving the ship for those ports anymore."

Cathy added her own claim to cruise-sophistication by telling us they only left the ship in those ports if they needed inexpensive drugs. "Not the illegal ones!" she interjected emphatically. "But you can get some very good deals on over-the-counter and prescription drugs in some of these ports, and you don't need a prescription in many cases. In fact, one time we booked a back-to-back while we were on this same itinerary. The second cruise was going to the Amazon River, so we needed to get the yellow fever vaccine. Do you know we were able to walk off the ship in one of these places, find a little local medical station and pay a twenty-dollar tip to the nurse on duty for two yellow fever shots? We didn't even need an appointment!"

The drinks arrived, and as the waiter was serving them a third couple joined us. They were wearing clothes too, no surprise.

"Looks like we all have at least one thing in common," the man said. He had a jovial smile. "We're the Alberts," he went on as he and his wife settled into a loveseat. "I'm Butch, and this is my wife, Sally. I don't even have to know you all to know we're all probably the cheapest couples on this cruise," he laughed. "I never met a good deal I didn't love, up until now."

Everyone nodded and laughed in agreement. Butch tapped the waiter's sleeve and asked him to bring us a couple of martinis. "I'm not picky," he said to the waiter, "but since it's free, make sure it's an expensive vodka." He laughed along with the waiter.

Everyone chuckled and settled in to sip their drinks and nibble on the munchies while looking around at the views. Inside the Paris Lounge, the chairs were fast filling up with guests. The fact that they were all naked was not as interesting as it might have been even an hour earlier. Of greater interest was the view outside the ship as it was sailing past the uber-rich Fisher Island, allegedly the wealthiest zip code in the country, and on its way to the Rickenbacker Causeway that connects downtown Miami with Key Biscayne.

"Oh, I can feel the tropical breezes," Annie suddenly said, fanning herself with her hand. "We just left Traverse City, Michigan, this morning, and it was snowing!"

"I love Traverse City," I said. "I'm from Michigan, too. I was on the prior cruise as a guest, and they asked me to fill a staff position if I could rejoin them for this cruise. It didn't take too much arm-twisting."

"So, you were commandeered without experience or qualifications to work on a cruise ship? How lucky is that!" Cathy said.

"My guess is, the staff person assigned to this sailing didn't want to work on a nudie cruise," Butch said. I wouldn't think they could force anyone to do that."

"Well, I filled a staff role on the previous cruise when they needed a cellist for their string quartet, and it turns out they needed an emergency fill-in for a social hostess for this one," I explained. It's a one-off, I'm sure, and besides, after this extended time away from my work, I will be more than ready to return to Michigan. Hopefully, it won't be snowing as much by then."

I did not add the part about the cellist going missing or the bit about the social hostess attacking me the last night of the cruise.

Max then said that he and Cathy came from Laguna Niguel, California. They weren't so much escaping bad weather as getting away from their routine and feeling coddled on a cruise.

"Laguna Niguel?" Butch and Sally said in unison.

"That's where we live!" Butch exclaimed. "What are the chances? We live close to The Center at Rio Niguel on Via Catalina."

"What a small world!" Cathy nearly jumped out of her seat. "We're practically neighbors! We're on Via Azul!" The two couples fell comfortably into a conversation about their neighborhood, favorite restaurants, stores and services and of course started digging around for mutual acquaintances, neighbors and friends. I smiled outwardly, predicting this cruise that started with so much apprehension was taking a definite turn for the better and would probably result in a friendship for life between these two neighboring couples. That's how it works on cruises.

As the Ringlers and Alberts continued to ramp up

their conversation, Ted and Annie started to talk with me with renewed interest. Where was I from in West Michigan exactly? As it turned out, they actually had lived for a while in East Grand Rapids, a couple blocks from Reeds Lake, while Ted was interning at Blodgett Hospital decades earlier. I was able to confirm that I lived within walking distance of the old Blodgett building and told them that I authored a girls' detective series. Annie said she had heard of the *Hope Dares* Detective Series and was certain one of her teenage nieces had mentioned it. I was feeling more like a cruise guest than part of the crew.

As our respective conversations went on, a lone man, elderly and wearing a boxy white shirt with a colorfully embroidered button placket, approached us. He could have been anything from a retired professor to a character actor in a small-town theater. Shyly, he asked if he might be able to join us since, as he put it, he felt more comfortable with us than with anyone else. We laughed in understanding and made room for him to join us in our circle.

I asked who he was and where he was from. The others stopped talking and listened with interest. "My name is Percival Turnkey," he said slowly and deliberately. Then he added, "Not Turkey, mind you, Turnkey." We laughed, appreciating the humor. He came off as a kind octogenarian. His ears stuck slightly out from a freshly groomed haircut. "I booked this cruise two years ago while my wife Millie was still with me," he said. "Or rather, it wasn't exactly this cruise," he smiled. "But when an offer came for me to switch to this one from the original one with such a reduced fare, I figured since I was alone now, why not? Now I can see why not!" He smiled again and looked around the room. I noticed a hearing aid as he turned his head to the side. "Not my style, which makes me more grateful to be meeting you all." He explained that he was a retired pathologist, who from time to time still gave lectures at the University of Miami, right there in Coral Gables where he lived. "We always liked this cruise line," he explained, "because it sails right out of Miami, so it's only a taxi ride away, or an Über these days."

"Well, we're glad you came over, Dr. Turnkey," I said. Then I added how unusual his embroidered shirt was.

"Millie got this for me in Guatemala years ago," he said. "It is a traditional Mayan shirt. I always travel with these shirts when I come to the Caribbean because they are cotton and loose and airy and go with the climate so well."

I invited him to order a cocktail and offered everyone else to order seconds to keep Dr. Turnkey company. Then I went around the group introducing the other couples to him.

My group of seven "solo" travelers was shaping up to be the "misfit" group of guests that weren't expecting to be on a clothing-optional charter. I made a mental note to send an email to Pauline with that information. I was beginning to understand what she had meant earlier about my function on the ship changing. She certainly got that one right!

4

Popular A-peel

ALONG ABOUT THE TIME we were finishing up our drinks and snacks, I invited anyone who cared to join me for dinner to meet me in forty-five minutes in front of the main dining room. Everyone agreed it sounded like a wonderful plan, and we separated to prepare for dinner. I knew with some relief that this was not going to be the posse of table mates I'd come to love and dread on the prior cruise. This was going to be a fresh start with "normal" guests that were considerably less colorful and hopefully less confounding than the last group. We decided after our pleasant first dinner to remain dining companions for the rest of the cruise.

Afterwards, I made a quick stop back to the room to freshen up and was greeted by the blinking red light on my phone. Wink had received my message and left a response. He said the MS *Aphrodite* was heading to

Cartagena in Colombia, and from there to the Panama Canal. He would call again, and hopefully he would catch me when we could talk. Then he added that he was supposed to join the MS *Athena* in Grand Cayman on the very same day the MS *Minerva* would be there and hoped we could spend that day together. Needless to say, I was disappointed how things turned out, but I was fast getting used to the unpredictable nature of life at sea.

The first night's opening show in the theater was once again "Neon City," the same opening-night extravaganza that had launched the prior cruise. As before, it was a full-fledged, pull-out-all-stops production with high-energy, nonstop dancing and singing and imaginative costumes against elaborate backdrops and ingenious stage lighting. I stopped in and stood at the back of one of the entrances. I was disappointed that it was so sparsely attended and imagined these naked cruisers opting to party in every other one of the ship's venues instead of enjoying the talent and labor that went into bringing this show to life. I also imagined the clothed guests avoiding the theater, afraid to be surrounded by naked strangers in the dark. Since there were plenty of seats for the taking, I selected one with a prime view and settled in. I was happy to see Natalia back on stage again, dancing in full throttle, her ankle bruise completely healed from our unfortunate run-in during the previous cruise. All hatchets were long since buried.

At the conclusion of the show, Pearl appeared on stage. She greeted everyone in her usual warm and gracious manner, welcoming the guests to the cruise of a lifetime. Her smooth skin glowed with the color of rich chocolate pudding, against the dramatic leopard print African gomesi that was tied at the waist with the same purple and gold obi-like sash she wore with her other gomesi the night she sang on the last cruise. She addressed the theater as if it were packed solid, extending full consideration and dignity to the paltry couple dozen people who showed up. She omitted the invitation she'd extended on the last cruise for the guests to visit her for lunch in Jamaica where she lived. I figured it was because we were really going to Jamaica this time, and she probably didn't want to cover all her furniture with plastic slipcovers.

She then turned to introduce a man standing off to the side. He was the man who had been sitting in her office when I stopped by earlier that day, the one I'd assumed was the assistant cruise director. Pearl said he was the charter host for this cruise and, before handing her mic over to him, added that he would be emceeing the shows and making the general announcements for the rest of the cruise. Apparently, he was well known to the clothing-optional community because when she said his name, the small crowd in the audience erupted into a frenzied explosion of whistles, whoops and cheers. "Let me present someone you already know and love dearly: your charter host, Perry Cardis!" With that, she graciously bowed out, escaping through a side stage exit to leave Perry Cardis alone in the spotlight.

From his opening remarks, it was evident that Perry Cardis was a magician. One trick after another excited him more than his audience. At one point, he complained how hot the stage lights were, and suddenly his clown-sized bow tie started spinning around and flashing gaudily like a fan. It was the best laugh he got all night. He said he was still too hot and took off his blazer, dramatically swinging it over his head before tossing it, striptease style. The drummer added a rim-shot. *Ba-Dum-Tis*! But Perry Cardis didn't stop there.

He started to unbutton his shirt. I thought, no, this cannot be happening. But it was happening, and his shirt followed his blazer to the same heap on the stage floor. There he stood in his white undershirt and navy pants. The audience was laughing and clapping and goading him on. Someone shouted out, "Don't stop now, Perry!" Someone else yelled, "Do your magic and give us a show!" Yet another yelled, "Make your pants disappear too!" And before I knew what was happening, he was standing there in white undershirt, striped boxer shorts and black knee socks held up by black elastic garters under the searing stage lights. He joked about the heat under the spotlights and closed off by inviting everyone to help him escape the heat by going upstairs to the Paris Lounge for a late-night dance and buffet to the music selections provided by Deejay Nude Jude.

I decided to skip the dance, but on the hunch Pearl was heading back to her office, I took the only shortcut I knew to get there fast. We nearly crashed into each other at the office door. "Why, Marianne," she said, "it's good to see you here again." She sounded weary. It was as though she had left all her energy and ebullience on the prior cruise. She invited me into the office where a young crew member was standing with his video equipment.

"Well, God bless this charter and let Perry Cardis take it over from here," she said to the stage manager, a handsome young man in a black, long-sleeved shirt and pants. His name badge read Dominic. "You don't know the relief that is for me. I'm also grateful that I don't have to be as visible for this cruise. Let's just give it our best so the guests have a great time. As long as they can bare their assets and parade their patooties, they should be just fine."

I was taken aback at this behind-the-scenes banter.

"Did they let you know who's coming to replace Samantha?" Dominic interjected.

"Samantha was going to give us two great trumpet performances," Pearl said. "She's always a sell-out crowd. She also wears one gown that is nearly transparent that would have swept this crowd off their feet. But a very privileged guest who happens to be on another ship in the South Pacific requested her and off they sent her! Now we're left with two open spaces that need to be filled by another entertainer, and I'm afraid it's not going to happen with such short notice. So the production team will have to go into overdrive with more shows. To make matters worse, this crowd doesn't even come to the shows. Did you see how few people were there tonight? I'd have guessed there were fewer than three dozen. All they want is their naked bacchanal."

Suddenly, Pearl looked at me and asked outright if I would play a solo cello concerto one night–in the nude. I was instantly wishing I had not chosen this moment to come and see her.

"Just kidding, Marianne!" she said, spouting with a laugh. "By the way, Marianne, not that anyone will even show up for your morning chat time, but what event did you have in mind? I'll make sure Perry Cardis gets the information since he'll be making the morning announcements instead of me."

"I'll be hosting Show and Tell," I said as I simul-taneously realized the double entendre that created in a ship full of naked people. We all burst out in sponta-neous laughter.

"Perfect!" Pearl said. "I might just stop by myself and see how that works out. Did anyone show up for your solo happy hour this evening?" she asked as she looked up, changing the subject.

"Only a few couples and one solo gentleman, an elderly widower. They were the only ones in the Paris Lounge wearing clothes. I think that's why they all gravitated over to me."

"They're wearing clothes now," Dominic said. "Later, they'll be trying the nudist lifestyle. It happens all the time."

"Oh no! They were positively scandalized," I protested. "Absolutely scathing!"

"Ha! The harder they resist, the sooner they strip," Dominic laughed. "You'll see," he said, smiling with confidence. "One day, one couple will stop showing up in your group. You'll look over and see them sitting and laughing and enjoying their dinner with a group of nudists. They'll fit right in, too," he said. "Anyway, they call themselves naturists these days."

Pearl looked up from her computer screen and groaned. "They took away my sure-bet trumpeter and are sending us Stella Laffer. She taught me everything I know," Pearl added with a deep sigh. "But the question is," she wondered out loud, "why did she agree to come onboard this particular cruise? Did they tell her Perry Cardis is on this ship now? Those two have been out to kill each other for years."

5

Show and Tell

Day Two: February 16, Tuesday
En Route to Cozumel, Mexico
Weather updates will be given by the captain.

UP AND AT 'EM by 7 a.m.

The sea was tossing and pitching with a fury outside my window, but I was holding steady, and besides, had no time to think about it. I showered, dressed and ran up to the Lido deck for breakfast. I hoped to beat the crowd, but the Lido buffet was already full of laughing, eating, joking and conversing naked people. They seemed like a great bunch of folks I'd like to meet under any other circumstances, but I honestly couldn't get past that part about wearing no clothes. I grabbed a small table closest to the exit, dawdled over some cold cereal and a banana muffin and fixed myself a coffee-to-go at the self-serve station. Then, I found a quiet corner on the pool deck to watch the morning sun mount the eastern horizon.

At eight-thirty, the loudspeakers crackled to life as the voice of Perry Cardis bellowed through the air. Some people nearby almost applauded at the mere sound of his voice, and you could hear more general laughter in the background. He greeted everyone to a "barely new" morning and ran through the list of activities for the day at sea, starting with my Show and Tell at nine o'clock in the Paris Lounge. Of course, he couldn't pass up the opportunity to add, "I'll show you mine if you'll show me yours!"

Fifteen people were already waiting for me in the Paris Lounge when I arrived ten minutes early. I greeted them and confirmed we were all there for morning Show and Tell. No one was wearing a stitch of clothes, but nearly all of them were balancing plates of muffins, danish or bagels smothered with cream cheese on their laps and sipping coffee or tea. The mood couldn't be more jovial or congenial.

"C'mon, Marianne," one man, who had more hair on his face than the rest of his body combined, challenged me. "You can join us. We're paying for this cruise, and we'd like everyone to try our carefree life-style. You'll never go back to binding underwear and confining clothes," he said.

"Not to mention matching outfits and making sure everything is pressed all the time," another woman with henna-dyed hair pitched in, smiling.

I started right in at nine. I introduced myself and thanked everyone for joining the morning Show and Tell, saying we would only meet on the sea-days but to check the *Tides* every day for other events I would host. While I was talking, a few more couples drifted in and joined us. We were up to nearly thirty people. All were naked except for me. I asked people to consider sharing any memories or impressions from their travels, especially if they had helpful tips or advice about our upcoming ports of call. I also asked them to introduce themselves by first name, and tell us where they were from and a little about themselves.

"Don't you want us to talk about how we started being naturists?" a man asked.

"Sure. Of course," I gulped. "It's your Show and Tell." I had to ask myself how I hadn't thought about that.

For the next forty-five minutes, people took turns introducing themselves, talking about their experiences with travel, but mostly gravitating back to how they came into being nudists. Some called it a naturist lifestyle, and a couple of times there were friendly but spirited debates over the difference. It was shaping up to feel more like a Friends of Bill W. meeting. The stories started to repeat themselves with one partner saying she agreed to try it to please her spouse or partner. Usually, it was the woman going along with the man. There were exceptions. Sometimes, it was a life-changing or traumatic event that sparked the interest in nudism. I didn't get the sense anyone was much happier for the effort, but they all seemed to be trying to prove that it was right for them. I wasn't convinced. There seemed to be a lot of energy and effort focused on persuading others, which told me they weren't quite convinced themselves. I sensed an elusive longing for something that wasn't quite defined or attained. Except for not wearing clothes, their aspirations, hopes and regrets were pretty much the same as everyone else's. What did become clear was that nudism cuts across a broad cross section of the population. In this group alone, people described themselves as college and university professors, scientists, researchers, doctors, truck drivers, teachers, contractors, business owners, childcare workers, bankers and even a Library of Congress librarian. There was less and less talk about travel memories or advice for upcoming ports of call as the session wore on. By the end of our time, I had to admit I felt more comfortable in the midst of this group and was getting used to looking at their faces and forgetting about what was below their necks.

By nine forty-five, people were fidgeting to proceed to the next activity, so we ended; in a matter of minutes, the space was emptied out. The housekeeping staff appeared with laundry bins full of fresh slipcovers to refresh all the chairs. Most of the folks were heading to the spa for a workshop about "Embracing Your Body's Perfect Imperfections." I thought I could live without that one, so I went to the excursions office to check into some of the shoreside adventures on the itinerary.

While I was standing there, the Clarksons came over. They said they were thinking about taking the Mayan culture excursion in Cozumel the next day. It was to make stops at an indigenous village and featured a reenactment of an actual Mayan ballgame. There would also be a chocolate demonstration. I didn't know what chocolate had to do with the Maya but agreed it sounded like fun, and we signed up together. What was even more appealing was that all the shore excursions were complimentary because they were included as part of the charter. I offered to call everyone else in our group and see if they were interested as well. I used the house phone in the nearby elevator bank, and within the hour, we were all ready to enjoy an educational tour together the next day in Cozumel. Once our plans were set, we all agreed to meet in the main theater, the Minerva Lounge, for the captain's welcome party that evening and proceed to dinner from there.

It was then I suddenly remembered that I was on duty for the captain's reception that evening and was supposed to be hosting the captain's table at dinner. I had not done any of the preparations for it and burst headlong into the cruise director's office.

6

Worst Nightmare

"Well, here you are, finally!" Pearl said, not particularly jubilant. "I'll ask you later how your Show and Tell went, but first you've got some work to consider here. There's that little matter of the captain's welcome reception and dinner tonight that I hope you didn't forget about. You're going to have a busy day preparing for it. But you're in luck, because the newly appointed DOSE, that is, director of onboard social experience, is with us this cruise. She'll be at hand to help orient you and get you situated." Pearl made a call on her phone, and in a few minutes, a tall attractive woman walked through the door.

Was I seeing things? I thought my eyes were playing tricks on me. Was this a bad joke someone was waging against me? Revenge? My mind was spinning in a hundred directions as my brain tried to grasp what my eyes were seeing. The woman standing there was none other than the ever-pouting Angela! When I'd been invited to take over the social hostess role on this cruise, it was to replace her for trying to push me off the ship. And here she was—back again—not only not in jail but now wearing an officer's uniform, still obviously in full employment of the ship. And the kicker was, this time she was my boss!

Angela started right in. She was terse and succinct. She sounded like a machine gun rat-a-tat-tatting out my marching orders.

"Captain Gurtigruten will be joined by four couples for his gala dinner this evening, and of course his personal guest. You will be paired off with and seated across from Chief Concierge Franklin at the big oval twelve-top table. It is the only one in the entire dining room. Oh, and by the way, you will introduce Captain Gurtigruten and his companion as soon as they arrive at the dining room after all the other guests are seated. Be sure to ask how he pronounces his name at the captain's reception this evening. You will stand in the receiving line next to him for that."

I was already overwhelmed. Angela went on without mercy. "You need to handwrite the place cards for dinner tonight because you waited too long to order them from desktop printing. You should have done that yesterday, but no one knew where you were. Take this list of names." She thrust a thick envelope at me. "Seat them formally, either as couples or alternating girl-boy-girl-boy. But Captain Gurtigruten's companion will be seated to his right since he is the host. His companion's name is somewhere in the folder."

She went on. "Many captains have some rotating companions along the various itineraries, or they ask to be paired up with staff members for the formal dinners. This is the pattern, except of course when the wife and children join the ship for the holiday cruises and during the summer vacation. We know our own captains, but Captain Gurtigruten is still an outsider until we get to know him better. He did not request to be paired with a staff member but submitted the name of his personal dinner companion instead," she said.

I opened the envelope and sat at the nearest vacant desk. All the desks were the same, and when they weren't being occupied, they were completely empty except for a computer. The drawers were supplied with pens and sticky pads and paper clips. This was efficiency on steroids. I sat down and pored over the names and studied the diagram of the big oval table, the only table that was not round in the entire dining room.

"Before you get too comfortable," Angela added, "here's the folder for all the names you're going to have to learn for tonight's reception line. The photos and names of everyone who is anyone on this ship are the ones you need to have lock-tight in your memory because you will be the one introducing them personally to the captain as they walk through the line. And you can't use notes!"

Was she serious? This was more like a mail pouch

than a folder. It weighed about ten pounds with full-color sheets showing the guests' pictures and names. Something like a cold sweat was starting to form at the nape of my neck and trickle down my back. I wasn't prepared for this onslaught of memorization for what amounted to a live and unrehearsed role to start in less than five hours. I took a deep breath as I riffled through the thick pad of papers with blurry copies of faces with names printed beneath. Most had titles too, like baron or esquire or the third . . . there was even a dame in there.

Back in my room, I Googled how to arrange seating for a formal dinner and filled the names in on the diagram. Then, I carefully handwrote the place cards with the calligraphy pen that was supplied in the big envelope. I double-checked to make sure all the names were spelled correctly and confirmed with the notes Angela had provided that the captain's companion was Miss Shirley Hempstead. I went to the dining room to hand-deliver the cards to the maître de', but the dining room was closed right then, so I made a mental note to return later. Back in my room, I sat down to learn the names and faces of about a hundred couples and hoped they looked exactly the same in person as they did in their boarding photos. The afternoon grinded on. I had to call my friends and tell them I would not be joining them for dinner because duty called me elsewhere but reconfirmed our plans for the next day's excursion in Cozumel.

In the middle of the afternoon, I remembered to take the place cards to the dining room. Just as I was leaving my room, the phone rang and Pauline greeted me. "You are already creating a stir," she said. "I have heard from two couples, appreciative and relieved to have you onboard. You know who I mean," she continued, "the Clarksons and the Alberts. They are very happy you are including them and offering a little oasis of comfort in this sea of flesh," she said. "I understand you arranged to join them for an island tour excursion tomorrow in Cozumel," she continued. "We're going to ask you to act as a ship liaison, accompanying our excursions for the rest of the cruise. We call the position a tour escort. Oscar will provide you with an envelope of instructions and details every day, and you'll be reporting back to his department on how everything went. You'll also have to take along a few injury forms, just in case. Be sure to stop by the excursions office today and get the packet for tomorrow from Oscar."

I decided to go right then and there on my way to the dining room, so as not to forget about it later. Oscar was waiting for me and handed me the packet telling me it was all self-explanatory in the note that was enclosed. He also issued me a staff shirt to wear on the excursion, explaining that the guests always identify staff by the yellow shirts. He said to wear black or white pants. He gave me a thick booklet of all the excursions on the entire cruise and invited me to consider all the options and sign up for my first and second choices. His team would do their best to book me on tours of my choice.

I headed directly to the dining room but realized I'd forgotten the envelope containing the place cards and dashed back upstairs to get it. Just as I was walking through the door, the phone rang. It was Wink!

"I can't believe we've finally connected," he said. I could hear a big smile over the phone. We filled each other in on our respective turn-of-events, and he said he was hoping to spend the day with me in Grand Cayman where both our ships would call at the same time. I remembered the fun day we'd spent on the beach at Grand Turk and was disappointed we'd only be together for one day this time. But I wasn't here for Wink, I had to remind myself; I was here to perform a job. I could tell things were going to be different this time. He had to hang up, saying another call was coming in, and I said goodbye and turned to prepare for the evening that awaited me.

I looked at my bed where all the names I had to memorize were spread out on little flashcards I had made. I went over to pop-quiz myself and became so absorbed in memorizing that the next time I looked at the clock, it was already time to get dressed. The dressiest thing I had with me was my red Valentine's Day dress from the last cruise. It was a little cheap looking, to be honest, with that light sprinkle of glitter, but would have to do. It was meant for the dance contest and had never been intended for an event as formal as the captain's reception, but it was all I had. I hoped the lights would be turned low.

7

Barely Visible

I WAS STANDING at the entrance to the ballroom in plenty of time for the guests to arrive, still running through all the names and faces in my mind as best as I could recall them. I had a new appreciation for the staff who performed these jobs for entire six-month contracts, as they were required to learn a boatload of names for every new cruise. As the guests were lining up on the other side of the entrance ribbon, their names and faces blurred into one big fog in my overworked memory. Frankly, with all the hair dye, false eyelashes, cosmetic surgery, teeth whiteners and Botox, they looked like cookie cutters of each other in blonde, brunette and red-haired versions. Whatever happened to character, I wondered, and people with memorable features like crooked teeth, dimples and chin clefts, imperfect complexions and furrowed brows? Then I saw a woman with a dark-green tattoo of a snake slithering down from her armpit and had to concede that character was still around, just in a different guise.

The general manager, Ivor, appeared, said hello to me dismissively, took his place militarily in the reception line and looked the other way, awaiting the captain who arrived seconds later and stepped into his place between us. Captain Gurtigruten was tall and trim and athletic and very pleasant to look at. I introduced myself, and he greeted me cordially. I asked how I should pronounce his name and he said Gert. Smart aleck! I guessed that was meant to be the extent of our conversation for the evening, and possibly for the entire cruise. As soon as the ribbon at the entrance was pulled away, the guests started to stream in. The overly floral smells of too many perfumes colliding with hairspray and men's colognes saturated my nostrils with an aromatic blend that approximated ammonia. I didn't think my memory could work very well under that condition, but there was no turning back now.

The first couple that came through was a tall gentleman, I would guess to be in his forties, and a nearly as tall woman who looked slightly older than he, with shoulder-length highlighted hair ringing a very high forehead. I recognized them as the Baron Kent Proulx and his wife, Melanie, from their photos. I reached out to greet them, and they bypassed me completely, walking straight to the captain and embracing him with European kisses on both cheeks. It was like a family reunion. Or a Mafia wedding. The same thing happened with the next couple, Dr. Boris and Professor Marguerite Simplington. This couple, too, ignored me as though I were a wall sconce and greeted the captain like familiar old relatives. I was beginning to wonder why I'd bothered working so hard to memorize all those names and faces all day.

One thing that hadn't even occurred to me as unusual was that these two couples got dressed up and were actually wearing evening clothes: tuxedos for the men and elegant formal-length black gowns for the women. But it was the next couple that took me by surprise. They arrived naked, except for the bright-red boa the woman was wearing around her neck.

I addressed them and reached out to shake their hands. "Dr. and Mrs. Preston and Deborah Trimingham," I announced, "please meet Captain Gurtigruten." They smiled right through me and moved on to kibbitz with the captain. Old friends, I thought. The captain must have made an inside joke because they all burst out in simultaneous laughter before the couple moved on to greet the general manager.

The couples rolled through, and I did my best to catch their attention while they made it painfully obvious I was completely invisible and unnecessary. I thought it curious that so many people on this charter seemed to be acquainted with the captain from before, especially since he was new to the ship. More and more were wearing nothing as they passed through the line, laughing gaily with each other and friends they recognized in the queue. I did my best to act as though I didn't notice the bare elephant in the room but found it more and more difficult to recall names of people whose photos were taken before they stripped.

The line dwindled after a half hour, and Pearl took the stage. People watched from the little tables set up everywhere as the spotlights focused on her.

Pearl welcomed everyone and said it was her pleasure to introduce the master of the vessel and general manager who then walked down the aisle through the center of the theater to the stage as the band struck up the cruise line's nautical theme song. She asked everyone to join her in welcoming Captain Gert Gurtigruten to the MS *Minerva* as he took the mic confidently, smiled in all directions, and then relayed how he'd learned the ropes of maritime life as a boy while fishing with his father in the cold waters of Norway's fjords. From there he worked his way through the ranks of piloting small ships, finally graduating from a sequence of elite maritime academies to become a ship's master. He smiled agreeably, expressing what a pleasure it was to arrive at Classica Cruise Line and take the helm of the MS *Minerva*. He paused while the audience applauded in approval. He added that he wanted to extend an extra-special greeting to guests who knew him from other cruises and followed him over to join him on this special charter. Another wave of applause swept across the theater amidst sounds of glasses clinking and low murmurs of guests conveying their drink orders to the roving waitstaff.

Ivor added some brief welcome remarks of his own, handing back the mic to the captain who introduced his staff of officers as they marched valiantly down to the stage in all their brass-buttoned and gold-sleeve-striped glory. At the end of the introductions, the officers were all offered a champagne flute and toasted a happy and safe cruise for everyone before retreating from the theater and returning to their duties with the same pomp and circumstance that had ushered them in. As they were marching out, Pearl invited the guests to linger and enjoy a magic act provided by the charter host, Perry Cardis.

This time when Perry Cardis took the mic, he stepped into the spotlight wearing a top hat and a big bow tie over his matching black satin undershirt and boxer set. Formal attire, I thought. His big bow tie started spinning and flashing dramatically. To be honest, he looked more like a circus act than a charter cruise host, standing there in all his black underwear with that ridiculous oversized bow tie blinking and strobing, and his black knee socks held up by those frumpy black garters. He reached into a cardboard box behind him and pulled out a white rabbit. He said he'd forgotten to put it in his top hat earlier, so he had to do it right then to execute the magic trick that went with it. Was he trying to figure it out as he went along? Apparently, I wasn't the only one wondering. He apologized that his trunks of magic tricks had missed the ship and promised that his acts would improve once the crates arrived later in the cruise. Most guests didn't want to sit around and wait. I marveled at how he kept going even as the room was fast hemorrhaging.

8

Hell Hath No Fury

From the ballroom, I headed directly to the dining room to start greeting the captain's guests at the dinner table. It was just as I arrived at the maître d's station that I suddenly realized with horror that I had completely forgotten to bring the place cards in earlier when I had been distracted by Wink's phone call. I was mortified and nearly paralyzed with embarrassment as Yves, the French maître d', rained down the full fury of hell on me with no end of recriminations, denigrations, threats and put-downs—all in his intimidating French accent to boot. It was too late to run back to my room for the name cards, and besides, he seethed that his exceedingly busy staff had done my work for me, arranging the place cards set at the table. He admonished me to head straight to the table and greet the guests as he would send them one couple at a time when they arrived; all the while, the points on his moustache twitched wildly to either side of his face like meddlesome handlebars. The captain and his companion would be the last to arrive, he said.

Burning with humiliation, I nearly dashed ahead on my own when one of the waiters extravagantly took my elbow and escorted me formally and agonizingly slowly to the table. All the place cards were set, beautifully handwritten, but as I circled the table, I noticed they were all unfamiliar names—not the same ones that were in the envelope Angela had handed me. What was going on here? Had I looked at the wrong list? Was there another list in that envelope I didn't see? Was it a setup? No matter how this happened, I had to figure it out on my own and work through it. For all I couldn't stand Angela, I was at that very moment wishing for her to show up and help me out of this mess. I could clearly learn from her experience.

With a whole new set of names spread out around the table and no time to learn any of them, I realized I would not be able to introduce these couples formally and properly to the captain. I walked around the table once more. Only my name and Franklin's, the chief concierge, were familiar. We had been placed opposite each other just as Angela had said. I tried to memorize names as I was looking at them, but they had been arranged in random girl-boy-girl-boy order, mixing up all the couples. This was a nightmare—fast devolving into a total calamity. I had a whole new respect for the degree of background work and meticulous planning that went into preparing for these events and was quite frankly questioning how Pauline had ever considered me qualified enough to take over without appropriate training and experience.

The first couple arrived and barely glanced in my direction. They were naked except for their expensive watches and rings. I was appalled. The waiter seated the woman directly across the table from her husband. She asked the waiter to move the elaborate bouquet centerpiece that was obstructing their view of each other. However, the waiter patiently explained the table had been ordered according to the captain's own specifications, and the waitstaff had no authority to change anything. The couple waved at each other as if to bid farewell for the evening and turned to study their respective menus. The second couple arrived. They looked at me expectantly, but I was at a loss as to who they were. I introduced myself and was about to ask their names when the third couple arrived right on their heels and heartily greeted the first couple. The fourth couple looked familiar, but it wasn't until after they were seated that I recognized them as the Baron and Baroness Proulx from the reception line. This time they were not wearing their evening wear. Everyone seemed to know each other, so I didn't know what I was even doing there. Shortly after, Franklin arrived and took his seat opposite mine. He was the only one wearing clothes besides me.

We were awaiting the captain when a blast of

horns erupted from the dining room entrance. Two trumpeters blared from either side of the grand entrance as the captain strode in, tall and confident, smiling to his right and his left and looking more like a politician in an election year. He was still impeccably dressed in the same crisp navy uniform he had worn at his reception. At his arm was a woman of nearly his height, thin as a cartoon, a long mane of highlighted brown hair bouncing down her shoulders and only partially covering her very endowed and very bare breasts. And look at that: she was wearing nothing at all other than shoes! Not even a watch! The guests applauded as the couple made their way to the table. A buzz of excited murmurs followed the applause. The captain's mysterious companion was all the rage!

This was my moment! While I had failed miserably up to now with everything that had been expected of me, I at least had this moment to vindicate myself. It was the moment for me to introduce the captain and his lady friend. With renewed confidence and a voice pumped-up from a mega-dose of adrenaline, I bellowed so loudly it even surprised me: "Ladies and gentlemen of the MS *Minerva*, please join me in welcoming the master of the vessel, Captain Gert Gurtigruten, and his lovely companion, Miss Shirley Hempstead!"

Complete silence. In fact, if I could have described the sound of the room, it would have been that of a black hole—a cosmic vacuum sucking all the air out of the universe. I stood there anticipating a wave of applause, but what happened next could be described as nothing short of apocalyptic. Because what I did not know was that the captain's companion *du jour* clearly was not Miss Shirley Hempstead, as had been in my package, but Miss Fantina Monaire!

Miss Monaire didn't miss a beat. Marching at me in high red strappy Manolo Blahnik platform pointed stilettos with no end of little charms and gewgaws bouncing merrily from the straps that probably set the captain back a couple grand, she sprang at me, her nostrils flaring and teeth bared as her impeccably shellacked talons nearly scraped my face off. All I saw were eyebrows so high they missed her forehead altogether. "You BEACH!" she screamed in a distinctly non-American accent. "You FOLKING BEACH!" she seethed at me. "I abhor you!" She was hissing like a cornered alligator. "Who are you to call me Miss Shirley Hemphair or whoever that hussy is? For your information, the captain and I are almost affianced!" she shrieked, holding up her hand that was distinctly lacking an engagement ring. "We were going to make our announcement in public later this cruise, and you spoiled it, you – you – you FOLKING BEACH!" I could feel her hot breath on my face she was so close. I guessed she'd had the garlic shrimp stir-fry for lunch. She thumped the edge of the table nearest her with the resulting effect that a glass of red wine bounced and shattered to the floor, spilling its contents into the rug. "You are a nasty, evil and ignorant BEACH!" she raged on, driving home her point all too well. "I never want to see you again! You have ruined my night and this entire cruise." Wet mascara was starting to clump and streak around her eyes, and her smeared lipstick looked more like blackberry jelly. She clenched her fists and waved them at me, making a sound that was a cross between a screech owl and a jackhammer. For some reason, I looked over at the captain right then and caught him sitting calmly in his chair staring blankly at the breadbasket.

I stood there, frozen in embarrassment and fear. I did not know which way to turn and felt like running out of the dining room, which in retrospect was probably what I should have done because two waiters came forth immediately, each one taking me by an elbow, and escorted me with record swiftness out of the dining room. Honestly, I don't recall my feet even touching the floor. I could hear the dining room come to life with a lot of nervous coughing, throat clearing, harrumphing and the general undertone of comments registering disapproval and indignation as my efficient escorts swooshed me through the exit. Suddenly, I went from an invisible no-name-nobody to the most famous person on the ship.

And I wasn't even naked.

9

About-Face

I BROUGHT OUT my suitcase. I knew there was no other recourse than to leave the ship and had every reason under the sun to expect they would send me packing in Cozumel the next day. At least I would be ready.

I really hadn't meant for things to go down the way they had and felt sincerely sorry for the scene I'd caused. But on any ship, the captain determines who stays and who goes, and by ruffling his fiancée's feathers–and in public–I already knew the verdict without having to face any judge, jury or executioner.

The phone kept ringing while I was packing. I couldn't have cared less who was trying to reach me. I didn't even give a hoot if it was Wink, to be frank. I wanted off the ship and out of this crazy life-at-sea for once and for all. It wasn't for me. I was fighting back tears. There it went again, that friggin' phone. I literally yanked the plug from the wall. I wanted nothing to do with the MS *Minerva* or any other cruise ship, boat, raft or rubber duck for the rest of my life!

❧❧❧

When morning came, I was up and ready before the sun. I was a woman on a mission: to leave the ship with as few people as possible seeing me or knowing about it. I didn't even say goodbye to Pearl or Pauline. I figured they both had bigger fish to fry, the biggest being the whale of damage control over the mess I'd created the night before. No, I concluded, best to remove myself quietly from the scene and end the wanton chaos I'd created, not only on one cruise but now on two.

I was first in line at the security station when Perry Cardis announced over the ship's loudspeaker that the ship had been cleared by local customs authorities. He welcomed us officially to Cozumel and said we were free to disembark for the day. The security guard motioned at me to approach.

"Where are you going with those?" he asked, pointing at my suitcases.

"Huh? I'm leaving the ship." I thought I was answering the obvious.

"Where are your disembarkation documents?" he asked. "Did you check out with the purser?"

"What document do I need?" I replied. "I don't

think I am welcome here after the scene I caused at the captain's table last night." I felt I had to explain.

"I have no information about a scene, and we have no instructions to disembark you, Miss Milliner." The answer was certain, succinct and strangely comforting.

I was stunned they weren't passing around a memo–all in caps, no less–to throw my sorry tush off the ship. As I stood there looking dumbfounded, he gently reminded me that I was blocking the way for other guests who wanted to leave the ship and explore Cozumel. He ordered me to take my suitcases back to my room.

On the way back, I detoured by Pauline's office. She had circles under her eyes.

"Gosh, I'm so sorry I screwed up like that," I said as I closed her door after me and helped myself to the chair in front of her desk.

"Oh, don't beat yourself up," she replied, never looking up from her computer screen. "We have bigger issues right now. Several members of the kitchen staff went AWOL in Miami, claiming nudism is against their religion, and now the executive chef is scrambling to fill the help he needs from other departments, insisting his emergency is everyone else's problem. He needs potato peelers and fruit slicers and dishwashers and bussers. On the other hand, housekeeping can't spare any of their staff as they are busier than ever, constantly replacing slipcovers in all the public venues."

I could feel their pain.

"Well," I said, "in any event, I would like to apologize to the captain and his girlfriend in person."

"Apologize? Are you serious, Marianne?" She looked up at me for the first time.

"Apparently, the scene that Miss Monaire created was more to the captain's disapproval than anything you may have done to precipitate it. He is sending her home from Cozumel, and I expect their engagement—if there ever was one—is off. For starters, he apparently was not overjoyed that she chose to join the captain's dinner at the last second in her birthday suit. There are certain lines that just aren't crossed at that level. Frankly, the officers were scandalized. They are wondering, if he can't control that loose cannon, how can he command an entire ship?"

I left Pauline and refocused on my plans for that day. It wasn't even eight o'clock yet, and my head was throbbing, probably from my unfulfilled caffeine addiction. The Mayan excursion was scheduled to meet on the pier in just over an hour, so I detoured by the Lido to grab a muffin and large coffee-to-go, still dragging along my luggage.

In my haste to leave my room that morning, I had thrown the escort packet from the excursion office into the wastebasket. I was hoping the housekeeping staff had not yet cleaned my room because now I needed it. When I entered the room, I noticed someone had been there, but not to clean. There on my coffee table was a bouquet of tropical flowers arranged beautifully in a crystal vase. The handwritten note attached said, "Sincere regrets," and was signed "Captain Gert Gurtigruten."

I emptied my suitcase, replenishing the closets and drawers and hanging all my scarves over the closet bar once more. Then I remembered unplugging the phone the night before and stooped down to reconnect it. I listened to the messages. There were five, and they were all from Angela. She sounded truly concerned and sorry and said the scene at the captain's table was not my fault. She kept asking me urgently to call her back. I thought a moment and then dialed her number.

"It's Marianne, Angela," I said, deflated. "Sorry, but I didn't answer my phone at all last night because all I wanted to do was to pack and get out of here. But they wouldn't let me disembark this morning. I just listened to all your messages now. I should have called you back last night."

"I was trying to reach you all night to tell you it was not your fault," she said urgently. "I found out that an updated list of names was submitted to the dining staff during the captain's reception, so the list I gave you would not have been useful even if you had submitted your name cards. Can I come to your room for a minute?" Angela pleaded.

She was at my door in two minutes flat. She started right in. "The list I gave you was the correct list of names," she said. "I have a strong suspicion that the last-minute list was submitted by the captain's companion while he was at his reception. Miss Fantina Monaire is a regular pain in the rump," she said. "The captain had intended to bring another woman, Ms. Shirley Hempstead, to the dinner and submitted her name well in advance. That was on the list I supplied for you. Miss Monaire probably wormed her way in and got the captain to bring her instead of Miss Hempstead at the last minute. There is no way she would have been allowed to board our ship with proper advanced notice. She slipped in through the cracks. She is a notorious drama queen, always causing scenes like last night. She has claimed to be 'affianced' to nearly every captain on the high seas and, believe me, I know because I have worked on virtually all the cruise lines over the years. It's too bad, because Captain Gurtigruten seems very nice. I bet he never saw this coming."

Then she looked at the bouquet on the coffee table. "From the captain, I take it," she said as she pointed approvingly.

"How did you know?" I asked, genuinely curious.

"I know them," she answered. "Take it from me. He has a dish of crow waiting for him and will have some answering to do for Miss Monaire's misbehavior. It isn't acceptable. Right now, he needs all the friends he can get. And I can guarantee *she* will be off the ship this morning, if she isn't already."

Then Angela looked at me with a totally different expression. "Are you interested in Captain Gurtigruten?" she ventured, studying my reaction. "You know, he is available, and he may be interested in you, Marianne. I think he is, in fact. This is an extravagant arrangement," she said as she pointed to the bouquet. "It wasn't just off the room-service menu, trust me there, I know. There might be more to these flowers than what you think."

"Not hardly likely," I laughed outright. The thought of it was preposterous. "I'm sure he's a very nice man and an excellent captain, but no, Angela, I'll leave him for someone else."

"So, you are still hopeful for Wink?" she asked. I had no idea she knew so much about me–us.

"That was the plan, actually. But we'd be lucky if we get to see each other for one day in Grand Cayman."

"Well, be careful what you wish for," she said. "Wink and Sorrenta have been very close in the past," she said as she crossed her fingers for emphasis. An unexpected stab shot through me at the mere mention of the name Sorrenta. It was evident she'd had her talons all over Wink on that last cruise. "Right now, Sorrenta is on the MS *Aphrodite*, probably working her own black magic to lure Wink back to her. She's really crazy about him."

When I heard that Sorrenta was on Wink's ship and actually working there, I almost felt my heart stop in my chest. I didn't know if the sudden reflex that took over was making me want to puke or gag. What was going on? Once again, I was knocked off balance and reeling from another left hook.

"Oh, you think Sorrenta really went to jail?" Angela went on, reading my mind. "Let me tell you something, Marianne, it is different out here. What guests see and what really goes on are usually very different stories. You didn't send Sorrenta to jail any more than you got me fired if that's what you're thinking," she said. "It doesn't work that way at all. I was on my way to this promotion all along. Even as director of human resources on this ship, Pauline doesn't have any control over my advancement at all in the cruise line because I have connections that are higher up in the corporate chain than she has. I've been here much longer, and it will take her a while to catch up." I almost detected a wink of her eye. "The same goes for Sorrenta. She is so talented and skilled, no one in their right mind would get rid of her. She may be temperamental and a floozy, but her desserts are legendary and bring people back to our ships—and that's the bottom line. Follow the money. Sorrenta is a cash cow.

"Anyway, you think you are not interested in pursuing Captain Gurtigruten right now, but that can change," she continued, a slow smile spreading across her lips. "I can tell you he is not going to keep Miss Monaire around here any longer. I can also tell you it's best to have some back-ups even if you think Wink is 'the one.' Leave it to me, Marianne. I'm going to find out for you if Captain Gurtigruten has his eye on you," she said conspiratorially. "Then, if you really want to stand by your Wink, you can make up your mind. But

I wouldn't rent the reception hall just yet! Consider Captain Gurtigruten. I mean, why wouldn't you? Right now, I know at least a dozen girls working in the boutiques and spas who would take a number to be next-in-line for him. But he has sent *you* flowers! Think about it." She picked up the vase and buried her nose in the flowers, taking a deep breath, as if the flowers themselves held a personal message from the captain.

10

Land of Swallows

Day Three: February 17, Wednesday
Cozumel, Mexico
Mostly Sunny: High: 86ºF/30ºC. Low: 67ºF/19ºC.

A SHORT WHILE LATER, I met up with my excursion group on the pier. In addition to our little dining clique, there were several nudists who had mercifully dressed before leaving the ship. We all boarded the bus, delighted to find it a brand-new one and hardly filled to half capacity. We could all spread out. The air conditioning worked, and the seats were clean and comfortable. There was even a bathroom at the back of the bus. It was going to be a good day!

Our local guide, Ramon, extended a warm welcome to his lovely island of Cozumel in the Mexican state of Quintana Roo. Then he introduced our driver, Miguel. Ramon said many of the people in Mexico were of Mayan ancestry, and he wanted to demonstrate why the Mayan descendants had so many reasons to be proud of their heritage.

As our bus left the pier area, Ramon told us Cozumel meant Land of Swallows and showed us a beautiful public sculpture of flying swallows along the busy street that paralleled the water's edge. He wove together a captivating story about the impressive accomplishments of the Maya, whose civilization stretched back more than four thousand years. By the time the Spanish conquistadors arrived in the early sixteenth century, Mayan people were still occupying parts of Mexico and Central America, including Cozumel. Over the millennia, the Maya undertook massive public projects that engaged their outstanding skills in the engineering and architecture of towering buildings and monuments. Intrepid observers of the natural world around them, they became accomplished astronomers and mathematicians. Ramon said their fascination with mathematics spilled over to the realm of time-telling, and they used calendars, still considered to be some of the most accurate in the world. In addition to their scientific accomplishments, the Maya produced incomparable art, leaving uncounted examples of beautiful and practical pottery, textiles, paintings and sculptures.

Then, suddenly and for reasons still debated by contemporary archaeologists, the vast and sophisticated Mayan city centers mysteriously declined almost simultaneously across the Mayan world. By AD 950, once bustling centers of trade and commerce and religious ceremonies were abandoned and left to the unstoppable forces of the ever-growing jungle that reclaimed and buried all they had accomplished for the next several centuries.

Ramon asked if we would like to hear some words in his native language. Everyone answered enthusiastically. He explained that there are nearly three dozen Mayan languages still spoken by the Mayan descendants. They are so distinct that they cannot be used or understood interchangeably. He said he grew up in a household with a Mayan mother and a Mexican father and learned Maya first and Spanish second. Still later, he learned English. He spoke a few sentences in his native Maya, called Yucatec, and said it was the home language of a significant portion of the populations in that part of Mexico. Other Mayan languages were more common in Central America. The Maya even developed a written language, using little symbols the archaeologists called *glyphs*. Literate scribes carved glyphs into stone monuments to record special historical events and glorify their rulers. They also developed a kind of paper from tree bark to make colorful, fully illustrated accordion-shaped books. The books recorded their entire culture, Mayan lifestyle, worldview, religion and great historic events. He called these Mayan books *codices* but said thousands were burned by order of a Spanish missionary in the sixteenth century. Only four of them escaped the destruction to find their way into European museums.

Someone asked if the Maya had anything equivalent to our Bible, and Ramon said as a matter of fact, they did. It was not exactly like what the Bible represents in our culture but a work of literature that contained the Mayan creation legend and explained the beginning of time in the Mayan worldview. He said it was called the *Popol Vuh* and considered the most important piece of Mesoamerican literature from the era before the Spanish conquest. While it was too complicated to examine in depth, he said it centered on the Hero Twins, young demigods. While symbolizing opposite forces in the universe like day and night, and life and death, their boyish antics resonated more readily as a modern-day action hero cartoon than a somber work of ancient literature.

I was getting excited about learning more about this amazing example of indigenous literature. I wondered if the ship library had a copy of the *Popol Vuh*.

Ramon said the Hero Twins faced off against the vicious gods of Xbalba, the dreaded underworld, outwitting their lethal traps and even playing the ancient ballgame against them. Mayan ball courts could be found all over the Mayan world, and nearly every Mayan ruin ever excavated had at least one ball court. The great temple at Chichén Itzá in Mexico had thirteen. The game was an essential element of Mayan life and culture, using a ball made from indigenous rubber that the Maya knew how to make bounce. Ramon said the rubber ball was an indigenous Mesoamerican invention that opened the floodgates to modern sports of today. He paused and invited us to run down the mental list of sports using bouncing rubber balls. It was hard to imagine a world of sports without balls that bounce.

The Maya called their ballgame Pok-Ta-Pok. It was a cross between our modern-day volleyball and basketball in playing and scoring. He said it was a ceremonial game, reserved for special events and sometimes staged as a replacement for a battle in war. But the Maya also enjoyed it as a pastime for leisure, and at those times, women could play too. Great rulers had to prove their leadership skills by excelling at the ballgame. The game required protective gear to shield the players from the hard rubber ball that weighed about ten pounds. Instead of hitting the ball directly with hands or feet or elbows, players hit it with a bone collar or girdle they wore under one arm or resting on a hip. They scored a goal by sending the ball through a stone ring, or tenon, protruding from the top of the ball-court wall. There were no quarters or halftimes or stretches in the game, and one goal was all it took to win. But since the diameter of the ball was only slightly smaller than the tenon hole, it could take all day to score!

Our driver, Miguel, slowed down and steered the bus carefully into a large parking complex where we saw a replicated Mayan village unfold with several circular thatch-roofed structures surrounding a large dirt courtyard. Plants abounded, either growing naturally or cultivated neatly around the huts in pots and baskets. He said we should feel free to stop in any of the Mayan domiciles where our gracious hosts would demonstrate some ancient skills like grinding corn on a heavy stone metate, flapping corn tortillas and playing indigenous musical instruments.

After a while, Ramon called us together and guided us along a manicured path with incense wafting at intervals, the haunting beat of a distant drum accompanied by the longing call of reed flutes beckoning us. We entered a modern arena designed to imitate an actual Mayan ball court. We settled into the bleacher-like seats on both ends of the long and narrow court as the reed flutes continued to pierce the air. The drums grew louder as a solitary drummer emerged from a thick cloud of smoke. His painted face and tattooed skin transformed him into the image of his own ancestor. As the music permeated the air, human chants added a shroud of mystery as we watched in total awe while a pageant of beautiful Mayans, young men and women, marched proudly in two parallel lines onto the ball court. They were dancing and stepping on bare feet, their ankles wrapped securely in wide cuffs adorned with little bells made from rattling seed pods.

At the onset of the game, two teams of men formed on opposite ends of the court, each player decked in exotic bird feathers and wearing lifelike animal heads of deer and jaguars and birds. Shiny silver wristlets glinted in the scorching Mexican sun as protective bone girdles and necklaces made from crocodile teeth and jaguar pelts flashed and swirled in timing with their quick-stepping feet. Their bronze skin was already wet and shining from sweating under the blistering sky. Their slick black long hair was pulled back into a dramatic ponytail, or scalp lock, in the ancient Mayan tradition. Smiling women tattooed with Mayan symbols strolled the perimeter of the ball court, holding up big clay bowls of incense as offerings to their ancient gods.

The game tested the players' athleticism. It also begged the spectators' patience because scoring a goal by getting the ball through a narrow stone ring required great skill. The teams smacked the ball back and forth, coming nail-bitingly close to a score every so often. We were completely swept up in the excitement. The same level of sustained energy and suspense that could galvanize a modern sports crowd overtook us as we watched this hair-raising reenactment. The only difference was that the ancient Maya played to the death because one team or the other would have ended up on the sacrificial altar.

The game continued in a fevered pitch of excitement that surprised us all. We watched on bated breath as the ball came tantalizingly close to the stone ring over and over again but only missed the mark by a hair. The crowd roared when it almost went through but bounced back a couple of times. The players retreated at intervals to hold their feet over a hot fire in a demonstration of bravura as dancers came out in costumes resembling deer and birds chased each other around the fire to the sounds of rattles and reed horns. The drummer thumped out his ominous rhythms continuously from his smoky perch overlooking the scene while more women covered in tattoos, their long hair embellished with colorful bird feathers, walked to the edge of the spectators' area, wafting bowls of incense.

It could have gone on for hours, but these teams were determined to make a goal for us. They were working very hard, and their bronze skin, oiled to protect them from the sun, glistened with their perspiration. Glistening rivulets of sweat were pouring down their foreheads and pooling in their collarbones. When they moved, the beads of sweat shot off and scattered wildly like liquid fireworks. They grunted and growled at their opponents, and yet that ball was not going through the ring. Ramon sat confidently talking with the guide from another bus. They were smiling and talking very fast.

Suddenly, the ball popped up and headed straight for the bleachers. Before anyone could see it coming, it found its target with a painful impact on the shoulder of one man in our group. I could hear the anguished yelp from the receiving end. I rushed over to help. Ramon was next to me in a flash.

"Are you okay?" I asked the guest. Of course he was not okay.

11

Balls and Chocolate

"I'M FINE," THE MAN SAID with a tinge of hostility. "And don't come after me with your damn injury report," he barked gruffly. I could see he was in pain, and the point of impact was already welting and red. Ramon asked if he would like to see an urgent-care doctor downtown, assuring him that Cozumel is very modern and has the best hospital facilities anywhere.

"Hell no!" the guest replied. "Did I make myself clear? I will be fine." He sat there in obvious discontent.

"Well, if you change your mind," I said, "I'll accompany you to the infirmary when we return to the ship. I do need to have your name and room number, though."

"The hell you do, lady!" he yelled. "That's the last thing I need or want on top of an injury—another monstrous bill from a blasted cruise ship doctor! I'm not even sure if it's a real doctor or some voodoo witch doctor shaman you scrounged up under some godforsaken scrub on some abandoned island somewhere in the Sargasso Sea."

Okay, now he was overdoing it. If he hadn't been in such pain, I think we both would have had a good laugh. I retreated respectfully, figuring it was better not to rub salt in the wound, but I really did need his name and room number. Ramon came up to me quietly and supplied me with the information based on his signature on the waiver we had all signed at the start of the bus tour.

"Dr. Elmer Spin," I wrote on an injury report. "Room #9609." I described the setting and the injury and the patient's response along with his option to decline assistance. I took a picture of the ball court where the impact happened, and made a mental note to take a close-up of the offending rubber ball after the performance.

The show ended on the very next play with a dramatic goal to the unrestrained cheers of the fans. It seemed to come off so effortlessly that I wondered if the teams were skilled enough to put on this extravaganza and come through with the grand finale at will. They certainly timed it right, I thought as I went to take more pictures of the accident scene and the ball.

On our walk back to the bus, the question returned just as to who exactly would have been sacrificed in the ancient days, the winner or loser of the game. Ramon explained that, by many accounts, it could be that the triumphant team went proudly to their deaths because the gods only wanted the best sacrificed to them – the winners! Ramon explained that the Maya believed there were seven levels in the underworld, and each level presented a challenge or trap that departed souls had to overcome in order to pass to the next level. It sounded like a rite of passage, only after you died. He said this was played out in the *Popol Vuh*, where the Hero Twins had to fend off vampire bats, voracious jaguars and talking mosquitoes. He said there were only three conditions of death that could override the traps of the underworld. They were dying in battle, perishing in childbirth, or being sacrificed in a ritual after winning the ballgame.

I thought it was stunning that a glorious victory could buy early death and a shortcut through the underworld and wondered if any Mayan teams had ever considered faking a loss, just to live.

At the bus, Miguel was handing out cold bottles of water from an icy cooler. That surely hit the spot under the Mexican sun-furnace, even though more than one guest asked if he had any Coronas in the cooler. Once we were seated and Miguel steered the bus out of the parking lot, Ramon continued with his narrative. He asked us what kinds of chocolate we liked. "Swiss!" someone shouted out. "Dutch!" was another answer. "Belgian!" came from another part of the bus. "French!" was yet another response. Ramon nodded knowingly and said everyone always answers that question the same way.

Then he asked, "Did you know that chocolate was never even known in Europe before the age of Columbus? Did you know that the plant that provides chocolate came from this part of the world, and it was guarded and protected by the Mayan royalty?"

He held up a strange-looking object he called a cacao pod. He said that some Maya worshipped a goddess of chocolate whose name was Ixcacao. The cacao pod was about the size and shape of a football, its surface fluted. He said these pods grow off the trees in many places in Mexico, especially farther south in Central America like Guatemala and Belize. He said inside the pods are big thick disks surrounded and connected by a white mucous-like film. These, he told us, were the beans from which we get chocolate. He then held up a cacao pod that had been cracked open. The shell was very tough. He pulled the beans away from the mass and started passing them around.

"Go ahead," he said. "They're not poisonous. In fact, they taste a little like chocolate. People in this part of the world actually suck on these beans as a snack." A few people reached out to try one. I wanted to see one close up, so I raised my hand too.

"The thing about chocolate to the Maya," Ramon continued, "is that it was only consumed as a beverage, and reserved exclusively for the royal families. They made a big deal about preparing it properly, and they used very tall and narrow clay pots that looked more like vases to pour the liquid back and forth until it worked up a froth. Archaeologists have found dozens of these pots in Central America that still contained microscopic traces of chocolate! The chiefs drank chocolate as a special treat for important ceremonies like ascendancy to the throne."

"When did chocolate candy bars come out?" someone asked.

"A good question," Ramon answered. "Solid chocolate was introduced in the mid-nineteenth century by a company in Bristol, England. In 1849, Cadbury introduced their first chocolate bar. There's also a difference between how chocolate tasted to the Maya and the way we like it today. The Maya added piquant flavors like chili peppers. Today, of course, we prefer it flavored with vanilla and lots of sugar."

Another question from the back of the bus. "Do they produce chocolate anywhere in Central America today?"

"As a matter of fact they do, and you will have the chance to sample some of the boutique brands of chocolate at our next stop. They are more expensive, to be sure, but they are high quality and come from the chocolate beans that the Mayan descendants grow right here. They cultivate them in small groves, just as their ancestors did."

By now, I was hankering for a piece of chocolate and happy to descend from the bus to watch the chocolate-making demonstration. We went inside a small building and took our seats on wooden bleachers surrounding a stage with a demonstration kitchen. Ramon got our attention once we were all seated and introduced his good friend, Pedro, who demonstrated how the cacao was ground and mixed to make a liquid drink. He showed us the tall vases that the ancient Mayans used to transfer the liquid chocolate back and forth to build up a froth the way they liked it. But he said these days the Mexicans use a wooden whisk. Pedro held one up, calling it a molinillo or a little mill. It looked like an ornately carved rattle on a long handle and worked like a beater when he whisked it through the liquid chocolate. In no time, the molinillo produced a frothy top. He said the Mayans savored that head and showed us an ancient painting that suggested a Mayan ruler discussing the froth on his chocolate beverage with his cook. After the demonstration, we sampled little cups of the liquid chocolate in various flavors in the adjacent shop and browsed among displays of locally made chocolate bars, interspersed with colorful bottles of Mexican tequila in a mind-boggling array of flavors.

By the time we returned to the bus, we were all chattering happily between enthusiastic bites of our chocolate bars. One man, who had been to my Show and Tell the morning before, introduced himself as Hal. He suggested people bring their tequila and chocolate to the next Show and Tell, and everyone share and share alike. I tried to remember Hal from the crowd of the morning before, but it was difficult to recall someone when the first time you saw them they weren't wearing anything at all. I was a little sorry that the nudism thing was such a barrier because I found these folks as engaging and delightful as anyone, and maybe smarter than most. I just couldn't get past the nudity.

Then, it suddenly dawned on me. Maybe it was my problem! I determined to soldier on and get to know as many of these wonderful people as I could and work my way past their lifestyle choice. I didn't have to join them, but I could still appreciate them for who they were, even if I had a hard time focusing above their necks. I determined to have a better attitude about it.

As we lined up to board the ship, staff members dressed as Mayan rulers wearing colorful headdresses and loincloths flanked our queue on both sides. They were holding up colorful signs that said, Afternoon Delight Happening Now! Mayan Body Painting Ritual! Get Your Personal Chocolate Tattoo!

Reinvigorated, guests eagerly ascended the gangway to check out this latest novelty.

12

A Little Favor

ONCE ABOARD, I stopped in the office to submit my trip report. Oscar was at his desk, so I explained the accident at the ballgame reenactment and told him the guest was not willing to let me write an injury report, but I hoped he would visit the ship's doctor on his own. I returned to my room for a shower and then went upstairs for some lunch in the Lido. We were in port for a very long day, so I still had time to explore downtown Cozumel.

When I returned to my room after lunch to collect my purse and camera, the phone light was blinking. The message was from the ship's nurse in the infirmary. Apparently, Dr. Spin did check into the infirmary upon his return from the excursion, and the ship doctor wanted me to supply some more details from the accident. Good thing I had taken those pictures. I went directly to the infirmary with my camera. The nurse at the desk asked me to take a seat, saying the doctor was with a patient but wanted to see me immediately after.

I couldn't have waited for more than five minutes before the nurse asked me to follow her to the doctor's office. There, I was greeted by a stout woman with short dark hair and oversized black-rimmed glasses. Judging from her portly stature, it was fairly evident that this woman liked to dine. She smiled warmly and beckoned me to the empty chair.

"I'm Dr. Messina Carver," she said hastily. "Everyone who knows me calls me Dr. Messy, and you should too," she said without cracking a smile. I had to restrain a smile because it was apparent to me that from the unkempt order of books, clipboards and file folders piled precariously on top of each other, not to mention soiled coffee mugs and assorted medical accoutrements I took for check-up and surgical instruments jumbled in random heaps, she quite aptly lived up to her nickname.

"You accompanied that tour this morning where Dr. Elmer Spin was accidentally smacked in the shoulder by that Mayan ball. Regrettable, but he'll live." She didn't sound very worried. "He's not a medical doctor, by the way. He comes on these cruises fairly often and keeps a low profile, but if you can keep this to yourself, he's actually a former diplomat for Vatican City. It's the smallest country in the world. Google it if you don't believe me. Go ahead, check my facts," she challenged. "Anyway, he stopped by for a social visit because we know each other from prior cruises, and he weaseled a free check-up out of me that way. I think he was more interested in learning who's who on this cruise. He was more surprised than injured, but those rubber balls can be lethal. The real ones, that is. They only use fake ones for the reenactment games. They have a lot of give, so while it certainly must have appeared that he was in a lot of pain, I can assure you he will survive."

This was all very interesting, but I wasn't quite catching why she invited me. She didn't have to tell me any of this. As if reading my mind, she asked, "You probably are wondering why I wanted to see you?"

"I'm glad to know Dr. Spin is okay," I said. "It did look like a pretty painful impact."

"The noise is much worse than the effect," she assured me. "But let me come to the point. I have a little favor to ask. I was planning to leave the ship to collect an order of medical supplies they're holding for me here in Cozumel. But there were a couple of injuries apart from Dr. Spin's that held me up, and now I have to fill out a rasher of reports. I won't be able to collect that order myself, so I was wondering if you would do me the honor. We're in port until nine this evening, and the whole errand shouldn't take you more than forty-five minutes round-trip. That should still give you plenty of time to explore downtown Cozumel because it's just past one-thirty now."

"Of course, I'd be happy to help, Dr. Carver," I

said. "We passed the hospital on our excursion, and I remember it's not very far from the port."

"Call me Dr. Messy," the doctor snapped. "And you won't be going to the hospital for this shipment. It's too complicated with security measures and all. The order has been sent to the Cozumel Island Museum instead. It's on the main boulevard that parallels the shoreline—the big building across from the waterfront. You can't miss it. In my earlier days, when I wasn't carrying around so much weight, I could walk it in twenty-five minutes from here and shop for souvenirs along the way. You'll have time to walk around Cozumel, do a little shopping, then pick it up and return to the ship in plenty of time. The museum stays open until six today."

I said I'd be happy to help and promised to have her package back in a few hours.

"No rush," she said. "Oh, and by the way, don't be surprised if you have to sign some purchase orders. It's the usual protocol. You know how things are in these dang foreign ports."

I guessed I was supposed to know how things were in these dang foreign ports, so I agreed as if I were an old hand at collecting medical supplies from museums in strange offshore places and signing for them. I was happy to help.

I took my time strolling down the same long pier I'd traversed earlier with my excursion, only this time observed the sights around me. The skyline of low-rise adobe-style buildings framed by palm trees looked charming in its tropical setting. A huge Mexican flag flapped lazily in the scant breeze on the water's edge. I rode the big outdoor escalator up to a platform suffocating with silver jewelry shops, one after another, and walked past friendly vendors assuring me their wares were so cheap they were "almost free." A catwalk took me over the street and past another village of shops selling silver, leather and souvenirs as well as several farmacias advertising Fosamax, Zoloft, Wellbutrin, Amoxicillin and the inevitable Viagra and Cialis. Another escalator took me back down to street level where I turned right on the sidewalk that paralleled the water's edge. On both sides of the busy street, the lineup of taxicabs and horse-drawn surreys stood at the ready to take visitors around Cozumel, the drivers chatting quietly together waiting for their next fares. Endless rows of shops selling leather boots, tequila, silver jewelry, clay pots, painted maracas and hammocks lined the street competing for the attention of throngs of milling tourists. Most would buy a couple trinkets and a postcard and end up at Señor Frog's or one of the sidewalk watering holes for margaritas and nachos. I stopped in one store whose front caught my attention with a metal sculpture of a comical burro wearing a sombrero.

Inside I found an inviting and colorful assortment of handcrafted home accessories. They were made out of papier mâché, clay, textile, stone and wood, and all very colorfully painted in typical Mexican primary colors—bright and happy. I gravitated toward a small display of kitchen utensils where there was an assortment of those wooden chocolate whisks that Pedro had used at the chocolate demonstration earlier that day. The little sign said *Molinillo 50.47 Pesos*. I asked the cashier how much that was in US dollars, and she said two dollars and fifty cents. What a deal! The hardest part about that purchase was deciding which one to select because they were all individually carved and slightly different sizes, each having a character all its own.

13

Sidewalk Spat

MY CELLPHONE came to life just as I was wrapping up my purchase. I was surprised, but then remembered my phone plan covered calls in Canada and Mexico. I answered it as I continued to the museum which was only a few blocks away. The familiar voice on the other end sounded like it was walking right next to me. "Wink!" I shouted. "Where the heck are you? You sound like you're right here in Cozumel!"

"So good to hear you, girl," he said. "I'm great now that I'm finally talking to you! By the way, before I forget, did you ever get my carry-on suitcase to a post office?"

God, he was annoying. What was in that thing he wanted back so badly anyway? I wondered.

"Well, I thought I could give it to you in Grand Cayman," I said.

"Okay," he acquiesced. "That's probably the quickest route now since you put it off this long."

This long? I thought. *Excuuuuse me, Your Royal Highness Bigshot, but I've been a little absorbed with other things since I was with Your Highness the last time. Like getting on a ship after a humiliating mix-up with the wrong ship, nearly causing an international incident at the captain's formal dinner, escorting a tour where a guest got smacked by a Mayan ball, and now picking up medical supplies from a Mexican museum for the ship's doctor. Oh, and yes, I also found out that you are back working on a ship with Sorrenta—let me repeat that—with Sorrenta! And you had the gall to deny you were ever close to her when I confronted you on the last cruise.*

I only thought that, though. The coward that I am said, "Sorry about that, Wink. I'll be sure to bring it to shore with me at Grand Cayman."

"Before I forget, I already mailed your carry-on to the address on your luggage tag," he said. "I don't know how the bags got switched like that." I remembered with a shudder that I had put one of Seth's luggage tags on my carry-on after the strap on mine broke at the last minute. Now the bag would be sent to Seth's house instead of mine. Talk about a mortifying mix-up!

"So, how have you been?" Wink jabbered on merrily. "I didn't even know they were bringing you back to the *Minerva*. That's really something that they swooped you up for a job so fast. You are really amazing, kid! It must have been a surprise!"

"You could say that," I said. "I don't know if anyone told you, but it's a charter cruise full of nudists.

They call themselves naturists, but either way they are pretty much not wearing anything."

"Well, it's a lifestyle," Wink said. I wondered if he'd ever tried it.

"I tried it myself once. Can't say I didn't like it either, to be honest. Feel free to try it during the cruise. Safest place in the world is right there on the cruise ship. No nicer people anywhere. If you like it, we might try it together some time," he said, laughing. "I could think of all sorts of things to do with you on a nudie cruise," he said and laughed.

"Maybe you'd like Sorrenta to join us," I blurted out. I honestly didn't know where the outburst came from.

"Wh-what?"

I didn't answer.

"Marianne? Girl, are you still there?"

I paused good and long before continuing, "Angela is back on the MS *Minerva*." I didn't know what I was planning to say next, but it all tumbled out anyway. "She wasn't fired–noooo. Instead, she's here at work, and now she's my boss! She told me you're on the MS *Aphrodite* with Sorrenta, and you two used to be *really close*. You never told me any of that, Wink. So now you don't have to go through this pathetic and tiresome act with me just to get your blanking suitcase back!"

Now he was the one pausing. I waited.

"I'm having a hard time with this connection, Marianne," he finally said. "I didn't hear most of what you just said. And the part I did hear didn't make any sense. Tell you what, kiddo, I've gotta run to a meeting right now, but I'll send you an email a little later. Bye now. Love ya." He clicked off before I could reply.

Love ya, my tuckus, I thought, as visions of Sorrenta's lacquered nails clutching his shirt and drawing his mouth to her shimmering red lips hijacked my imagination. I hung up and figured, good riddance.

Besides, I had a backup.

తతత

Just as Dr. Messy had described, the museum building was big and hard to miss. I checked in at the registration desk, explaining that I was there to pick up an order of medical supplies for the doctor on the MS *Minerva*. The young male attendant appeared confused and got on the phone, asking me to wait for a moment. Before long, a gentleman appeared, inviting me to take my time looking around the museum while they prepared the order. I found that curious because Dr. Messy seemed to imply it would be ready and waiting for me. But then again, this was one of those dang foreign ports where everything is done on a different agenda. I took the man up on his offer and walked along the exhibits. He assured me they would find me when the package was ready. The museum was not too big, he smiled.

I made my way through the various rooms and

exhibits. It started with the earliest geologic emergences of Cozumel and segued to the early indigenous people with exhibits that showcased incredibly old artifacts, tools and implements made from stone and bones. Gradually, it moved through the era of the Maya to the early Spanish explorers and Hernan Cortes, who used Cozumel as a jumping-off point before heading for the Mexican mainland where he conquered the Aztecs in 1521.

There was also an exhibit about Ix Chel, the patron goddess of women and weavers. In ancient times, Mayan women made a once-in-a-lifetime pilgrimage to worship at her temple right there in Cozumel. I was in another world completely as I gravitated back to the entrance and walked by the gift shop display. There, I saw a display of the *Popol Vuh*, the book of the Mayan creation legend Ramon had referenced a few times during our excursion. Without a second thought, I bought a copy.

The man who had greeted me earlier showed up and said they were ready for me to take Dr. Messy's order back to the ship. I held out my hands, expecting to receive a small box. He smiled and motioned for me to follow him to the parking lot behind the museum. There, he told me the order had been loaded into the back of a truck. I had to wonder how much stuff was in that order. He said I could ride up front with the driver, but first I needed to sign the purchase order form. It was about five pages long and in tiny Spanish text. It required my home address, phone number, date of birth, citizenship, passport number, email address, ship's name and my room number. They only fell short of asking for my social security number and college GPA. I remembered Dr. Messy assuring me this was "protocol" in these dang foreign ports and signed everything they asked of me. The man passed the signed papers to the parking lot attendant sitting in the little booth near the exit. From my fleeting glance, he could have been Dr. Percival Turnkey's identical twin, except for a big, bushy moustache.

The ride back to the ship was quick and the driver jolly and friendly. He talked about his granddaughter, who was turning nine the next day, and the party he and his wife were planning for her. He laughed softly as he anticipated the surprise on the girl's face the moment she was to see all her friends. He planned to dress up like a clown and give the children balloons and little gifts and help them break the colorful burro piñata his wife had purchased. His childlike excitement was touching. I marveled at how we take ourselves too seriously as adults sometimes. He never stopped smiling, lost in his sweet thoughts about making his granddaughter happy, until we arrived at the pier. Then he instructed me to leave the truck because he had to take the order to the cargo loading area where guests weren't allowed. I climbed down from the passenger side and watched as he drove on. When he stopped, the cargo door opened on the ship and, from my angle, it looked like the profile of Dr. Messy waiting there. The next thing I saw was a crate being heaved by two crewmen and carried into the ship.

From where I stood, it looked like a coffin.

14

Bravo! Again

I PUT THOSE CRAZY THOUGHTS aside and went back to my room to examine and admire my beautiful new molinillo. Even though I couldn't predict the next time I would be stirring Mayan chocolate into a froth, pretty things always made me happy, and this simple kitchen implement was a handmade work of art. Besides, it might come in handy to whip up a cup of Nesquik. I placed it on my coffee table, where I could continue to enjoy seeing it for the rest of the cruise.

The phone rang just then. It was Dr. Messy.

"Thanks very much for helping me today," she said. "I wonder if you'd care to join me for dinner tomorrow evening."

"Very much so," I said, reminding myself to inform my dining companions that I would not be joining them the following night.

"Great!" she said. "Eight o'clock in the Taipei Room on Deck 12. Have you dined there?"

"Actually, I have not," I said, recalling that I'd

meant to try some of the ship's so-called special restaurants on the last cruise, but was too enmeshed in the drama that awaited me every night at my own table. I'd privately named it Gilligan's Table because everyone there resembled someone from the old TV series.

"Well, it'll be my treat," she said, alluding to the fact that there was a nominal charge in those restaurants. "Oh, and by the way," she added casually, "things being what they are in these dang foreign ports, there was something that didn't make it in time for the Cozumel pickup. They promised it will be waiting for us in Costa Maya tomorrow instead. Same country, different port. I'm wondering if you'd help me one more time in bringing that order back to the ship too. Same protocol as today, except you can collect it right at the farmacia on the boardwalk in the little village of Majahual. It's a quick trolley ride from the ship, just two miles from our port, and they will arrange your return trip with the supplies. Won't take twenty minutes, so you can spend the day doing whatever you want and have plenty of time for it before all-aboard. I checked, and we don't leave until six o'clock, and that's well after everything closes up."

"Sure," I said. "I'd be happy to help," although I was wondering if I meant it.

With that, I suddenly remembered that I had not made any plans for the following day in Costa Maya. I went directly to see Oscar in the excursion office. He appeared as though he'd been waiting for me. "We already booked you on the Chacchoben Mayan ruins excursion," he said. "It's our most popular excursion at this port, and there will be seven busloads. If you can get your friends to book it too, we'll make sure you're all on the same bus together. All the buses leave the ship and arrive at the site together, so if there are any incidents, you will be the staff representative to handle any of them. Hopefully, tomorrow will go better than today did, though."

I thanked him and noticed the early starting time of seven-thirty. It would run until noon and that should still leave me plenty of time to collect Dr. Messy's order. I returned to my room to drop off the escort packet and still had a couple hours before dinner, so I checked the *Tides* to see what might be going on right then. It was four-thirty, and there were still lots of afternoon activities in full swing, including bingo, trivia, pool deck contests, a lecture and afternoon tea. Aha! I thought—perfect timing to catch a spot of tea and see my friends in the string quartet that I'd come to know so well on the last cruise. Hopefully, they were all there and no one was mysteriously missing this time around.

I entered the Paris Lounge to the welcoming sound of that beautiful and gifted foursome of classically trained string musicians hailing from places like the Ukraine, Serbia and Romania. They were playing an upbeat rendition of "New York! New York!" They had about fifteen minutes left in their program, and I wanted to greet them in the moments after they finished before they went to the next venue. I wasn't sure any of them knew I was back on board the ship. The room was loud with the festive chattering and clickity-clacking of people stirring tea in china cups and sampling tempting sandwiches and sweets. What caught me by surprise this time was that I'd hardly noticed the public nudity. Bareness and skin everywhere were starting to become visual white noise, and I was happy to accept that I was subliminally working beyond my issues with it. Everyone seemed to be having a wonderful time, and as I searched for an empty seat, a couple motioned for me to join them.

"You probably don't recognize us like this," the man said, waving his hand, "but we were on your bus this morning." I'm Burt Smothers, and this is my wife, Lily."

"Pleased to meet you," I said. "And no, I did not recognize you, but I'm happy you called me over here to join you. What did you think about our excursion?" I asked.

"Not bad," Burt said. "A little heavy on the chocolate and tequila hawking . . . but that was at the end, and it didn't take away from the ballgame. That was sensational!"

"We also really liked our guide," Lily added. She had a very pleasant voice, the kind you wouldn't mind listening to in an audio book. "What was his name, honey?"

"Raul?" Burt said. "No, wait a minute. Raymundo, I think."

"It was Ramon," I offered. "I only know because I had to write it down in the report I submitted."

"Did you find out anything about that guy who got smacked in the shoulder with that Mayan ball?" Burt asked.

"Yes, and fortunately he'll be okay," I said. I didn't want to add any details, uncertain if HIPAA laws applied at sea. Better to play safe, I thought.

"Well, that was a shock. But other than that, we thought the whole thing was at least a four-and-a-half stars out of five."

We chatted lightly for the remainder of the tea. They were from Baltimore where he ran the family business of printing big signs for billboards, marquees and sport arenas. They wanted to share how they became involved in the nudist community and dove right in to tell me their story, without my asking. Burt said it was a client of his that turned him on to it in the very beginning. That was when he was married to his first wife. "She went along and tried it but never felt comfortable," he said. "I never understood why not," he added, shaking his head. "She'd putz around the house in huge, puffy pink slippers with nothing on but her underwear. She'd cook and clean and tend to her garden in the backyard like that. Once I came home and found her vacuuming the floor totally nude. It was a turn-on for me, I'll be honest. But she could never quite jump the line to feel comfortable about it with strangers. On the other hand, I loved it from the start!

Nothing like feeling comfortable in your own skin and not wearing binding clothes that chafe and pull and tug and only remind you that you're enjoying your meals a little too much. Nothing wrong with that!"

"No, there's not," Lily said, tweaking his stomach playfully. I noticed her fingers dusted lightly below his paunch, and their eyes met.

"Ooh!" he said. "Maybe we should go straight to our room." They laughed, and he went on. "That's what I love about this. It's so spontaneous and direct. And we're all adults here, right?

"Anyway, Julia—that was my first wife's name—couldn't adopt this lifestyle, no matter how much I tried to help her. I think she wanted to accept it for a while, too, but in the end, we both had to make a decision. I mean, there was no way I was letting go of this scene, and I absolutely love the people in this community. We've come to know so many, and they've become very close friends. Then he looked at Lily and repeated, very close, "Right, honey?"

"Right-o!" she said as she patted his hairy chest.

"Well, in the end, I guess I made a decision about my own life. I figured I couldn't live without my new lifestyle, but I could always get a new wife." They both laughed. "And you know what? I was right! And here's the proof!" He hugged her. "Lily and I met at a naturist meet-and-greet in Punta Cana about six months after my divorce. And gosh, it was love at first sight. We were playing on opposite sides in a big beach volleyball match. In fact, I can remember exactly what she was wearing that first time I laid my eyes on her, can't I, baby?" They both exploded in laughter.

"Tell her the best part!" Lily urged, nudging him with her shoulder.

"Well, come to find out, a couple days later, we were playing another beach volleyball game with a new group from the resort, and guess who was playing on the other side this time?"

I couldn't.

"None other than Julia, my ex-wife, and her new husband! Turns out, they had been getting it on from our very first naturist meet-and-greet. In fact, they got married a month before we did." He slapped his knee and started laughing. "And to think she had me so fooled to believe she didn't like being undressed in front of strangers."

"I just love it every time you say that story, babe," said Lily. "It always makes me think of how we met that first time at that volleyball game."

"Well, to answer your earlier question, Marianne," Burt said, turning away from Lily as he kept a tight grasp on her forearm, "we loved that Mayan ballgame, but we're probably a bit biased because we met playing volleyball. In fact, I'm getting a hankering for a little ballgame reenactment right now," he added as they left with hasty goodbyes.

The string quartet lingered over their last note before collecting their music from the music stands. They were smiling and talking quietly amongst themselves. I walked over and stood there to watch their expressions when they saw me. "Oh! Marianne!" Sabrina was the first to look up. Danita and Valetta saw me next, and everyone jumped up for one big group hug.

"I'm baaaack," I said. "But, happily, I will be leaving the real professionals to create their beautiful music without me. And please, let's keep it that way this time," I joked. You all look stunning, and I'm so happy to see you all together!"

"At least you're not seeing us in the altogether!" quipped Mario, the only male in the group. "I've been on these clothing-optional charters before. It all gets a little old after a while," he said. I told him I was already getting used to it, and it frankly was starting to feel like yesterday's news.

I asked them what was new, and they said, aside from starting a new cruise with no one mysteriously missing from their group, not much. Except for the fact that now they had a new name for the quartet. "Bravo! String Quartet," Valetta said proudly. "They're making us a little tripod sign to put in front of us while we are playing around the ship."

I wished them well for the cruise and promised to stop by now and then to see them. Then I went to the piano lounge to watch Guess the Song. The pianist, Nolan, was apparently playing up to the baby boomers in his audience. Today's guessing game was all about identifying those old tunes from the popular TV sitcoms from the 1960s. I could identify them because they were still playing the reruns when I was growing up. I had no problem recognizing theme songs from *I Love Lucy*, *The Andy Griffith Show*, *My Three Sons*, *Bewitched*, *Green Acres*, *Leave it to Beaver*, *Mr. Ed*, *Flipper* and of course *Gilligan's Island*. By the end of the game, I'd wished that I had joined a team. I aced all the songs. I thought back to the miserable display of ignorance I'd exhibited during the trivia games of the prior cruise and regretted that I'd chosen to play trivia instead of joining a team for Guess the Song.

Back in my room, I went to my laptop to check my email and, sure enough, there was a long message from Wink. This time, instead of obsessing about that suitcase of his, he sounded more like the old Wink I had come to know and grown to love once upon a time. He started out by saying how excited he was that I was back on the ship, and he was trying to switch things around so he could actually join the MS *Minerva* in Grand Cayman and stay through Cuba and Key West. I was starting to feel relieved that he had not heard my outburst on the phone when he added, "Just so you know—and in case anyone tells you secondhand—I don't want you to think there's any more to this than there is, but Sorrenta is on the ship here. I honestly didn't know or even notice until we were seated together for the officers' night dinner."

He had a lot of explaining to do.

15

Matchmaker! Matchmaker!

DINNERTIME CAME and I joined my friends at a round table by a window with a lovely view of Cozumel. The setting sun cast a golden aura over the entire skyline and water's surface. Another cruise ship was departing, and we could see it slowly break its way across the water while it blew a farewell honk.

I started by saying that Oscar had booked me on the Chacchoben Mayan Ruin excursion and invited everyone to book the same one, and they would be sure to seat us on the same bus.

"We've already figured that one out," Annie said. "We all showed up together at the excursion desk, asked where you were going, booked at the same time and told them we wanted to be on your bus."

"Awww, that's just fantastic," I said. I was genuinely flattered. I looked around the table. We were all present: the Clarksons, the Alberts, the Ringlers and Dr. Turnkey. I tried to imagine him with a bushy moustache but threw the thought aside, feeling altogether silly for even entertaining such absurd notions. I complimented him on the Mayan shirt he was wearing, this time with various shades of blue embroidery down the front placket, and he said it was another shirt Millie had given him. I thought I detected a price tag dangling inside his sleeve but couldn't be sure. While our waiter was passing around menus, another waiter ushered a new couple to our table, introducing them as Russ and Sonya Cook. Both waiters scrambled to squeeze two more chairs and place settings at our table as we welcomed the newcomers.

"What next?" Russ exclaimed as soon as they were seated. "I never in my life would have believed it."

"We had no idea. When we boarded the other day, we had to go directly into quarantine," Sonya explained. "We'd just come from an African safari, and there was a virus the CDC thought we may have been exposed to—so the ship allowed us to board only if we agreed to self-quarantine for forty-eight hours. Once we emerged from our room and realized we were in the Garden of Eden, I swear we headed straight back to our quarantine.

"I thought we'd have to stay in our room the entire time, but we called the concierge, Franklin, and he very helpfully told us there was a small group of mainstream guests onboard and to look you all up for dinner," Sonya said. "He didn't quite say 'normal,' but we read between the lines."

"You weren't hard to find once we got here," Russ

added. "Thank goodness! I've heard of cruises from hell, but this is ridiculous. No warning about it whatsoever when we booked."

Annie interrupted suddenly. "No, I have to disagree. They did tell everyone this was a charter cruise. They just didn't explain the nature of it, but fine print said that charters are customized to the specifics of the paying charter host and may not always be to everyone's tastes. I've done a lot of thinking about this, and I think these nudists or naturists or whatever they want to call themselves certainly have their rights, even if we may disagree. Where else are they supposed to go as a community if they can't buy their own cruise and go out to sea, for crying out loud? Let's be fair, guys."

"She's right," Sally chimed in. "There are conventions, websites, support groups, magazines and communities for every kind of hobby or interest or personality type or other self-defined identity on the planet. Why should these folks be denied that same consideration? They're not violent; they just want to walk around without the restraints of clothes. Let them have their day and their cruise."

I was stunned. It sounded like Annie and Sally were taking a second look at things and—dare I say it—coming around to a new point of view.

Then Max pitched in. "It's not as if they are hostile or unruly. They've been very pleasant, and you'd have a hard time coming by a more educated and cultured group—lifestyle choice notwithstanding—randomly. I don't think any of us could complain about the ones that were on our excursion today."

"Say what you will, I think it's disgusting. Now, let me say words can't express how pleased we are to join your table," Russ said.

"Well, we are glad you're here, Russ and Sonya," I said. We went around the table introducing ourselves for their sake. At the end of dinner, we walked, *en famille,* the length of the ship to the theater where the evening show was to start momentarily. Along the way, we passed couples and groups browsing in the elegant boutiques, admiring expensive watches and designer perfumes in the sparkling windows and examining outlandish handbags with prices that you would only find in an exotic port or in a cruise ship boutique. We passed the freshly incorporated Bravo! String Quartet, their new little tripod sign placed politely to one side. I waved, but no one noticed me as they were absorbed in playing "Flight of the Bumblebee" right then.

Inside the theater, we easily located an entire row of empty seats because there was only a sprinkling of people in the audience. I assumed everyone else was reveling in the nonstop parties, dances and games arranged by Perry Cardis and happening simultaneously in venues throughout the ship and out on the pool deck. I recalled the prior cruise when even ten minutes before showtime the theater was already stuffed to standing room only. You could count this audience on your fingers and toes.

The energetic production team presented "High Tide Meets Broadway," their costumes shimmering in glitter and glitz that sparkled like a roving disco ball as they moved around the stage singing and dancing like clockwork in time with the band. They acted as one cohesive organism and kept us in their thrall the entire time. I recognized all of them from the last cruise but had to admit, I couldn't remember all their names. The show ended with a thunderous shower of applause from a small but appreciative audience. Perry Cardis appeared on the stage instead of Pearl to introduce the cast for their curtain call. He was wearing another over-sized bow tie blinking with bright yellow and red lights, his fluorescent green undies and black knee socks held up by those ridiculous black elastic garters. He invited the audience to another party-and-midnight-buffet in the Paris Lounge. I'm not really sure if anyone from our group ended up going, but as we filed out of the theater, we all agreed to meet at the pier the next morning for the excursion to Chacchoben.

Just as I turned away from them to head for the staircase, Angela sprang on me from around the corner as if she'd been scoping me out. "There you are!" she whispered, smiling as she accompanied me back to my room. "I saw you with all your friends, but I need to tell you something in private." She was brimming with a smile and looked like the image of victory. "I was right, and you should know it. But now I will tell you why. Can you guess?"

I couldn't.

"Because Captain Gurtigruten is going to invite you to have dinner with him!"

I stood there in stunned silence.

Angela continued like a meddling matchmaker as I opened my door and we went inside. "He wants to ask for your friendship, so be sure you at least go and get to know him." She beamed as if it were all her own doing, which it probably was.

"I–I don't know what to say, Angela," which was the truth. "I mean, what about Wink? I'm not really sure about any of this. What does he mean by friendship? I live in Michigan." I wasn't even making sense to myself.

"Don't think about those things," she said, laughing. "But when he asks you to join him, be sure to say yes and go. It's an honor, really. All the other girls are lining up for that invitation, but you'll be the one to get it."

Then she looked in the corner by the bathroom where Wink's carry-on was still standing. "Don't you have room for storing that?" she asked.

"It's actually Wink's," I told her, explaining how I ended up with it. "I will return it to him when we rendez-vous at Grand Cayman."

"I'll take it and put it in his office. Save you the hassle," she offered. I didn't object.

She reminded me to be sure to respond to the captain's invitation, which should be coming any day.

I promised I would, and she fairly skipped her way down the hall, trailing Wink's carry-on behind her.

16

Place of Red Corn

Day Four: February 18, Thursday
Costa Maya, Mexico
Sunny: High: 89ºF/31ºC. Low: 71ºF/21ºC.

By 7:15 THE NEXT MORNING, we were greeting each other in the organized chaos of the tour bus depot at Costa Maya, having walked the very long pier from the ship. Costa Maya was a tourist spot. No one really lived there. It was designed and built to bring the cruise ships to a central location from which the tours could depart for several Mayan sites. For guests who just wanted a relaxing day off the ship, the terminal area had a great deal of lively offerings: a pool, shops, entertainment, restaurants and even a sea-quarium with dolphins.

Already it was steaming up to be another hot-ta-male Mexican day, and the long walk from the ship to the meeting place reminded everyone how vital sunglasses were in this part of the world. If the water looked blue in Cozumel the day before, it was reaching new dimensions of azure in Costa Maya, appearing in dazzling shades from aqua to teal to azure, the deep blue of lapis lazuli. We were the first ship in port that day, but two more, off in the distance, were lumbering their way in. Oscar and his excursion team were hell-bent on getting us on our buses and on the road before the next onslaught of tourists came off those ships.

Our young Mexican guide, Juan, greeted us in Spanish on a spanking-new bus. When no one respond-ed to his questions, he switched over to English, joking that he'd be happy to turn our Maya excursion into a Spanish lesson instead. He introduced his driver, Car-los, and explained that our trip to the site would take a little over an hour of driving on mostly flat roads. Flat roads were so important for trade they were considered sacred to the ancient Maya. Pack animals simply did not exist in the New World until the Spanish brought over their horses, donkeys, mules and oxen in the early sixteenth century. Before then, everything had to be transported on the backs of humans. Flat roads were certainly a blessing!

The name of our destination, Chacchoben, meant The Place of Red Corn. Indigenous to the New World, corn was not known in Europe until after the time of Columbus. Juan said a great exchange of cultures and crops happened in the sixteenth century when crops were introduced for the first time across the Atlantic in both directions. Coffee, sugar and wheat came from the Old World to the New World for the first time as beans, tomatoes and chocolate went in the other direction. Corn, not wheat, was the Mayan staff of life, and any meal in Mexico right through to the present day was nearly impossible to imagine without the corn tortillas that mothers have been patting out for their families for eons on end.

"Did the Maya eat popcorn?" someone asked. Juan smiled and said, "A great question. Archaeologists have evidence that the Maya popped corn kernels in hot sand, probably making it the earliest all-American snack!"

The Mayan civilization lasted for many centuries and flowered into a patchwork of prosperous and culturally sophisticated city-states that spread over present-day Mexico, Guatemala, Belize, Honduras and El Salvador. The far-flung city-states of the Maya never organized themselves into an administrative union as the Romans did, for example, but remained as disparate kingdoms, their rulers continually vying for power over each other with frequent wars. One of the remarkable features of Mayan society was how far and wide their trade networks reached. In addition to basic necessities like salt and honey, they seemed always to be on the lookout for precious metals, gems, feathers, pottery and other exotic acquisitions to glorify their rulers. The Maya embodied a prestige-based society. The impressive architecture of their enormous buildings and tall temples, and the exotic stones, shells, feathers and other finds from faraway sources, all showcased the power of their rulers and kingdom. Their expertise in masonry, mathematics and writing were all touchpoints of pride that their kings liked to show off to other rulers in their bid for eminence and respect.

Juan said the Maya were vain about their looks and considered being slightly cross-eyed an attribute of beauty, so they trained their babies' eyes to cross by hanging little beads from their foreheads. They also pressed the still-forming soft foreheads of babies between wooden boards to create a sloped forehead, also considered beautiful. He held up a photograph of a Mayan skull with a sloping forehead and passed it around.

"Why did they think that flat foreheads were beautiful?" a woman asked.

"Possibly because their corn god was often depicted with a sloping forehead in their art, and they wanted to emulate him," Juan said.

"But," he added, "their obsession with personal beauty in no way stopped there. The rulers liked to dazzle their subjects and admirers with some bling in their smiles. The Maya were not only adept at dentistry," Juan said, "but accomplished at cosmetic dentistry as well." He held high the picture of a gem-studded set of teeth in a skull, then passed it to a set of eager hands. He said they used rubber to help hold the gems in place and knew how to administer numbing allspice leaves for anesthesia.

Knowing more about the Mayan traditions, we were excited to explore the ruins as Carlos guided our bus into the big parking lot along with the other buses from our ship. Juan told us to take a few minutes to stretch out, use the restrooms and then meet him at the entrance to the path at nine o'clock to begin our tour of Chacchoben.

As we started down the wide footpath, a glorious sun broke through the canopy of jungle above. Our first close-up glimpse of a Mayan ruin came very soon, and we would have scattered to take photographs if Juan had not called us together to warn us about the red fire ants. He said they were not harmful but could sting, and especially warned one couple wearing open Birkenstock sandals. He told us to join him after taking some pictures. I was intrigued by the stepped configuration of this ancient pyramid. It wasn't quite a pyramid because the top was flat, but Juan explained that unlike the Egyptian pyramids that tapered to a point, the Mayan pyramids were flat on top to accommodate a temple. We climbed the narrow steps as far as the barrier tape allowed us, taking selfies and group pictures from different angles of that imposing mass of ancient temple, dark and weatherworn against a cloudless sapphire sky.

Suddenly, a sound that could have been our ship's whistle pierced the jungle air. Everyone looked for the source—it was Juan blowing into a conch shell signaling us to regroup. We all met at the foot of the pyramid where Juan explained that while Chacchoben was occupied as early as 200 BC, the structure we were looking at probably dated from about AD 700. By about the middle of the tenth century, the entire Mayan world across Mexico and Central America experienced a mysterious demise and Chacchoben was abandoned. Over the next two thousand years, the jungle grew around and over it, and it was left undisturbed until the 1970s when an American archaeologist flying over the site noticed bumps on the ground that were not part of the flat natural terrain and went about unearthing the site. The temple we were standing near probably served as a ceremonial center with a complicated network of residential, administrative and commercial structures nearby. We visited more temples and a residential "neighborhood" that seemed like what we today call a planned city. Foundation remains of ancient domiciles were connected like urban townhouses, and everything seemed to blend organically with the natural surroundings.

At one stop, he pointed at a tree. The trunk was scored with X marks gouged into its gruff bark. He asked how many people liked to chew gum and told us this tree produced the substance that made gum before synthetic components came along. In fact, he said, the Maya chewed gum from this sap to clean their teeth. He said the sap was called chicle, meaning "mouth movement" in Maya. I thought of Chiclets chewing gum.

We stopped at more temples and milled around in small groups when suddenly a loud screech stopped everyone cold. This was not the sound of Juan's conch shell. It was more like something between a honk and a holler, human and animal. Everyone stood still and looked to Juan for an answer.

"That is a howler monkey," he said. "It is the loudest creature in the jungle." He walked over to some tree branches and pointed directly above him. We all hurried over, pinning our eyes to the place he was pointing.

Slowly the responses were coming in. "I see it," someone whispered.

"Look! There it is! You can see his tail!"

"Shhhh! You'll scare him away for the rest of us."

In the end, nearly everyone was able to see the howler monkeys playing in the trees and calling down to us. We felt very satisfied, especially when Juan told us they don't always appear and it had been about a week since they last came out.

By the time we completed our tour, we had walked a big circle to explore the handful of stately old structures that comprised the part of Chacchoben that had been excavated. Juan assured us it was only a small fraction of the entire complex. We boarded the buses again for the hour-long ride back to the ship.

When we approached the terminal, Juan said that there was much to see and do at Costa Maya, but to get a taste of real life in a sleepy little Mexican coastal village, all we had to do was hop on the trolley to Majahual, about two miles away. I was grateful of this reminder, or I might have forgotten completely about my promise to deliver the package of medical equipment back to the ship for Dr. Messy.

As soon as our bus arrived back to the cruise center, I bade farewell to my friends. I found the trolley stop and bought a ticket and was on my way to town, as they optimistically called Majahual. I felt like I was stepping back in time, walking along a boardwalk that paralleled the bright-blue shoreline with hucksters in every direction beckoning, cajoling and bribing me to get a cheap massage on the beach, buy handmade silver jewelry, eat a red snapper or drink a tequila. The food looked delicious and fresh as waiters emerged from the restaurants with tray after tray for the awaiting hungry humans at the outdoor tables. But I was on a mission and made my way down the boardwalk to the little farmacia Dr. Messy had described. As soon as I announced myself and started to walk into the little shop, I glanced through an office door and saw a man sitting at a desk. He looked for all the world like the very same man I had seen the day before in Cozumel: a Dr. Percival Turnkey look-alike, only this time, instead of a moustache, he had bushy sideburns. I squinted, blaming the bright Mexican sun for playing tricks on my eyes.

Before I had the chance to look again, the pharmacist whisked me out of the line of sight of the office and hurried me to an awaiting truck on the main street. The motor was already running. I realized I was not going to have any time to explore Majahual and gave up any hope of a fresh red snapper lunch on the beach that day. The driver quietly and quickly stepped into the truck and motioned at me to jump into the passenger side. We were almost off and running when the pharmacist dashed out of the farmacia with a clipboard clamping some forms down. He pointed to the lines that required my signature and information. Once I signed the last sheet of paper, the pharmacist grabbed the clipboard out of my hands and the truck squealed away, conveying me back to the port in ten minutes flat. As soon as we arrived at the ship, I was instructed to leave the truck while the driver navigated through the throngs of tourists to the back of the ship. I maneuvered my way through the pressing crowd to get a view of the cargo door. I was fairly sure that I briefly saw Dr. Messy's silhouette as a trunk was loaded into the ship.

It looked like a coffin.

17

Just Friends

BACK ON THE SHIP, I went to see which excursion Oscar's team booked for me the next day. When I arrived in the office, Oscar wasn't there. Pearl, who could see me from her desk in the adjacent office, called me over. She was on the phone. She handed me a packet mouthing the words, "It's from Oscar. You're booked on one of the Mayan excursions tomorrow."

I took the packet and was about to leave the office when she motioned for me to come back in and mouthed the words, "Wait a minute." As soon as she hung up from her call, she asked how things were going. She assured me I was helping them by focusing on the non-charter, non-nudist guests. She said many of them were feeling like they had been tricked into booking a nude charter cruise, and she conceded the terrible oversight with the booking department could give it that appearance. Then she said Perry Cardis had stopped by wondering if she had any spare staff to help him host his game shows.

"We're all stretched quite tightly, so I offered you!" she laughed.

I laughed too. Then I asked, "He won't need me for his magic acts, will he? I'm not sure I could trust him sawing me in half."

"No, not at all," Pearl laughed. "But do your best to play along with these interactive games he's concocted. He wants to do them in the theater in place of the regular production shows because this group isn't attending the productions."

That was an understatement. "Yes, of course. I'm happy to help. When do I start?"

"Plan on starting tomorrow and every night thereafter until I rejoin the ship in a few days. He will call you with more details."

I looked up.

"I'm actually going to leave the ship tomorrow and run home for a little emergency. No one will miss me between Belize and Jamaica, where I'll rejoin you.

I remembered that Pearl lived in Jamaica.

"I hope everything is okay back home," I said, curious about the nature of her emergency.

"Yes, there are some window boxes that need emergency weeding," she laughed. "Perry Cardis wants to handle everything here without me and, frankly, he's paying for this dog and pony show, so I don't have much of a say. He said I'm free to go, but it was more like an order. He's already gone ahead and canceled not just all the rest of the production shows, but all the headliner entertainers we had scheduled for this cruise. Some of them are on the ship right now, and having been told they can't perform; they will just sail to the next ship. For them, it is a paid-for cruise. For the guests, it's a missed opportunity. From here on out, it's all charter entertainment all the time, which apparently means Perry Cardis and his assistant. So, I'm handing you over as his personal Vanna White. And," she added, "you have my official permission to keep your clothes on."

"Aye-aye," I laughed, snapping a salute. "Let the games begin!"

Later, two envelopes were waiting in the mail slot on my door. The first was from Perry Cardis thanking me for helping out. It said simply to join him on the stage the following night for the first game show yet to be determined, and to feel free to come *au naturel* or else wear something simply black. Perfect, I thought. It's all I have anyway.

I opened the second note, expecting it to be another invitation to the jewelry sale in the boutique. It was from Captain Gurtigruten, and it was handwritten. "Please to come for dinner–Just Friends–on 21 February at eight o'clock. Captain Gert Gurtigruten, #12001."

I looked it up, and that was the day we would stop in Roatan. I didn't know if the number he left was his room number or his pager. In any event, he didn't tell me where to meet him, and I was hoping it would be in one of the restaurants. This was something I had to ask Angela about. I left a message for her and put the invitation aside.

Meanwhile, I sat on my bed and pored through the description of the next day's excursion. It was to be a long day that included a local lunch. I was very excited about this particular excursion because it included a water taxi down the New River to the Mayan archaeological site, Lamanai. I wasn't sure if I was pronouncing it in my head right. I said it out loud, and it sounded okay. The summary said that it had some very big stone sun masks and a ball court. I called the other couples, one after the other. No one was in, so I left messages for each one that I was going to Lamanai the next day in Belize. I suggested that if they wanted to join the tour, we could meet at seven-fifteen and sit together. Then I pulled on my handy black dress, twirled a colorful yellow scarf around my neck and rode the elevator up to Deck 12 and the Taipei Room to dine with Dr. Messy.

I checked in with Sung-ho, the maître d', about five minutes early. He said Dr. Messy was already seated and waiting for me. He motioned for a waiter to escort me to her table. She was sipping a glass of sake and greeted me with a cordial nod. The first thing she asked was if I ate meat.

"I think everyone in Michigan eats meat because it's so cold up there," I laughed as I sank into the upholstered chair and the waiter draped a linen napkin over my lap. She said that was a relief because she'd already ordered our dinners for us and, almost on cue, the appetizers arrived. The gorgeous presentation was enough to make my mouth water like Niagara Falls, and the courses kept coming out from then on. I realized by the time we were finished with our appetizers alone I would never make it to the show in time.

I looked around the dazzling restaurant with its dark carved-wood posts and rich paneled walls separated by deep crimson curtains. The tables were set with fluorescent-white tablecloths. Stunning live orchid plants in modern bone china vases served as centerpieces. The seats were an artsy combination of upholstered benches and chairs with complementing patterns of crimson, gold and eggplant upholstery. Replicas of ancient Chinese tapestries hung on the biggest walls. I could have imagined the room full of guests dressed in elegant evening gowns and dinner suits, but Dr. Messy and I were the only diners wearing anything at all: I, in my trusty black dress, and she in a pine-green dress with three-quarter sleeves that she'd probably acquired in the seventies but it still was a timeless and classic style. In fact, I mused that it well could have been purchased in the seventies because the extra pounds she accumulated in the intervening years were starting to press noticeably against the seams.

18

Doctor's Orders

THE APPETIZER PLATTER included crispy wontons, pork dumplings, shrimp and vegetable spring rolls and a dollop of what looked like kimchi sprinkled with some sesame seeds. I helped myself to two of everything since there was enough to go around for four people. It could have served as my entire dinner.

I complimented Dr. Messy on her choice so far and added that I hadn't eaten anything since breakfast. I wanted to do some preemptive damage control because it was almost guaranteed I would spill something. As soon as we wiped our mouths from the appetizers, the next course arrived. It was a savory red curry noodle soup.

Dr. Messy talked about growing up as a missionary couple's only child and living in many places around the world. She said her mother's favorite place was a little town in Italy called Messina. That was how she got her name. She had the advantage of living amongst different cultures until she went away to college. Her early experience instilled in her a love for travel, but after she became a medical doctor, she was not able to do much of it until recent years when she started working on cruise ships. She laughed, "Now I travel the world, but I don't have time to step outside of the ships, and I have to see most of these dang foreign ports from my porthole. I'd see more of the world on TV back home in Dayton. A ship doctor is much busier than people might realize. Guests come onboard too sick and frail and old to travel and need constant monitoring. And then there is no end to the trip-and-falls and other accidents. Just yesterday someone broke his big toe stumbling into his bathroom. He forgot about that little raised ledge under the door." I could relate, having stubbed my own toe on that raised lip a few times myself.

"People forget and let down their guard when they are on vacation. They walk into traffic looking at their maps instead of the street; sample unsanitary food from street vendors; forget to bring sun hats, sunscreen and water bottles on their tropical excursions; and let themselves get sunburned and dehydrated. Mine is a constant job of mostly mothering adults perfectly capable of taking care of themselves, but they just go into a different la-la-land mindset on vacation, and there you have it.

"I'm looking at a case in point," she said, suddenly pointing her spoon at me as she talked. "You were like the cat with nine lives on that last cruise, and after being dropped, bitten, dragged, smacked and nearly drowned, you still never once came to see the medic. I know because, while I wasn't officially on duty, I joined the ship in Grand Turk and the doctor on duty filled me in. You have quite a little rap sheet in the office, I might add," she said, scooping up another spoonful of soup.

"I appreciate your help with these medical supplies," she went on after pausing briefly to allow one waiter to take our soup bowls and another to deposit a salad made of crispy chunks of duck meat and watermelon garnished with fresh mint. I was intrigued by that combination but after my first taste said only one word: "Heaven!"

"And I'm not going to beat around the bush because I will need your help again tomorrow. Of all the ports, this is the most important one. The past three times this ship has sailed into Belize, we weren't able to connect with the supplier of this particular stock of meds, so it's imperative that it gets to us this time. I know Oscar went and booked you on that all-day trip out to Lanai or whatever the blazes it's called, so I don't want to mess up your plans to go there. But I am going to ask you to part ways with the excursion the minute you return from the river cruise and from that point get a taxi to beeline you back to Belize City. You will be in a place called Orange Walk, and the driver will need to take you directly to Belize City from there at top speed. I've arranged for the package to be waiting for you at the Bank of Belize building because they post security there around the clock. The security guard will be expecting you. Tell the driver to drive as fast as he legally can to get you to the Bank of Belize in Belize City," she repeated, as though I were taking notes. Maybe I should have been. "Tell the taxi driver to wait while you collect the package and then have him bring you back to the tender platform for the ride back to the ship. Oh, and be sure to get a receipt for reimbursement because that taxi ride won't be cheap."

How many more hoops was I to jump through? I wondered, as I saw the promise of an exhilarating day turn into a complicated fiasco. "How do I get a taxi from the river launch?" I asked.

"Good question. That's the point where all the buses will converge before you take the river ride to the ruins. There's a restaurant there where you'll have lunch before you take the river ride. Sometime during lunch, while everyone is eating, go into the parking lot and get a taxi driver to agree to meet you back there when the boats return from Lamanai. You'll have to ask your guide what time that will be, so do that before you go to the parking lot."

"But what about my duties as escort for the excursion team?" I asked. "What if they need me on the ride back to the ship? What if there is an injury on the bus, or the bus is delayed?"

"Have you met these people?" Dr. Messy laughed. "After a long day of busing, river cruising, exploring an expansive Mayan ruin, and a big lunch to boot, they're going to be singing one chorus the whole way back, and it starts with Zzzzzzz. And I wouldn't bother telling Oscar about this, either. He's a worrier like you. Just secure that taxi ride while they're having lunch, and everything will work out."

I wasn't convinced. Moreover, I found it very unsettling that I might be doing something in secrecy that could get me into trouble or cause some problems to others down the way. But I didn't know how to word the question without sounding like I didn't trust Dr. Messy. Just then, our next course arrived, and we eagerly dove into our steamy pad thai spiced with aromatic curry and piled high on top with a generous dousing of crunchy crushed peanuts.

"Don't worry, the ship won't leave without you, if that's what you're thinking," Dr. Messy said. "This captain is under some scrutiny after that unbecoming tantrum his girlfriend exhibited that night. You were the epitome of class. It's all over the ship, you know. Everyone realized you were not at fault, and even if you had said something to provoke Miss Monaire, she acted like a bully. Out of line. Captain Gurtigruten isn't going to leave anyone behind on this cruise, least of all you, trust me. Besides, it's in the contract for the charter. They were forty-five minutes late departing last night, if you happened to notice. A couple returned to the ship late from a private excursion to Tulum.

The waiter swooped up our dishes and handed us each a dessert menu.

"I am stuffed as the Christmas goose," I said. "I don't think I can have anything else."

"Then I'll eat it," Dr. Messy said, laughing. "I mean it. Don't you dare not try one of these desserts. I already ordered them. Take one bite, and if you can't finish yours, I will finish it for you."

Our desserts arrived. Not two, but three. "I thought we could share the chocolate crème brulée with lemongrass. That goes between us. You get the bounty cake with coconut, chocolate chips and vanilla bean, and I get the caramel tapioca with mango and ginger cookies," she said, claiming a corner of the chocolate crème brulée for herself. I liked her style.

As we savored the sweet delicacies, Dr. Messy asked if I knew why Pearl was leaving the ship for a few days. I said she'd told me something about needing to go home and weed her window boxes. Dr. Messy had a jolly laugh over that and said it was more likely because Stella Laffer was joining the ship. "Frankly, this ship's not big enough for Stella and Pearl onboard at the same time," she said, "and Pearl knows it. Perry Cardis and Stella Laffer go way back, and they loathe each other more today than they did the first time they met. How Stella even got assigned, let alone agreed to come on this cruise, is a mystery to me. My guess is, corporate hid from her the little fact that Perry Cardis was here when they booked her." She said Perry Cardis was going to be sweating and fretting the whole time. She waved a chop stick at me and said, "You'll see."

Back in my room, the message light was flashing. I knew it had to be from Angela. She sounded excited and said definitely to RSVP at the number the captain provided and to assume dinner would be in his quarters served by his personal butler, room-service style. She said also there was a good probability there would be other officers joining us as well.

I dialed the number and left a message saying that I looked forward to joining the captain for dinner. I made sure to include "just friends" somewhere in my message. Well, I figured, if nothing more, it will be one more adventure to write home about.

19

Submerged Crocodile

Day Five: February 19, Friday
Belize City, Belize
Rain: High: 79ºF/C. Low: 69ºF/20ºC.

THE EXCURSION to Lamanai started uneventfully enough the next morning. Rain clouds were gathering as we boarded the tender for the five-mile transfer from the ship to Belize City. Belize used municipal tenders that were large and airy, more like sightseeing boats. Instead of the few dozen people that the ship's little tender could accommodate, the tenders in Belize held a couple hundred people. The boat was delayed, turning what would have been a half-hour's ride into nearly an hour because of unruly seas and near-zero visibility. The massive tender slapped and smacked down, bouncing noisily on the turbulent water while frequent wild sprays punished us with cold ocean water. The rain continued to splatter from every direction as we boarded the buses in Belize City. Elison, our local guide, assured us we were driving away from the rain in the direction of Orange Walk, one of Belize's handful of regions. Our ride, which typically took an hour and a half, was an hour longer due to a mudslide on the main road. We sat in the bus doing our best to cling to Elison's convoluted play-by-play narration of the Maya Hero Twins' escapades through the various tricks and traps in the underworld.

We watched the dismal view outside the windows as the road workers labored to remove the muck and debris while traffic backed up and came to an agonizing halt. Two guests had to use the bathroom, but there was not a restroom on our bus. My mind kept reverting to that tenuous connection I was to make, expecting some yet-unknown taxi driver in a dang foreign port to race me back safely to Belize City. I was fast losing faith in Dr. Messy's harebrained scheme. By the time we arrived at the water taxi launch in Orange Walk, we were ready for lunch. There was no sign of life at the adjacent restaurant though, and Elison announced a change in plans. The people who ordinarily would have had our lunch all ready for us had been held up by the mudslide too, and now lunch would have to wait until our return from Lamanai that afternoon. As soon as we deboarded the bus, I scanned the big parking lot for a taxi. Nothing in sight. I started to panic, wondering if there would be any taxi drivers at all when we returned, let alone one willing to rush me back to Belize City on a moment's notice so late in the day. All

I could do was go on with the excursion and hope for the best.

We boarded the little water taxis two dozen at a time. These were open-sided motorboats, and even on the sunniest day, we would have been doused with spray. That day we were going to get rained on as well. Sure enough, not five minutes into the ride, the thick gray clouds above us burst wide open and dropped all the rain in the heavens on our little group. The water was fast filling up the boat, so we took turns bailing it out with the cutaway bleach bottles at our feet, kept handy for that reason. No one was smiling. Once or twice, Elison slowed down the boat on our journey along the New River and detoured into a mangrove lagoon here or there where he pointed at a monkey or a sloth, but no one else saw them. We urged him to skip the sightseeing and get us to the ruins. By the time we arrived, the entire morning had been lackluster at best. We were dripping, slipping and hungry as we alighted from our boat and walked a small muddy path to meet Luis, the archaeologist waiting to show us the ruins. After a brief restroom break, we convened with Luis and started on our way.

The rain never stopped, and a soggier, more forlorn group of tourists would have been hard to imagine as we traipsed over muddy puddles and waded through slippery rivulets. It was hard to hear Luis through the driving rain and frequent thunder, and we were starting to grow uninterested and ornery from hunger. People passed around breath mints, gum, even forgotten Tums lurking in the linty corners of their pockets. Anything to stave off the growing gnaw of hunger.

Lamanai, or Submerged Crocodile, as the name meant was reputed to be one of the longest continuously occupied Mayan settlements ever discovered. Evidence claims that corn was grown as far back as 1500 BC in the area when settlement started. It continued as a thriving trade center into the sixteenth century, with the Spanish arriving in 1554. A collision of cultures inevitably followed as missionaries converted two erstwhile Mayan temples into Catholic churches with the aim of converting the Maya. But the Maya revolted and burned one of the churches in the 1640s.

Lamanai covered about nine hundred acres. It had been strategically located along the bank of the New River, which provided the access that made Lamanai a major trade center. Among the artifacts that archaeologists uncovered, many were made of metal, including copper and copper alloys, a surprising find. In fact, Luis said that by AD 1150, metal tools and implements were manufactured right in Lamanai, where more copper implements have been found than at any other Mayan site. A small display contained little copper bells, rings, needles, fishhooks, pins, tweezers and even axes and chisels.

Coming from Michigan, I knew about the copper mines in the Upper Peninsula. I asked Luis if the copper could possibly have come from that far away. He said it probably had come from western Mexico, underscoring the wide trade networks that Lamanai had developed. He said other trade goods included things made from obsidian, jade and the red mercury—cinnabar—which was used in pigments. Other commodities traded commonly throughout the Mayan world included salt, honey, cacao, textiles, jade, obsidian and clay cooking vessels.

But Lamanai also served as a ceremonial center with religious temples adorned by enormous stone carved masks representing important Mayan icons. We walked past several temples and buildings. One of these was the Temple of the Jaguar, built on seven levels with two enormous jaguar masks flanking the stairway. Then we came to the Temple of Masks where two carved limestone masks of the sun god Kinich Ahau, topped with crocodile headdresses, stood sentry on opposite sides of the temple staircase. I wondered what it would feel like to grow up in a place with so many imposing monuments of mythical and whimsical characters and considered that the Maya, like ancient cultures all over the planet, were steeped in mythological searches for answers we still seek today. Luis said in their heyday, these monuments, temples and structures would have been covered by thick stucco and decorated in bright colors, primarily red.

Luis took us to the ball court. Unlike the one we had seen at the ballgame reenactment in Cozumel, it was smaller and had a different configuration altogether. Luis said at Lamanai the ball court used a flat, round rock in the center of the court as the goal marker instead of stone rings protruding from high side walls. He said no one was certain how the Maya played the game on this court, but the goal may have been scored by hitting the stone marker with the ball against the opposing team's efforts to prevent it. He said when archaeologists excavated the site, they found something of singular interest buried beneath the center stone as an offering to the gods: a lidded bowl that contained mercury!

Saturated with new images and impressions of the remarkable Maya, and even more thoroughly saturated with the rain that never let up, we trudged back to our boats and resigned ourselves to a sloppy return to the other side of the river. The hour-long ride seemed to go more quickly because Elison did not stop for any sights along the way and seemed to be going full throttle, except when slowing down to make hairpin turns in the narrow bends. I couldn't imagine how these pilots knew their way around this jungle maze of water, trees and mangroves.

I half-dreaded the completion of this journey, knowing that I still had a full adventure ahead of me and not knowing if there would be a taxi available to help me make that crucial link. Any thoughts about staying for lunch fell away as the boat came to a stop and the guests piled out. From the little dock, I could see the tables had been gaily decked out with colorful centerpieces, and the gloomy expressions on the guests were soon replaced by smiles as they looked up and saw the promise of an inviting lunch served on picnic tables under the shelter of a sturdy thatched roof. I said goodbye to my group, telling them I had to be back on the ship, and went to find a taxicab in the parking lot. The driver of the only cab there said he could take me to Belize City for about three hundred Belize dollars, quickly adding it was about a hundred fifty US dollars, as if it were a deal. I had no other choice and no time to bargain, so I accepted his offer and let myself into the back seat. The driver said his name was Jims.

As soon as we cleared the driveway and I was too far out to change my mind, Jims said the mudslide from earlier that day posed a problem and he might have to take another route that would cost more. I was seriously wondering if I had enough cash on me to go much over the one hundred fifty dollars he'd quoted. He said the landslide might have been cleared by now, or might have returned, and instead of taking the risk of getting there and having to turn around and double back, he judged it safer to take the longer route around. He said it would take a little longer but was a better bet than the risk of the shorter route. I sighed audibly and wondered why I always had to be so fast to do favors for people. This was clearly out of my hands, and he barreled the cab forward down a remote and untraveled side road that seemed never to end. I was curious how many cars we would pass in the next ten minutes, and it wasn't until we had gone over forty minutes that someone came from the opposite direction. And that wasn't a car. It was a horse and buggy!

I did a double take. "Is that what I thought it was?" I asked Jims. "I didn't know there were Amish in this part of the world." Jims laughed and said that there were, in fact, many Mennonites in Belize. They still lived by their traditional lifestyles, driving their horse-driven carriages and wearing their old-fashioned styles. He said we were passing near a Mennonite community and to watch for more. It wasn't long before another horse-drawn buggy trotted toward us. Jims explained that the Mennonites came to Belize in waves over different times in history and were always welcome because of their woodworking and home-building skills, something very necessary in Belize where they are frequented by devastating hurricanes.

I complimented Jims on his excellent English, and he answered me with another question. "As opposed to what?" he asked. "English is the official language of Belize."

I had never considered that a country in Central America spoke English instead of Spanish. Jims went on to explain that Belize was once known as British Honduras. Its roots—quite literally—were in mahogany, which early settlers harvested for a hungry lumber market in the days before steel construction. He said Belize might be Spanish-speaking today, but for a battle played out between the Mexican Spanish and the so-called Bayman, lumbermen and assorted outcasts of British descent, living in a settlement called St. George's Caye. Jims said a battle there in 1798 settled the question for good when Belize fell to the British. Jims said Belizeans still celebrate the Battle of St. George's Caye every September.

The road meandered on and on. I tried to avoid glancing at my watch while simultaneously wondering if lunch had ended and the excursion bus was heading back to the ship. I was hoping against all odds that they would make it back to the ship later than I would, so if the ship had to be held back, it would not be for me. It was getting dismal though, and my watch seemed to be going backwards with every passing mile. I asked Jims at one point if he had any idea when we might arrive in Belize City. He did not answer, and I suspected he was preoccupied with something. Then I looked over his shoulder and realized what it was. He had offered to take me to Belize City and on a long detour without considering how much gas was in his tank. The arrow was hovering over empty! I knew I would never make it back in time for the last tender.

I was screwed!

20

Guardian Angel

I DIDN'T SAY ANYTHING, but I was feeling plenty! This driver had not only offered to take me to Belize City on a nearly empty tank but was now tootling down abandoned country roads in a land unfamiliar to me, and we hadn't run into another car since we left the parking lot. I was fuming, but more than that, I was worried. And afraid. Who knew who this person was and what malicious intentions he might have! I had nothing but a little over a hundred eighty dollars on me, no working phone in this dang foreign port and no idea where I was on the map. I was at his mercy. I had heard of instances where drivers simply dumped outspoken passengers from their taxis in foreign ports, and I was not going to let that happen. At least I still had a chance of making it back to Belize City with Jims, even if I had to miss the ship altogether. I rued the day I ever met Dr. Messy and vowed never again to rush in where angels feared to tread.

"You know what they say here in Belize?" Jims asked suddenly.

I wasn't interested in any local sayings. It was the last thing on my mind. I had a few sayings of my own but didn't think he would appreciate hearing them. I didn't answer. He filled in the void. "It's an unBelize-able day!"

"Well," I answered, "I certainly would not have 'Be-lized' this could happen when I woke up this morning."

We laughed together, and somehow the humor helped calm me down. He passed me a cold bottle of water from his cooler. I did not reject it and started to drink it greedily. I was not only hot and annoyed, but hungry and thirsty.

"I will simply call a replacement," he said. "You can pay me up to this point, which is about sixty-five US dollars. No need to tip me, either. I know you're going to need the rest of your money to get to Belize City."

"You mean we're not even halfway there?" I asked.

"Maybe less. We had to take that detour, remember?"

I was really in a panic.

He tried making a call on his cellphone but said there were no towers this far out, and no one around here needed them anyway because the Mennonites didn't use cellphones or computers or need Wi-Fi. He told me to stay in the car and wait a few minutes while he walked down the road in search of anyone with a car. I waited a few minutes. I waited a half hour. I waited just under an hour with no sign of Jims and nothing in sight but a Mennonite approaching in his horse-drawn carriage.

I put seventy dollars on the driver's seat and hailed the Mennonite buggy. The driver stopped, and I explained what was happening. Then I said I was desperate to get to the Bank of Belize and from there to the cruise tender station. I asked if he could at least take me to a place where I could hail a taxicab. He looked at me with steely eyes. His thistly, gray beard twitched slightly under a pronounced jawbone as he was considering something. He slowly raised a weatherworn hand in a "come aboard" gesture, and I clambered into the spindly contraption and sat in the seat next to him. At least the horse didn't need to stop for gas, I reasoned.

I figured I wouldn't be back in Belize City until noon the next day. All I heard the entire journey was the steady clop-clop of the horse's dainty hooves and the rhythmic creaking of the surrey. It didn't help to check my watch because it was already getting dark, and I had long given up hope of making the last tender to the ship.

When we came closer to town, I told the driver that when we got to the Bank of Belize, I would need him to wait for me to get a package. I was dreading the inevitable explanation about finding a way to load a coffin-sized crate on the spindly surrey. I smiled at the driver as I shakily lowered myself from the buggy and headed for the front door of the bank building, its architecture inspired by a Mayan ruin.

Inside the door sat a lonely white-haired guard.

He looked bored and didn't raise as much as an eye-brow when I walked in but was evidently waiting for me with a sheaf of papers to sign. I scribbled my name and information on all the requisite lines, dated everything and handed back the papers. He handed over a square box about the size of an apple crate and shrugged as if it were all in a day's work. Forgetting for the moment that English was the official language in Belize, I said, "Gracias," to which he swished his hand at me and said, "You're welcome." He assumed the same uninterested stare he had when I walked in moments earlier.

Thankfully, my ride was still waiting for me, and words couldn't express my relief to be holding a box this time instead of escorting a coffin. The driver deposited me at the tender station. I turned around to pay him, and he was already on his way, a little cloud of mud and dust kicking up under his horse's obedient hooves, his back license plate disappearing in a cloud of dust. It simply read "Gabriel." I tried chasing him, waving all my remaining bills at him with my free hand. He waved me off with that big, weathered hand and continued on his way. I had never seen such an unexpected act of kindness. It was humbling to receive it.

I was the only one on the tender platform returning to the ship. It was already dark, and the lights coming from the ship were the only sign of life out on the black water. By now, the rain had stopped completely. Thin clouds were veiling timid stars.

Once we were in motion, I asked the tender pilot if

I could take his photograph while he piloted the tender with no other passengers on board. He agreed to let me take his photograph as soon as we started heading toward the ship. Wind and spray added a lively and delightful effect to the photograph, and I gave him a few dollars for the memory. Then, when we were in full throttle halfway to the ship, he offered to take a picture of me at the wheel. I was elated! What an adventure! I hastily gave him my camera and took to the wheel, feeling my hair beating back in the wind and the ocean spraying at my face as the tender accelerated. I didn't know who was in charge for a moment and certainly didn't know how to drive the thing, let alone stop it, but for those fleeting moments, I was enjoying the caper of piloting a tender. Mercifully, the pilot took the wheel when we were within wake distance of the ship. As exciting as it was, I wondered if taking the wheel of a marine craft without proper license, training or clearance made me technically a pirate.

I was about to board the ship, the package under one arm, when a whistle caught my attention. It was the kind of whistle that someone makes by blowing between teeth. I looked up, and one of the crew offered to take the box from me. I happily relinquished it. Then I suddenly remembered I did not ask for a receipt from the taxi driver for the seventy dollars I left on his seat, but I was so grateful to be safely back on board before it sailed, I didn't care. I figured I would have paid twice that much anyway.

21

Lady in Red

BACK IN MY ROOM, I was relieved to find no messages from Dr. Messy. I was determined to decline any future requests for these favors. This last escapade came too close for comfort.

I took a few minutes to collect myself, lying on top of the freshly made bed and flipping through the news channels on the TV. As I clicked along, I caught one announcer saying something about a robbery in Cozumel and thought it was a coincidence we were just there.

I had to turn off the TV and run down to the office to pick up my escort packet for the next day in Guatemala. Oscar was smiling brightly when I arrived and did not mention anything about skipping the bus ride back to the ship, if he'd even found out about it. Dr. Messy was probably right in predicting that everyone would nap the whole way back. I submitted my report and was on my way out when a loud voice and a thud came from the cruise director's office next door. One voice was that of a woman's, but it was not Pearl, who had left the ship that day.

I went to peek at the goings-on and acted as if I were reading some charts on the wall outside the office. Perry Cardis, wearing his signature underwear and one of his gaudy bow ties, was standing opposite a woman. She was wearing a red power suit and no-non-sense pointed black stiletto pumps. The two were in the throes of what could only be described as a knock-down-drag-out confrontation. Sizing it up, I would have chosen to be on the woman's side in this face-off.

"I certainly intend to give not just one of my comedy acts, but both of them," she roared. "The nerve of you to cancel all the production shows and redline all the scheduled headliner acts. If you thought for a second it would keep me off this ship, Perry Cardis, you'll have another thought coming!"

"I still don't know how you even boarded this ship," he fired back. "I should have stood sentry at the tender station and never allowed you onboard!"

"Ha!" the woman in red retorted. "You don't know what you are doing by changing the entertainment schedule like this. You don't know what it takes to run a ship's entertainment department, and I don't care if it is a charter or even how much you paid for it. I don't care how much you think these guests want everything around here to be a nudist orgy. I don't care if everyone on this ship is wearing clothing, skin, moose pelts or beer barrels around them. I am here to tell you, there are some lines that are not to be crossed, and cruise ship entertainment is one of them."

Perry Cardis started to say something, but she cut him off.

"Another one is professional deportment, and you really ought to be wearing more than your boxers and that tie that looks like a pathetic cry for attention!" she scoffed.

"You have no experience with this community," Perry Cardis retorted. "You'll see, no one will come to your comedy act. No one will come to the production shows, and no one will come to anything you schedule because you are out of place here and completely out of touch." He was pointing his finger at her in a threatening way. "I'll get you off this ship yet, and you will never tell one more solitary joke on stage here or anywhere else. In fact, I might just tell security to escort you down the gangway tomorrow in Guatemala, and you can find your own way home! It'd serve you right to thumb your way home on a banana boat," he huffed.

"I'm shaking! Look at my knees! Let them just try," she challenged. "Not only am I here to do my comedy acts on this ship's stage, but you will see how well-attended they'll be, and you will also see how your charter group will love the other ways I am going to turn the entertainment on this cruise around. You had some nerve to cancel all those great headliner acts! What were you thinking? That you're a cruise director?

Ha! In your dreams, Perry Cardis! In your dreams! I think your brain turned off along with your logic when you ripped off your clothes."

She looked directly at me, and I realized I was in full view and obviously eavesdropping. I had to save face and simply said, "See you later for that game show, Perry Cardis," and turned to go. How I regretted that slip-up in the next moment!

"Wait a minute!" she bellowed, pointing at me. I froze outside the door. "What game show is she talking about?" she charged at Perry Cardis. "What cockamamie idea do you have for tonight's headliner show?" She picked up the copy of the *Tides* lying on the desk and tore through it. "This is the night for the production show 'Star-Spangled Spectacular!' she said. "Every other ship in the fleet is featuring this brand-new all-out revue. It cost over a million dollars to produce, not to mention all the untold hours of practice, rehearsal, costumes and stage set preparations. I am not reading 'Star-Spangled Spectacular' here, Perry Cardis, but instead I am seeing words that say 'The Nudely-Wed Game!'" She took a breath and asked, "The Nudely-Wed Game? Are you out of your mind? What is this?" she nearly shrieked.

"For your information—and it really isn't your business—this is a fun interactive game based on the old *Newlywed* TV game show," Perry Cardis rattled off, "but instead of sharing their first date, couples share the first time they joined our clothing-optional community."

"Over my dead body!" the lady in red retorted vehemently. "You can play that with the three couples that might show up on the pool deck next time they cancel the Hairy Legs Contest because of rain. No one else is interested in the Nudely-Wed Game because it's all anyone ever talks about around here anyway. They want to see the shows, not play your juvenile, perverted and asinine games!"

"Did you say asinine, or Ass in Mind?" Perry Cardis flipped back. "Sounds like a name for a new game! I can actually use this! You're finally making yourself useful here, Stella!"

So, this was Stella! Stella Laffer! I was starting to see what Dr. Messy was talking about. There was not room enough for Pearl and Stella on the same ship. And Stella had the last word with Perry Cardis. She sat down taking over the cruise director's desk as if it were her divine right. She opened the computer screen and went to work clicking, moving and arranging schedules. "It will take me all night to fix the mess you made, you perfect Neanderthal," she said to him. Then she mumbled to no one in particular, "At least he's a perfect something."

He dropped his arms to his sides and shook his head, defeated, as he walked out, mumbling that it was no use arguing and how she was barely on the ship an hour and already taking control.

"And you should count your lucky stars!" her voice chased after him as he slinked through the door.

I slipped away and headed to the dining room to join my friends for dinner.

ৡৡৡ

I was almost the last to arrive for dinner. The table was a ten-top to accommodate our larger group since Russ and Sonya Cook had joined us, but two seats were unoccupied. I looked around, greeted everyone by name, remarked I'd hoped they'd had a pleasant day and started glancing over my menu.

"Before we order," Sonya said, "I have a little present for everyone." Then she proceeded to hand out chocolate bars. "One for every couple, except for Marianne and Dr. Turnkey who each get a whole candy bar to themselves," she said. "I bought these in Belize today—Moho chocolate, locally made. They even gave us a tour of their little factory. Don't worry, I got a discount for buying more than three bars," she added as everyone laughed.

We looked at our chocolate bars and read out the various flavors she was distributing. Mine was chocolate with whole roasted almonds. I couldn't wait to finish dinner and bite into it!

"How did you know we love hot peppers?" Ted asked as Annie held up their bar of Moho chili-pepper chocolate.

Butch and Sally Albert showed off their bar of milk chocolate with ginger as Dr. Turnkey held up his bar flecked with cocoa nibs and gave the thumbs up.

"What did you get for yourself?" I asked Sonya. She held up two bars and admitted she got a chocolate with lime for herself and a dark chocolate with coffee nibs for Russ. "Actually, they're both for me, but it looks better if I tell you one is for Russ," she confessed as Russ nodded and rolled his eyes comically.

Suddenly, Annie broke in, looking directly at me, "Do you notice someone's not here?" she asked with a twinkle of mischief in her eyes.

"Well, I assume Max and Cathy are either on their way or sitting out dinner tonight. I almost ordered room service myself, it was such a long day," I answered.

Annie jabbed me lightly in the side. "They weren't here last night either."

I looked up. "Are they okay? They didn't come down with something, did they?"

"Nothing we can figure, unless they came down with a new mindset," Ted said.

"I looked around the table. All eyes were on me. Suddenly, I noticed Sonya pointing subtly to her left, her manicured, white fingernail almost level with the table. She nodded when our eyes met. I followed the trajectory of her pointing finger, and there in unmistakable technicolor were Ted and Cathy Ringler sitting at another table stark naked. I thought back on Dominic's prediction and marveled at how fast it happened. Someone at that table said something funny, and when Ted and Cathy joined the laughter, they looked up and saw me. They waved enthusiastically, smiling widely and pointed at themselves. I waved back and smiled.

"They're having fun for sure," I said. "But on the other hand, they're missing out on some good choco-late."

22

Stella Ha! Ha!

PERRY CARDIS'S game show was an unmitigated flop. Just as Stella had predicted, hardly anyone showed up, and all the talents of the dancers and singers went into greeting about a dozen couples that bothered to come to the theater out of curiosity. Perry Cardis tried to make a go of things, but a few minutes into it, he was fast losing traction. His bubble had been burst by Stella. Even a lame attempt at a dusty magic trick fell flat, and he cut his losses, inviting everyone to the Paris Lounge to sit around with him and kibbitz. We all followed him upstairs like loyal lemmings, but what greeted us there was a show no one could have anticipated. Stella, still in her red power suit and black stiletto pumps, was leading a country line dance on the dance floor while twirling a lasso over her head. She had a following of at least sixty guests dancing enthusiastically along with her, and the overflow crowd had to dance between the tables. Many were wearing the cowboy hats and bandanas Perry Cardis had supplied and stacked on tables near the entrance for the taking. Stella was laughing and stomping her feet wildly to the tune of "Tush Push."

From what anyone could clearly see, Stella was both completely in place here and totally in touch.

"What the hell is she doing?" Perry Cardis wondered out loud. I couldn't tell if he was impressed or threatened. He couldn't take his eyes off the scene and sat in his own world as the rest of us arranged ourselves into a lopsided circle.

"Who is Stella?" I asked. Perry Cardis turned and looked squarely at me.

"That is the most legendary female comedian at sea. She makes her own rules, runs her own show and everyone else's too . . . and she doesn't know how to be anything but in charge. Meet Stella Poughkeepsie, aka Stella Laffer!" he said, floating his arms out toward her. "Stella is rip-snort mad that I canceled all the other acts, but it didn't stop her from bulldozing her way onto the ship anyway and taking over things, even though she was actually paid not to show up. I shouldn't be surprised."

I couldn't help wondering if Pearl left the ship because she was complicit with Stella's coup against Perry Cardis. Hadn't Pearl said that Stella taught her everything she knew?

"She started as a cruise director, and that's why she knows so much about the drill," Perry Cardis said. The waiter set down a Samuel Adams and glass for

Perry Cardis, who took a long swig right from the bottle. "No one gets in Stella's way."

"How did she progress from cruise director to comedian?" I asked.

Perry Cardis took a deep breath and another long pull from his bottle and looked at me, his absurd tie blinking and flashing annoyingly in mocking contrast to his weary expression.

He said he was probably to blame for it. It all started on a bet several years earlier when he was booked on Stella's ship. "I used to be a comedian myself in those days," he said. "I got a little carried away one night. The audience was in the moment. They were laughing hard, so I didn't stop and maybe I went over the line a little. What the hell. You don't get too many nights like that, so you milk it a bit. At least I did. It goes like that. So, I went past my time slot and pissed Stella off. Later, she said that parts of my show were insulting, and that the women were complaining, so I had to watch my language. I guess I didn't bother taking her advice. In fact, maybe I added a little smarm because the men were laughing so hard. Hell, they're my audience too. One day when Stella had enough complaints from some of the women, she said I wouldn't clean up my show because I didn't know how. I told her to try standing up for fifty minutes doing comedy and keeping it clean the whole time and expect an audience to sit through it and see how it'd go over for her.

"You know what she did? She actually took me

up on a dare. Next thing I knew, she scheduled her own act and went out on stage as a comedian with a full fifty minutes of clean jokes. I don't think she even said 'darn' the whole time. She was such a hit with the audience, she could have been booked all over the country. Her audiences couldn't get enough of her, and as soon as her contract as cruise director ended five months later, she got herself an agent and went all over the country as a comedian. She even appeared on Conan O'Brien once."

I asked how long Stella was supposed to stay on board. Perry Cardis thought a moment and said, "As long as she wants to," shrugging his shoulders. "That's how it goes with her. I'm finished for the rest of this cruise, that's all I know. Look at that!" He pointed at a flash of red power suit spinning, whirling and twisting in a dizzying blur to the rhythmic thumps of "Ride, Sally Ride!"

He sighed, turned to look at me again and said she was scheduled to leave the ship in Grand Cayman for a booking she had in Vegas the following day. "We'll see if it actually happens," he added.

❧❧❧

The next morning, the ship's loudspeaker came alive with a woman's voice. Stella had taken over Perry Cardis's gig and was greeting the guests to Guatemala. I looked outside and saw that we were the only cruise ship docked alongside a very big and busy cargo port with corrugated container boxes stacked on top of each other as far as the eye could see. They were the same big metal boxes you see loaded on trains. Most were stenciled with the Chiquita brand. They must grow some bananas around here, I thought.

When I came out of the shower, the phone was ringing. Angela went over details about my dinner date with the captain. She said the night of our dinner date a security officer would collect me from my room and escort me to the captain's quarters. I would have to be guided through the security doors to enter that area. She said after it was over, she wanted to know every-thing that happened, from what was served to what we talked about. I assured her I would let her know.

Just as I started dressing, the phone rang again. I picked it up saying, "Yes, anything else?" expecting it to be Angela again. But it was Wink. He sounded cheerful and funny and carried on as if he hadn't heard my cat-swipe comment the other day. He was sounding more like the old Wink I had come to love. I was starting to miss him again.

"Gosh, I miss you, girl! Can't wait to see you and give you a good squeeze. You miss me too?" he asked.

"I really do, Wink," I said, believing myself. I could feel his breath on my face and his big arms pulling me close to him. I remembered the carefree time we had spent together in the luscious waters of Grand Turk be-fore that blasted barracuda bit my neck. I remembered the soft lingering smell of his cologne the last night of the cruise after I'd been attacked and almost made into fish food and how he came to my room to calm me. This was the Wink I knew and loved—kind, reassuring and doting.

"If I can cross over to your ship in Grand Cayman, we can have an evening together in Havana. We could stroll along the Malecon under the shadow of all the statues and monuments along the way."

I didn't know what he meant by the Malecon, but it sounded romantic—and I was hoping more than ever he could find his way over to stay on our ship. "I wish there was some way I could help you get over here," I said.

"Only if you can muster up another mystery like you did on the last cruise," he said, laughing. Then he shouted, "No! Don't do that!" and we both started to laugh. He said he knew I had to run and asked if anything was going on he should know about. I started to open my mouth. I almost told him about joining the captain for dinner but stopped short.

"No," I said. "Just a typical nude charter cruise over here." We said our goodbyes. As I hung up, I wondered what kept me from telling him about my dinner date with Captain Gurtigruten.

He doesn't have to know about it, I convinced myself. After all, it's "just friends."

23

The Jungle Kingdom Quirigua

Day Six: February 20, Saturday
Santo Tomas, Guatemala
Partly Sunny: High: 88ºF/31ºC. Low: 80ºF/26ºC.

AN HOUR LATER, we were on our way with our local guide, Yolanda, who confirmed that Guatemala was an important banana-growing nation. She told us to watch for Chiquita trucks on the highway along our way to Quirigua. She said that the banana was not indigenous to Central America or even the New World. Dominican missionaries introduced banana plants to some of the Caribbean islands from Africa in the decades following Columbus, and the fruit grew and spread rapidly in the hot and humid climate. She invited us to look out of our windows as the bus was passing rows and rows of banana trees, each one with a blue plastic bag covering the banana bunch growing inside. Our driver, Manuel, slowed down so we could see the neat rows of stubby-looking trees with dark-green fringed leaves. She said to look closely at each banana plant to see a big red pod. Every banana plant—and she emphasized it is a banana plant and not a banana tree—produces one bunch of bananas that emerges from that red pod, or flower. The banana workers cover every banana bunch with blue protective bags that protect the maturing bananas from UV rays and tarantulas, she explained. "When you see those blue bags on the plants, you know you are passing a banana farm."

Yolanda said the historic importance of the banana industry could not be overemphasized in this part of the world. Regimes rose and fell over control of the humble banana. She also said that the Mayan site we were about to visit, Quirigua, a UNESCO World Heritage Site, was once owned by the United Fruit Company—an enormous and influential fruit producing conglomerate in the nineteenth century that eventually became Chiquita Brands.

Unlike the flat terrain in Costa Maya and Cozumel, Guatemala was hilly. Yolanda said if our ship had called on the Pacific coast of Guatemala instead of the Caribbean coast, we could have seen the active volcanoes there. She said on a recent tour on the Pacific side of Guatemala, her group was able to witness streaks of red lava streaming down from the cone of Volcan de Fuego. She said it is that rich volcanic soil that nurtures their major export crops of coffee, sugar and bananas.

Her attention shifted to the Maya, and she said she was not of Mayan ancestry but was an ardent scholar of

Mayan culture and had studied the Mayan civilization at Vanderbilt University. She said many modern-day Maya were well educated but still opted to live in their traditional domiciles, eating food that came from their own small gardens and embracing a lifestyle that closely resembled that of their ancestors.

Yolanda said the majority of Mayan descendants lived in Guatemala and many still clung to ancient Mayan traditions around the use of their calendars, saying they used different calendars for different purposes. Their calendar that most closely resembles ours was based on the annual revolution of the Earth around the sun, essential for the cycles of planting and harvesting in an agrarian society. But instead of twelve months with thirty or thirty-one days as we have, the Mayan solar calendar had eighteen months with twenty days each. That made three hundred sixty, so they also had a little span of five "extra days" before the new year started. Yolanda said the Maya avoided doing anything important on those five extra days in order to ward off bad luck. No one got married, started a war or traveled during those days. If a baby was born in that interim, the shaman might change the date of the baby's birth, and the parents would never tell the child to prevent a stigma.

It was not the first calendar the Mayan people used, though. An even earlier Mayan calendar was the so-called ritual calendar, still observed by Mayan shamans, or calendar-keepers, who protect these traditions in our modern times. She said the calendar was derived by combining the thirteen day-numbers with the twenty day-names to reach a span of two hundred sixty days. Unlike our numeric calendars, the Mayans reckoned their days with both names and numbers. The function of the ritual calendar had more to do with naming babies and keeping Mayan traditions than following planting and harvesting cycles. In fact, she said two hundred sixty days is about the average length of time for human gestation. She added that the ritual calendar emerged at the beginning of the Mayan creation legend, the *Popol Vuh*. There was no escaping that book, I thought. I chided myself to start reading the copy I'd purchased in Cozumel.

"But the Maya didn't stop with two calendars," Yolanda went on. "They combined the two hundred sixty days from the ritual calendar with the three hundred sixty-five days in the solar calendar, interlocking each to the other day by day—until each day from one calendar was joined with each day from the other." She said this new calendar cycle took fifty-two years to complete and compared it to all the possible pairings of suits in a deck of cards. She said fifty-two years was just about the time the Maya liked to refresh and rebuild, too. They built bigger temples right over the ones already standing there. This fifty-two-year calendar, she said, was called the Calendar Round and it was always engraved on a round stone to symbolize the continuous nature of time.

But even three calendars apparently weren't enough to satisfy the Maya. They invented a fourth one called the Long Count. This calendar started on the first day of creation and assigned a specific date to every day from then on. Unlike the earlier calendars, the Long Count was strictly a linear record of time—not given to repeating annual cycles. In our calendar, any given date like October 25th can recur an infinite number of times because it returns every year. But the Maya calculated that creation started on August 12, 3114 BC, and from that point on, assigned a unique date to every day that followed with no repetition for five thousand one hundred twenty-eight years. Yolanda explained that this length of time was considered the measure of a dynasty.

She asked if we could remember back to December 21st of 2012. We didn't at first remember what she was talking about until she reminded us it was the day the Earth was supposed to end in some cataclysmic apocalypse, according to popular culture. People were making pilgrimages to Chichén Itzá, Copan, Tikal and other famous Mayan sites to witness the end of the world. Then she looked around and said, "Looks like we're still here. So, what happened?"

She went on to explain. "The end of the world was just the end of one Long Count calendar cycle," she said. "After five thousand one hundred twenty-eight years, it was time to throw out the old calendar and start a new one."

We arrived at Quirigua and stepped down from the bus. The look was markedly different from all the previous Mayan sites. Instead of the temples, ziggurat pyramids and great looming face masks of the sites we had visited earlier in Mexico and Belize, Quirigua was spread over a wide-open campus. A manicured path allowed visitors to walk along the entire stretch and stop at the various standing stones and boulders along the way. Everything was intricately carved, and our local guide, Rodrigo, compared it to a three-dimensional book carved on rock instead of printed on paper.

Towering stones, or megaliths, stood in small groupings, each one under its own thatched covering. Rodrigo said these enormous rocks were hauled from a sandstone outcrop farther down the Motagua River. Reaching as high as thirty-five feet, the biggest weighed in at about sixty-five tons. He said these carved standing stones were also called *stelae*.

Rodrigo drew our attention to a pattern engraved around the edges of one of the stelae, saying it was inspired by the exotic quetzal bird with its disproportionately long tail feathers. Considered sacred, the bird was protected by the Mayan royalty who reserved its tail feathers for the ruler's massive ceremonial headdress that could weigh over a hundred pounds! He said the quetzal is still fiercely protected and is commemorated as the name of Guatemala's currency.

We strolled at a leisurely pace as Rodrigo pointed out what the carvings meant. In one case, there was the depiction of what looked like a dancer with one foot placed firmly on the ground and the other foot elevated and pointing to the ground. He said this was the dance of death, and the Maya at Quirigua would have believed that the nearby Motagua River led to the departed souls' entrance into their underworld, the dreaded Xibalba.

Rodrigo took us to one of the monoliths and showed us a configuration of bars and dots, explaining that this was a Mayan number. "The Maya," he said, "used only a bar and a dot to denote their numbers." Three horizontal bars were stacked in a pile topped by three dots. "Each of those bars represents five. And each of the dots represents one. So, what number are we looking at?" he asked.

"Eighteen," most of us answered.

"Yes! Look at you, you have just arrived and are already counting in Maya!"

"What did the number eighteen signify here?" one of the guests asked.

"I'm glad you asked," Rodrigo said. "Quirigua started out as a small trading outpost along the Motagua River. It was ruled by the king at the great Mayan center at Copan in present-day Honduras. His name was 18-Rabbit. It sounds funny to us, but his name was derived from the ritual calendar with its day-names and day-numbers." Suddenly I was seeing what Yolanda was explaining to us earlier.

"But Cauac Sky, the leader of Quirigua, wanted

to break away from Copan's rule and grab more power for himself. He ambushed 18-Rabbit in AD 737, then kept him in custody, delaying his execution until later. You could call it a Mayan coup. Once Quirigua was independent of Copan, Cauac Sky commissioned scribes to carve the stones to commemorate his achievements and document that part of Quirigua's history." Rodrigo said the story of Cauac Sky's rise to power and the events that happened during his sixty-year reign were carved in intricate detail on the stelae and boulders scattered across the site.

He guided us to an enormous, engraved boulder. He called it a zoomorph for the animal depictions of Mayan gods. These carvings of phantasmagoric jaguars, crocodiles, toads, deer, turtles, two-headed serpents and birds represented the gods in the Mayan creation legend and recorded the historic events that showcased parts of the creation myth and glorified Cauac Sky. He said the largest zoomorph boulder weighed twenty tons, and every inch of its four hundred thirty square feet of surface was intricately covered with carvings. Rodrigo said to consider these zoomorphs as ornately illustrated books, only recorded with engravings on boulders instead of print on pages.

Another guest asked if there was a ball court at Quirigua. Rodrigo said there had been one, but at one point it had been covered over. He led us to the wide, flat acropolis at the farthest end of Quirigua. He said it was one example of Mayan earthquake engineering.

Earthquakes were not unknown in this region, and the structure was designed to roll with the earth's movement, avoiding or minimizing its effects and destruction.

Back in the parking lot, Yolanda and Manuel were handing us chilled bottles of water as we boarded the bus.

Yolanda talked on for a while about local politics in Guatemala, something that seemed to be her favorite subject. She told us how their current president was a comedian by profession. He won the election and probably would have won a second term, in her opinion, but for a relative who was caught in some corruption scheme or other—so typical of this part of the world.

I mused over the notion of a comedian for president, which sent my thoughts back to the antics going on between Stella and Perry Cardis. I started to nestle comfortably in my seat for the long ride home, for once relieved of any medical-supply-gathering duty, when suddenly Yolanda ended her narration, walked to the back of the bus and stood over me.

"While we were touring Quirigua," she whispered, "I received a message to convey to you from the ship's doctor."

My heart sank. I just knew what was coming next.

"So, we are going to make a quick stop at Puerto Barrios to let you get off the bus where someone will be waiting to give you something for the doctor." She smiled as if this were welcome news.

I looked up at Yolanda in disbelief. Then she

explained, as if I even cared right then, that Puerto Barrios was established by the United Fruit Company in the nineteenth century specifically to serve as its own port for the distribution of bananas grown in Guatemala. She said I would see Chiquita containers everywhere. I'll alert the media, I thought. She also said that other than that, Puerto Barrios was a bit "unimproved" and not to wander too far off. She said under no circumstances were they to let anyone else disembark there with me, so not to mention it before we arrived. I got her point.

I also got that I'd been snookered once again by Dr. Messy.

24

Dashed Aspirations of Jaguar Scroll

THE PORT TOWN of Puerto Barrios that Yolanda characterized as unimproved was more like a Brazilian favela with dilapidated corrugated ship containers serving as buildings and stores. A small butcher shop with a freshly slaughtered pig hanging from a wire was being visited by emaciated dogs sniffing for any unclaimed scraps of entrails curling on the ground and covered with flies. Rows of floppy and sun-faded displays of the myriads of kitchen utensils, clothing, shoes, household appliances, toys and tools promised to supply the locals with the needs for everyday life. It was a colorful sight but tired, dusty and uninviting.

Someone came around from the port area behind me. He asked, "Are you here for medicine?" in Spanish. I answered in my fledgling Spanish, and he motioned to follow him into a little Quonset hut where a woman at an old wooden desk was engrossed in a heated conversation on an old dial-up phone. She thrust a pile of papers in front of me and placed a pen on top while never taking her ear off the phone. She was speaking in rapid-fire Spanish.

I signed the papers and turned to collect the box, expecting it to be the same size as the one they had given me in Belize the day before. The first man took me back outside and to the curb where a limousine awaited me. At least I thought that was what it was. It was so old, it had to be from someone's vintage collection. It could have used a wash and a wax on the exterior and a deep cleaning inside.

The driver—short, round, jolly and hidden behind reflective sunglasses—came around and opened the door of the front seat for me. I already knew what was taking up the entire back without even looking. It was a funny thing, but as we were returning to the port, a taxicab passed us heading in our same direction. I could have sworn the passenger was yet another Dr. Percival Turnkey look-alike, but this time, instead of a moustache or sideburns, he wore a beard. I rubbed my eyes, but before I looked again, the taxi was gone. It had sped up and was already a block ahead of us and gaining speed as it wove through the stream of old cars.

By the time we arrived at the ship, I already knew the drill and let myself out as soon as the car stopped, a couple hundred feet short of the cargo door. It was already open and waiting to accept the coffin that rode back with me.

Dinnertime came up fast, and before I knew it, I

was back with my friends–minus the Ringlers who were comfortably sitting with their new friends enjoying the freedom of no clothes, I surmised, except Cathy had a light shawl hanging loosely over her shoulders. I noticed the dining room was cooler than usual, and a quick scan told me more people, especially women, were wearing light cover-ups against the chilly air conditioning.

"Tonight it's my turn to share something from our shore stop," Sally said as she half-stood and held up some packages. "I have something for everyone from Guatemala," she announced triumphantly as she passed around the bright vacuum-packed pouches of Guatemalan coffee to everyone. The pouches looked inviting and festive with their colorful illustrations of tropical birds perched among lush exotic leaves. I held mine up to my face and smiled as the aroma of freshly roasted coffee tickled my nose. "Mmmm!"

Ted said his favorite was a good French roast, but Annie said she tested him from time to time with regular old Maxwell House, and he could never tell the difference.

"That reminds me," Sally said, "we will be dining at The Fussy Frenchie specialty restaurant tomorrow." She teased that they might try going *au naturel*. "I'm seriously considering it," she said. "I'm running out of things to wear, and it might save me from having to pick up something in one of these ports." I took that opportunity to mention that I, too, would be absent. I did not give away my plans to dine with the captain, though.

"Have you seen that amazing robbery in Cozumel on the news?" Sally asked as soon as we placed our orders with the waiter. "Someone actually stole a Mayan mummy in Cozumel the other day. It might have been the day we were there, but I can't keep track of days of the week when I'm on a cruise."

I thought back to my errand for Dr. Messy in Cozumel and the image of that casket-like crate that was loaded onto the ship.

"How'd they get away with that?" Ted asked. "You'd think someone would have seen someone walking out with something that big. Guard was probably asleep at the switch," he went on, musing to himself out loud, "or someone rubbed his palms with some green payola."

"These are complicated plots played out by professional thieves," Russ broke in. "I caught a corner of the story on the news. Apparently, they were restoring a newly uncovered Mayan mummy they discovered somewhere in Mexico. They said something about a ritual sacrifice that may have been performed on it."

Butch said, "I went to the lecture about the Maya the other day and learned that they performed sacrifices on victims after their ceremonial ballgames to appease the gods. They slit the sternum open and pulled out the victim's beating heart. They were anesthetized and all, but still it was gruesome."

As the waiter placed our appetizers in front of us, Butch continued. "This mummy that was stolen was apparently some Mayan rebel who had set his sights on taking power in a place called Palenque. His name was Jaguar Scroll, and he allegedly attempted to wrest power away before twelve-year-old Pacal could claim the throne. But Pacal's mom, Lady Sak K'uk, was the reigning monarch following her husband's death. About the time Pacal turned twelve and was about to receive the kingdom from his mom, Jaguar Scroll mounted a coup. It failed, and he was later sacrificed—and they are speculating that the stolen mummy might be Jaguar Scroll."

"Oh. What colorful names they had," Sonya remarked. "So how did they sacrifice him?"

"He wasn't sacrificed outright but kept in custody and finally forced to play a high-stakes ballgame a couple of years later. He was probably ritually sacrificed right after the game. That little twelve-year-old Pacal, with the help of his mom, Lady Sak K'uk, went on to rule for the next sixty-eight years, building Palenque up to rival the most splendid Mayan kingdoms."

Sally took over as Butch dipped a colossal shrimp in sauce and raised it to his mouth. "There is an archaeologist out there postulating that this uncovered Mayan mummy almost changed history. The thought of a little twelve-year-old taking over the entire rule of a place would give me pause, too. Lucky for him, his mother was so politically savvy and watched out for her little guy."

"But this matter of legitimacy was serious and so

important to the Mayans that they went to some pretty bloody extremes to prove their claim to the throne," Butch said, taking over the conversation so Sally could eat. "Our enrichment lecturer said they enacted ritual blood sacrifice." He lowered his voice and added, "The lecturer actually showed pictures of some terrifying implements made from obsidian that the Mayan rulers used to pierced themselves in a very squeamish part of the body." He looked at all the exposed flesh at the dining room tables and said, "Enough to give these folks something to think about, I'd imagine."

He paused while we took it all in. Then he sat back as Sally started in anew.

"The women drew a thorn-studded string through their tongues because the ruler didn't go through this ritual by himself," Sally said. "His wife joined him in the fun. And if the ruler was too young to be married, as in Pacal's case, his mother did the honors."

"Well, as we try to digest those images over our meal, and thank you very much for that, Butch and Sally," Russ said, "I'll conjecture that they will find the perpetrators of this major violation, and I hope they will prosecute them to the fullest extent of the law."

This was where things started getting scary for me. I mean, I had accompanied something that looked like a coffin back to the ship from the museum in Cozumel. I saw what looked like a coffin, or at least a big black trunk, loaded into the ship. The timing seemed to corroborate the robbery. I sat as all these comments were going on around me, wondering if I had inadvertently aided and abetted a grave robber and helped smuggle national treasures onto our ship. I started to say something, then thought the better of it until I had more facts.

My mind flashed back to that afternoon I walked around the Cozumel Island Museum waiting to collect the medical supplies. I tried to recall every detail of the museum, the office and the people I spoke to. I remembered the Dr. Percival Turnkey look-alike and turned to Dr. Turnkey, sitting one seat over in another white Guatemalan shirt, this time with embroidery in several shades of purple and pink. I was trying to imagine him in a bushy moustache. I asked him if he had ever seen a mummified body during his career as a pathologist, and he said no and smiled. He said he had only ever dealt with tissue samples from living people. He added that mystery writers love to glamorize the work of pathologists because their testimony can go a long way with juries in murder-mystery cases and be compelling enough to influence verdicts. He said it was pretty much routine work for the most part, but the pay was steady.

I couldn't imagine this gentle little widower involved in any kind of a major international grave robbery and chastised myself for entertaining such baseless thoughts. As the conversation reverted to more mundane issues, I excused myself before dessert. I had to check back with Perry Cardis in the office about plans for the evening show. I had not heard from him and assumed things were still in turmoil. The *Tides* had slated the evening entertainment as a "Surprise!" Evidently, Stella and Perry Cardis had had another showdown that resulted in a stalemate.

෮෮෮

I got to the office just after Perry Cardis walked in. He didn't see me outside the door and left it slightly ajar. Before I could count to three, he and Stella were at fisticuffs again. It was as if they were continuing an ongoing argument, and I couldn't pull myself away from the fireworks. I was actively eavesdropping while I pretended to be reading some graphs on the wall outside the office that I didn't understand. Stella told Perry Cardis that her comedy act was going to happen that night, and she had already set up the stage for her show and directed the stage manager to remove the game-show chairs and lectern she found when she arrived in the theater. "You must be crazy! You honestly think these people are interested in wasting an hour watching 'Let's Make a Peel?' You couldn't even get anyone to participate in your game last night." She was fuming at him and told him he looked ridiculous parading around the ship in his boxer shorts and undershirt and that goofy flashing bow tie. "You look like a one-man freak show," she admonished. He activated his whirring bow tie just then and some papers fluttered off her desk.

"You secretly like it," he said. "In fact, you probably wish you could wear your underwear too."

"You scoundrel, Perry Cardis!" Stella roared. "There are lines of decency you don't cross, which you used to do whenever you told that revolting joke about the hippopotamus's deadly gas emissions. How desperate could you be for a laugh?"

"Ha!" Perry Cardis spouted. "Deadly but not silent!" He smiled, reminiscing fondly. "That's the problem with you. You can't laugh at things most people find funny. What's not to love about a hippo cracking a big noisy air biscuit? The only ones not laughing were the whining old biddies."

"And do you know why those nice ladies protested?" Stella provoked. "Because your joke went over the line of decency."

"So, you've never visited the buffet? C'mon, Stella, face it! It wasn't the hippo's butt burp that annoyed them, it was that the hippo reminded them of their own husbands."

"Get out of here right now, Perry Cardis!" Stella exploded. I could hear her pounding the desk with her fist. "You disgust me! And from now on, I don't want to have any more conversations about underwear or nudity. Am I making myself clear? It's off the table! All I know is that at nine-thirty tonight, you are going to introduce my comedy act in the theater, and I am going to be on stage as the curtain goes up for my show. After my show, you will invite everyone to join me in the

Paris Lounge for a Twist and Shout dance party. Is that clear? Furthermore, I will *never* strut around this or any other ship in my underwear. I will not laugh at your disgusting jokes either. Do I make myself clear, or do I have to start rummaging through one of your trunks to find something that will make you disappear?"

"Rummage through my trunks any time you want!" Perry Cardis laughed as he approached the door.

"What did you just say?" Stella asked sharply. "You know what I meant! No, you get right back in here right now, Perry Cardis! I'm not through with you yet!"

I slipped out at that point. I saw all I needed to know—the glaring fact that everyone seemed to have missed. Those two couldn't get enough of each other. Perry Cardis and Stella Laffer were in love!

25

Monkeyshines

Day Seven: February 21, Sunday
Roatan, Honduras
Mostly Cloudy: High: 86°F/30°C. Low: 77°F/25°C.

THE NEXT MORNING started with Stella's cheerful voice bouncing through the loudspeaker welcoming us to Roatan. By the time we arrived at our meeting spot on the pier, Stella was the talk of the ship as much for her uproarious comedy act the night before as for her Twist and Shout dance marathon, all the rage in the Paris Lounge until the wee hours of the morning. Everyone took it for granted that she was the new sheriff in town, and no one even mentioned Pearl or seemed to miss Perry Cardis.

I had stopped up and joined the dance party for a little while, amazed at the number of people dancing to the sixties generation rock-and-roll music and drinking enough to sink the ship. I left just after midnight as a squadron of waiters rolled in an entire banquet and spread it out on a row of long white cloth-covered tables.

What was most noteworthy, though, was Perry Cardis's reaction as he took it all in. He never glanced away from Stella. And those were not eyes of despise or loathing, but eyes of admiration and respect and...*love!* I knew there was something between those two, whether they admitted it or not. Now I was more curious than ever to see how this was going to play out over the next few days.

∿∿∿

Our group met on the pier, and we were ushered to the parking lot where they divvied us up into small van-sized buses. Roatan is a long and narrow island a few miles away from the coast of Honduras. Mojita, our guide, gave us a little time to chuckle about her name as she joked about her mother's favorite cocktail while the driver guided us out of the parking lot.

Mojita told us how a common sight along the beaches was of people leading metal detectors over the sand looking for lost pirate treasure. She said there was a decent chance of finding old coins, buttons and buckles from the pirate days since Roatan was a notorious pirate "Hell Town" and a popular pirate hub by the seventeenth century. She attributed it to its ideal location along the main routes of the Spanish galleons and for all the nooks and crannies along its ragged shoreline that offered hideaways to bury their treasure.

Roatan was the stomping ground for some very famous pirates like Captain Henry Morgan, who may even have attended a real honest-to-goodness pirate convention that attracted about a thousand swashbucklers to Roatan in 1683.

Someone asked if there had ever been a significant treasure find in Roatan, and Mojita said there were a couple she was aware of. One British adventurer in the 1920s uncovered buried chests containing coins worth about six million dollars. He "got out of Dodge" with the loot and went back to England where he bought himself a castle. Following that, in the 1960s, a self-described treasure hunter from Texas found a decaying wooden box full of coins near the place where the earlier treasure had been discovered. He emptied the coins into another container, and just as he was about to toss the old crate off his boat, he hesitated because it felt too heavy for its size. Sure enough, when he examined the box, he found a false bottom concealing sixteen Peruvian silver ingots worth sixty thousand dollars. Mojita said in those days, if you found treasure, you hightailed it off the island before the authorities caught up with you and confiscated it. But more recent treasure finds have changed the laws so that nowadays, treasure must be conceded to the landowner.

For a very small island with nothing comparable to the Mayan ruins we had seen in Mexico, Belize and Guatemala, there was still a lot to do in Roatan. We headed off for a visit to an iguana farm where hundreds of lazy, leathery and loathsome prehistoric reptiles loitered leisurely, crunching on the palm fronds left around the grounds for guests to pick up and feed to them. When we had our fill of those miniature monsters, we headed to Gumbalimba Park, a nature reserve that held the promise of exotic tropical birds, listless sloths and playful Capuchin monkeys. Mojita warned us the monkeys would steal anything from buttons off our shirts to backpacks to our very glasses and strongly advised us to place everything that wasn't permanently attached in the lockers provided. "Last week one ran off with someone's videocam," Mojita warned.

Nothing can quite reduce an adult to a child as fast as a monkey, and these monkeys did not disappoint: jumping on heads, sitting on shoulders, grabbing our ears and pulling on necklaces. Guests were laughing and posing for photos in little groups and taking selfies as the mischievous monkeys ratcheted up their attention-ops with every trick they knew. One reached out and grabbed a full bottle of Fanta Orange from a guest's hand. Off he scampered, leaving the guest sorry he'd brought it along. Another monkey touted her fuzzy little babies riding on her back and clinging to her fur for dear life as she jumped from the shoulders of one delighted guest to another.

Suddenly, a shriek. We all looked in the direction of the scream and saw a woman standing there, blood spurting out of her earlobe and saturating her yellow polo shirt. She was trying to sop it up with a tissue.

"Ahhh! Ouuuch!" she cried. The sight of a hoop earring dangling from the other ear told us that a monkey had grabbed her shiny earring and tore it right off her earlobe. Fortunately, the flap of skin was torn on one side but the earlobe was still attached, so with any luck they could stitch it back together. I offered to escort her back to the ship right then—an offer she readily accepted—and cut my own excursion short, bidding everyone else goodbye.

We grabbed a taxi in the parking lot. As I was filling out the injury report, the injured woman kept sopping up the blood with one hand and holding her earlobe with the other and crying. "Oh, it hurts so much," she said.

"Try not to touch it so you don't infect it," I cautioned her, wondering just how dirty a monkey could be and thinking it was probably very dirty.

The driver did his best to speed us back to Coxen Hole, bumping over potholes and scraping by overgrown brush on the edge of the road. Coxen Hole, the island's little capital, was named for a pirate, John Coxon,[*] who used Roatan as his corporate headquarters in the seventeenth century for a while before disappearing at sea and from the pages of history.

We eased into a light conversation along the way. The guest said she was Patricia Willisten from Boca Raton. She said she had been on these nudie cruises before. She wasn't one herself, but took advantage of

---

[*]   The pirate and the town's names are spelled differently.

the good deals they offered and, while she was on the cruises, always went the way of the majority. "What the heck," she said, "when in Rome and all the rest, you know." Patricia assured me there were many like her on the cruise who weren't actual nudists but didn't mind the "cover" to "uncover" every now and then.

When we arrived back at the ship, the taxi driver had to weave around a bottleneck near the cargo hold caused by some local pickup trucks loaded with freshly caught fish on ice. It looked like they were going to transfer the fresh fish into the ship. I asked the taxi driver if he knew what kind of fish they were, and he said they looked like red snapper and yellowfin tuna. I was hoping it would be on the captain's menu that night.

I escorted Patricia to the infirmary, grateful for the unexpected "official" excuse to stop by because I'd been meaning to ask Dr. Messy if she'd heard anything about the robbery in Cozumel.

The nurse greeted us and said the doctor would be right out. But the doctor that came through the door was not Dr. Messy. Instead, a man was standing there. He said he was Dr. Gerome and he had been called on short notice to replace Dr. Messy who had disembarked that morning!

26

Grave Robber Strikes Again

ALL KINDS OF UNSETTLING doubts were starting to crowd my imagination: the biggest question being, why did Dr. Messy leave so abruptly? Did she think someone might be pursuing her? I left Patricia in the capable hands of the medical staff and went to my room intent on finding a news station on TV to see if there was anything new about that missing mummy in Cozumel.

The light was blinking on my phone when I entered the room. It was Stella, asking me to drop by the office for the next day's marching orders. It was to be a day-at-sea, as we would be en route to Jamaica, and she wanted to fill it wall to wall with fun activities for the guests. I knew that was going to be a tall order after she essentially fired Perry Cardis from having any part in arranging the entertainment. Leaving the TV on, I went to the office where she was sitting alone at the desk tapping on the computer keyboard. I congratulated her on her fantastic comedy show the night before and the rousing dance party that went on all night.

She looked up and smiled. "Thank you. It would have been nice to offer the singer, ventriloquist, guitarist, impersonator and all the other qualified entertainers that had been booked on this cruise but were stricken off the agenda by a certain nameless person," she said.

"He also started a scandal of sorts by directing crew members to dress up as Mayan rulers one day, and now some guests are complaining that it was insensitive to the indigenous." I remembered seeing them that day, holding up "Chocolate Tattoo" signs as we reboarded the ship after our excursion in Cozumel. No one seemed to mind it at the time.

"Now, I'm steeped in damage control over that too. Some days I would like to shoot that man to the moon."

I thought to myself, only on those days you're not head-over-heels in love with him, and stifled a smile.

"Fortunately, for tonight's entertainment, we have a very special and unexpected surprise. The local Garifuna tribe has a dance troupe, and they've offered at the last moment to come onto the ship and present an entire show of their native traditional dancing. I'm working out the details right now, including a later departure time.

"By the way, Marianne, I liked the way you jumped in and twisted and shouted with the rest of us last night," she said. "You should have stayed until the end of the party, though. You're really here to pitch in. I'll expect more of you, and I'll need you up there dancing every night until the party ends. The production team is going to be stretched pretty thin with all the daytime activities they host around the ship, and I'll need them to fill the headliner productions with so many spaces open now. So, I'll need your help greeting our guests at the theater entrance every evening as well. Report twenty minutes before curtain."

She continued, "This evening, I want you to start hosting those solo happy hours again, but instead of doing it in the Paris Lounge, let's take it to the Monkey Bar. They're not getting enough people in there for some reason on this cruise, so we can at least try to fill more seats." I couldn't repress the image of more bare bottoms sinking into the upholstered chairs.

"In fact," Stella continued, "let's switch Perry Cardis's games to the Monkey Bar as well," she thought out loud. "I'll let him know," she said, jotting a note on a pad of paper. I'm putting Perry Cardis's games in the half hour before dinner from now on, so as soon as you tie up your solo happy hour at six o'clock, stick around to help him from six to six-thirty."

I mentally calculated that would only give me a few minutes to run back to my room to be ready in time for dinner with the captain at seven.

I left her office feeling good to have a new purpose and a sense of belonging to the team. I was looking forward to the rest of the cruise and putting aside any thoughts of my mounting work at home and the pile of mail waiting for me inside my front door.

Entering my room, my eye caught a text scrolling

along the bottom of the still-running news show on TV. It read, "Ancient civilization violated! Mayan mummy robbed from Costa Maya!"

I froze.

The reporter's eyes widened as she relayed that someone had stolen a priceless archaeological treasure from one of Mexico's Mayan ruins. I was transfixed and listened on. "The mummy of a little-known Mayan ruler had found its way out of Mexico at the hands of a modern-day grave robber through a complicated network of conspirators. The last time this mummy was seen by the archaeological staff was when it left Chichén Itzá for Costa Maya, where a prominent Mayan archaeologist was scheduled to receive and study it and report his findings to a blue-ribbon panel of Mayan scholars." She went on to explain that archaeologists were up in arms over the disappearance of this incredibly important piece of Mayan history, and the reporter added that it was so delicate from its age that even slight movement could disturb and destroy the remains completely.

I had stopped hearing everything that followed "Costa Maya."

I stared at the TV in a cold sweat as the camera panned the cruise port at Costa Maya, exactly where our ship had been. I was relieved there had been no mention of a connection between the abduction of the mummy in Cozumel and the disappearance of the other one in Costa Maya, only a day apart. Just then it came.

The reporter turned to her colleague who asked her about a possible connection between the two events, and the first reporter answered that nothing had been established but authorities were certainly investigating that possibility.

I didn't know what to do or where to turn. I tried to convince myself that it was just a coincidence. The conspiracy was probably way too sophisticated for any professional theft ring to leave the last and most crucial step to a totally innocent amateur and a proven klutz at that. But maybe that was the genius of it and Dr. Messy already knew what a klutz I was. I was already implicating and accusing her.

I calmed down and reasoned with myself. Dr. Messy may have been a little eccentric, but she most realistically wasn't involved in anything that far-fetched or illegal. I chastised myself for creating my own paranoia and quickly thought back to the trouble my self-imposed paranoia had brought me on the prior cruise.

The TV news shifted to a big sea turtle migration sighted along the Pacific coast of Costa Rica, and I switched the TV off to focus on my work schedule. The busier, the better, I thought.

❧❧❧

Wearing a lavender and yellow scarf with my black dress, I sat alone for nearly forty-five minutes in the Monkey Bar single-handedly consuming the bowls of mixed nuts and potato chips and chasing after it all with two servings of ginger ale. From where I was seated, I could pick up bits and pieces of nearby conversations. One group had joined a submarine excursion in Roatan. They were laughing because their most exotic marine life encounter was a scuba diver. Another group cheered as one of their members passed around Honduran cigars he had purchased from a vendor on the pier. Their conversation drifted into a comparison between Cuban and Honduran cigars. I had to keep reminding myself that the little resort-like island of Roatan was part of mainland Honduras.

The time dragged on. I was acutely aware of sitting there conspicuously alone, not even attracting a casual bystander. I looked at my watch and swore it was going backwards. I started fidgeting with my scarf, trying different ways to tie it around my neck. I could only do two things with scarves and wondered if there were more ways to arrange them. To kill time, I tried arranging the scarf artfully on my shoulder only to realize I could have used a third hand to prevent self-strangulation.

As I reverted to tying the scarf in my usual boring way, the loudspeaker crackled to life and Stella's cheerful, upbeat voice rattled through the bottomless list of evening activities. She mentioned that a happy hour party was in progress on the pool deck with music provided by the Latin Swingers guest show band. Then she said Chef Marcel had gone fishing in Roatan and was preparing to serve freshly grilled, freshly caught red snapper and yellowfin tuna in the Lido buffet. Finally, she paused dramatically and announced that the ship's departure would be delayed until ten-thirty because a very exciting and unexpected surprise awaited us in the theater that evening at nine o'clock. Our showtime extravaganza was a local dance troupe from Roatan in their debut production of "Garifuna Goes Bare-ifuna!" I thought that was sure to grab this crowd's attention.

She said the ship would wait for the conclusion of their performance to sail and encouraged everyone to enjoy the bonus time in port at Roatan. As soon as Stella finished, the conversations around the room reverted right back to the fantastic comedy act she had given the night before, and people were hoping she'd be back with another show soon.

I didn't get any action with the solo happy hour and stayed right there in the Monkey Bar waiting for Perry Cardis to show up for Skin-Opoly. A member of the stage crew was setting up an easel with a hand-drawn sketch of something vaguely resembling a Monopoly game board. But instead of streets and places, it had titles of movies, books and songs. The point of Skin-Opoly was to advance through the spaces; players had to know the actor or character that appeared without clothing in the book or movie or song. Instead of Monopoly money, players started with a cutout doll of a celebrity and a pile of cutout clothes. Each article had a different value attached. A sweater was worth five points and a pair of socks worth one point. You "bought" your way around the gameboard with these by taking off pieces of clothing while moving closer and closer to the goal of total nudity. A wrong move could "cost" you by putting a garment back on. First one to shed all their clothes won the game. I had to admit it was kind of a clever adaptation and was equally aware that I probably didn't know too many answers. I didn't have to. My part was to keep score so everyone playing and watching could relax and have fun.

Fair enough.

27

Love Letter

By 6:45 P.M., I was back in my room dressed and ready for security to pick me up and escort me to Captain Gurtigruten's quarters for dinner. It all seemed otherworldly as the knock on the door came five minutes before seven o'clock. The smiling security agent led me by the elbow down the corridor and up the elevator, making small talk about the cruise and the fish catch at Roatan. Apparently, freshly caught grilled fish was on the captain's menu!

I was led through a sequence of security checks involving what looked like some red laser lights and a couple of echoing pongs, like sounds you would hear underwater in a scuba dive; but the sliding doors responded quickly, and I was admitted with ease. Captain Gurtigruten was right there to greet me. I looked around hopeful to see more people, but the dinner table was set for two. Captain Gurtigruten was wearing his navy captain's suit. He looked distinguished and smiled easily. I had to admit, he looked very nice, and like a nice person too. He welcomed me in and showed me around. There was a lot to take in because his suite was enormous compared to mine. There was a proper dining area and living room and a balcony so large he probably could have steered the ship from there. Everything was polished to a glistening reflection, and he proudly showed me his collection of models of all the ships he had ever worked on. There were dozens, and each one had been meticulously labeled with its name, the time he'd spent on it, his rank and function and all the itineraries. He was very proud of his collection and exuded contagious enthusiasm.

When a little bell tinkled, we made our way to the dining table gradually, talking as we went. I had a lot of questions for him, and he seemed to enjoy answering them all. He answered slowly, with a great deal of deliberation, but there was always a twinkle in his eyes. He liked to laugh, which made the whole thing less awkward. His steward met us at the table and held my chair for me, dropping a linen napkin on my lap as I sat down. I noticed it was a black napkin because my dress was black. Captain Gurtigruten called him Montalban, and I got the feeling they had known each other for a very long time. There was no menu, and everything was served first by the waiter, then left on the table in serving dishes family style. We could help ourselves to seconds. There was no alcohol in sight because, after all, the captain was driving.

The grilled red snapper was the freshest I'd ever

tasted and utterly sublime. It was served with assorted steamed vegetables and a fragrant rice pilaf. I could have gone for another heaping helping but didn't want to seem as hungry as I actually was. When I was done asking the captain about seventy-seven questions that he answered patiently and graciously, he started asking questions about me. I wanted him to know that I'd played the cello with the string quartet and solved the mystery about Sabrina's disappearance on the cruise just prior to the one he joined. He was fascinated by the circumstances under which I'd found the missing Sabrina and started a playful interrogation of his own.

Thankfully, he avoided any mention of the whole incident at the captain's dinner and never brought up Miss Fantina Monaire. I took it we both considered it closed and forgotten. He said he was enjoying our dinner more than one time and—without my even asking—started serving me a heaping second helping of the rice pilaf and more of the red snapper. He said perhaps next time I dined with him, I could serve the seconds.

He hinted that he wanted to hear my opinion about "certain things" and that he was already trusting my judgment. I said I'd be happy to be his sounding board.

"You see, Marianna," he said, leaning over the table and drawing closer to me, "I am *in amour* with a woman who never answers my pleas. I try, oh I try to win her attention just to have dinner with her once. But she is so sweet, so shy. I love her so much, but she can't get herself to write to me. It makes me so sad."

"How long have you been *in amour* with the lady, Captain?" I asked, suddenly very interested in this unexpected soap opera.

"Oh, maybe three years. Esmeralda! Ach! She is so beautiful! Her eyes! Her lips! I really love her," he said, grasping his heart.

"Where is she now?" I asked. I was eyeing the desserts calling out to me from the counter on a shiny silver tray and hoped he wouldn't forget to serve me some. "In Cartagena with her family, of course," he said, as if defending her.

"Esmeralda!" he said again. This poor man was hurting. I stared at the desserts, but he didn't catch my drift. I had a mind to get up and start serving our desserts myself, but luckily I hesitated. Because just then, Montalban reappeared with a silver coffeepot. He tilted his head as he hovered the coffeepot over my cup, and I nodded. The stream of coffee poured into the white porcelain cup, and I helped myself to sugar and cream as Montalban poured the captain's coffee. Then he came back to the table with the tray of desserts, an irresistible selection of delicate, pastel-glazed petit fours and a sumptuous mound of coconut macaroons. With polished silver tongs, he transferred three morsels to my plate and then served the captain. One bite of one of those chewy macaroons and I was transported.

Captain Gurtigruten took a slow sip of his coffee. His eyes were upturned as if he were deep in thought.

"I like that you are my friend," he said, suddenly looking at me as I was stuffing an entire macaroon in my mouth. Now the challenge would be to answer him with that thing taking up my entire mouth. I drank some coffee, hoping to melt the macaroon a little faster.

"You have lovely eyes, Marianne. Do you want to go to bed?" he asked as casually as though he'd asked me to pass him the salt.

I literally almost choked on the macaroon, a chunk flying out of my mouth and skipping over the tablecloth. It was hard to play down my reaction after that, but I just said, "Nope," as if he'd just asked me if I liked pineapple pizza. "But I would like another macaroon," I said, chewing the one already in my mouth and pointing to the tray on the counter behind him.

"Oh, yes, of course, Marianne," he said, twisting around to reach the tray.

"Good. Just friends," he said, patting my hand. I nodded as I stuffed the next chewy macaroon in my mouth.

"You are a writer, Marianna, yes?" he asked.

"Yes."

"Will you help me? I am trying to write a love letter to Esmeralda. Can you read what I wrote and tell me how to make a change?"

What was going on here? I wondered. Did he bring me in for dinner to help advance his romance with another woman? Who the heck did he think I was, anyway, Cyrano de Bergerac?

We went to his desktop where the letter was open and ready for me to see. It was brief and left much to be desired.

"My dear, beloved Esmeralda, you are so beautiful, and my heart longs for you more with every passing day. Why won't you answer me? Why? Why! Why do you ignore me so long? Please don't be so shy. Think of me as your Adonis, yes? When will you come to me? Esmeralda! Esmeralda! Esmeralda! I need you, Esmeralda! Yours in waiting, Captain Gert Gurtigruten."

What could I say? What could I do to help? I looked at Esmeralda's email address. EsmieXXXon-call@loveplay.com. It told me everything I had to know. I shook my head.

"Where did you meet Esmeralda?" I asked the captain.

"Oh, it was a beautiful day in Cartagena!" he said dreamily. "I'll never forget it. It is a long story. I will tell you next time."

I guess that meant I'd be back for dinner. I was already thinking about those macaroons.

I sat down and composed a letter I thought would placate him. He thought it didn't express his longing enough. I told him sometimes it's okay to play a little hard-to-get. He reluctantly agreed when I reminded him his approach had not worked. I sent the email. He said he would let me know when she replied. I wasn't holding my breath.

Our dinner was officially over by nine o'clock. Captain Gurtigruten had to get back to the bridge to prepare for that late departure, and I had to get to the theater doors. We talked briefly about the local Garifuna dancers coming on board for the evening show before we parted. He said local entertainers at ports of call were always an exciting change for the guests. If he could not get to the theater, he at least planned to watch it from the TV screen on the bridge where he could see what was going on in any part of the ship at any time. Then he said he was always a little uneasy any time someone came on board without prior clearance from the corporate office. We left it at that as he saw me out, taking my hand and kissing it gently. Then he said he would arrange for us to have dinner again soon.

"Just friends," he added with a smile.

"I'd like that, too, Captain Gurtigruten," I said. "And next time, I'll serve the seconds."

28

Garifuna Goes Bare-ifuna

I EMERGED from the security door and made my way back to my room. I had just a couple of minutes to run a toothbrush over my teeth and grab a sweater before heading for the theater to greet guests at the doors. I beat Stella to the entrance by a hair's breadth.

Stella was all smiles, and we delighted in the turnout, watching the couples and groups pour in. By curtain time, the theater was filled to capacity, and more people were pressed against the side and back walls. Several were either fully dressed or draped with a shawl against the cool air in the theater. I suspected Stella had more than a little to do with the plummeting temperatures in the theater and dining room over the past couple of days.

The stage was lit up with "Garifuna Goes Bare-if-una!" I had to marvel that someone had so cleverly tweaked a title to fit the theme of this cruise and credited Stella with doing her homework. The houselights turned off and a bright spotlight followed Stella down to the front of the stage, where she welcomed everyone to the theater and said she was excited and proud to introduce the local dance troupe on board the MS *Minerva*. "And now, ladies and gentlemen, a once-in-a-lifetime extravaganza! 'Garifuna Goes Bare-ifuna!'"

The drums rolled while a deep voice emerged from the dark as smoke drifted across the stage. The voice called himself Aboulef and said he was of the Garifuna people. As images were played across the screen, the curtains opened to reveal dancers and drummers in colorful costumes caught in a frozen stance. Aboulef explained the origins of the Garifuna people. He said they were shipped almost two thousand miles away from their homeland of St. Vincent and the Grenadines in 1798, deposited at Roatan and told to make a new life for themselves there. The Garifuna were a racial blend of African slaves and indigenous Caribs, adding that the Caribbean Sea derived its name from the Carib tribe of indigenous people. "The Garifuna have come to be known for their traditional ethnic dance, the Punta," Aboulef said. He added it took a great deal of practice that was helped by a genetic predisposition.

"Not anyone can do the Punta. You have to be Garifuna from birth to do it." He enunciated the word Garifuna slowly for emphasis and followed up with a deep and loud belly laugh.

The dancing started to the insistent beat of the drums. The first group of dancers swirled and swiveled as more dancers poured onto the stage, joining them with exotic costumes of mostly yellow and black that shimmered in the strobing stage lights. Some of the men were brandishing machetes and decoratively carved wooden clubs as they danced. Aboulef said the machetes symbolized the cutting of sugar cane, the African slaves' primary task on plantations across the entire Caribbean region in the Colonial Era.

In no time, the entire audience fell under the enchantment of the dizzying motion, mesmerizing music and Aboulef's hypnotic voice. A serene smile fairly stretched from ear to ear on every face in the audience. I couldn't imagine any other ship's stage coming alive like this and dismissed the captain's earlier apprehensions. I thought maybe the cruise lines should do it more often if this was the reaction from the guests. Hard to believe, but this act was even outdoing Stella's comedy act from the night before. The sounds grew so loud they spread beyond the theater's entrance. Guests strolling by the shops or heading to the elevators heard the music and beelined for the theater that was so full at one point that Stella mumbled something about the fire code. The music and dancing went on. Women in yellow and black gowns were streaming matching scarves in the air, forming hypnotic helices that morphed into diaphanous braids and wafted into dissipating clouds. Men wearing yellow loincloths danced as if in a trance, their bare feet working together with strong, purposeful steps in effortless synchrony, their black skin shining from perspiration under the blazing spotlights as smoke wafted across the stage. They were showing no sign of slowing down or stopping but seemed to feed on the increasing energy from the audience. They were all stepping and chanting in unison as the music mounted, and the entire stage seemed to writhe with the excitement of an impending grand finale. As the last notes were struck and the dancers swept around in their final bows, the audience rose as one unit and burst into unrestrained applause. The performers danced their way off stage and came out for an appreciative curtain call. They acknowledged the audience and each other and waved. A couple of them blew kisses, and they marched back out of sight.

Stella was heading back to the stage with her mic as she called out for another curtain call. The audience could not get enough of these performers, and she wanted to milk the moment for all it had. The performers did not come out and she called for them again, smiling and saying she knew they were not shy. Another awkward moment as no one appeared. I began to wonder if they already had started to disembark the ship.

But suddenly they appeared. Only this time they were dressed far more scantily, as if they had been in the middle of changing out of their costumes when they decided to return for a final curtain call. Some of the men had machetes between their teeth and others were holding long javelins or spears. Two were holding scythes and several of the women wielded hoes. The one defining difference this time was that their faces were covered completely by gorgeous African masks. I marveled at how clever this was, thinking they probably were very modest about being nearly naked and the masks hid their identities. More performers streamed onto the stage, and I was beginning to realize their numbers had increased. I wondered why all these dancers had not appeared earlier as part of the main show. The men bowed and the women curtsied, but there was no music from the band, whose instruments all lay at the back of the stage with no musicians to play them. Instead, the music came from the performers themselves, blowing through conch shells, rattling dried-out gourds and tapping javelins and hoes against the floor and chanting. They made intriguing sounds by clicking their teeth as they crossed from one side of the stage to the other. It was almost as if they were sending each other coded messages, and I got the impression that the performers were starting all over again with a whole new show.

The audience clapped and stamped their feet for more, not caring that it was going well past ten forty-five and the ship was not yet sailing. The performers seemed to have forgotten that they were supposed to end the show before our ten-thirty departure. They revved up their music and bodily swirls, but there was no synchrony this time. Whatever they were doing now was completely unrehearsed and impromptu. One by one they stepped off the stage and spread out into the audience. The spectators were transfixed! This show was going into overtime and becoming interactive! It felt like a party was starting. A conga line formed spontaneously as guests streamed out of their seats and headed to join in. People were singing out, "one-two-three-four Conga!" as they grabbed each other by the waists and snaked through the rows and aisles of the theater. Simultaneously, several new conga lines were starting up from different directions. The Garifuna leaders led them all in the same direction to merge into one big line. In the midst of this festive frenzy, some of the dancers started selecting random dance partners from the audience, showing them simple steps and dancing them to the exit and through the doors. The audience dance partners were picking up the steps and following their leaders eagerly.

The conga lines followed everyone else noisily and happily to the exit and through the doors. The rest of the audience started to leave their seats and follow the entire entourage to the doors. This had to be the best ship performance ever, and the most unforgettable curtain call in the history of ship entertainment. But by the time the audience reached the doors, the dancers, now on the outside of the theater with their audience dance partners, suddenly closed the theater doors, trapping everyone else inside. For a moment people thought it was part of the act, expecting the doors to open—but that didn't happen. The doors were shut from the outside and didn't budge. Stella and I tried shaking them but realized with increasing alarm that they had been barred from the other side. At the same moment, frantic screams and shouts sounded from outside the doors. We heard javelins and hoes hitting the walls while someone was blowing a deafening blast with a conch shell. The heated commotion intensified as voices kept rising. It sounded like the conga line dancers were yelling at the performers in a struggle to escape from them. But whatever was happening, we were trapped inside, unable to help.

Stella said to stay where I was and keep trying the door. She was going to escape through the backstage exit and would come around and open the door from the other side. The audience inside was panicking and pressing up against the blocked doors. I could see I was going to be smooshed by a delirious crowd trapped in a space too small for everyone, and all trying to escape together. Men were pounding on the doors shouting, "Let us out! Open these doors!" Women were scream-ing. I could hear as much turmoil on the other side of the door. I could barely see past the frightening throng that had collected at the door. I waited for Stella to get to the other side and simultaneously was afraid for her.

Then I heard the word from someone in the crowd. "Pirates!" a man yelled. "They're goddam pirates!"

Someone else screamed, "We've been taken over by pirates! The ship is full of pirates!"

Another man shouted, "They'll kill us all!"

A woman nearby sobbed, "God help us!"

29

Pirates Avast!

I FROZE. My first thought was of Captain Gurtigruten. I hoped he had been watching the performance from the bridge and doing what he could to head off a takeover by these pirates. So, this was why he was anxious about anyone coming on board without advance clearance.

Everyone stopped talking and shouting simultaneously as the reality started to settle into our brains. We had been cleverly seduced and were even complicit in our own capture by these pirates masquerading as performers. The evening had started out so beautifully and was now heading toward a very bad end. I was afraid for our lives and our ship. I was afraid for Captain Gurtigruten. Piracy at sea is no laughing matter. I was hoping someone would clue the captain in and that the officers on the bridge locked their doors in time. I was wishing Wink had been on board. He would have known what to do.

One man was talking to someone behind me. He said everyone knows pirates take hostages against their wills. But these pirates had cleverly gathered up willing hostages by selecting their dance partners from the audience.

Another woman screamed, "My husband is one of their captives! He's a hostage, and he's out there with those murderers right now! I warned him not to dance with that strange woman and all her jiving and gyrating! It was obscene, but he wouldn't listen to me!" She started frantically pounding the door while sobbing, "Herb! Herb! You answer me now! What are they doing to you, Herb?" until someone pulled her away from the door.

The scene was fast disintegrating into one of utter chaos and despair. I noticed the stage lights were still on high beam and thought immediately of Dominic alone up in the control room. I made my way over, squeezing through all the people that were pressing against each other in their frenzied attempt to reach the doors. Dominic was nowhere in sight when I climbed the four or five stairs in the dark and entered the little booth. I knew he would not abandon his post, and I also knew he had direct telephone communications with the rest of the ship. I looked around in his small space, but there was no sign of Dominic. Then I saw something stir on the floor. It was rolled up and tucked away underneath a console, but it twitched enough to catch my attention in the dark. It was Dominic!

I quickly took the gag out of his mouth and untied the colorful scarves from their own costumes they'd used to bind his hands and feet. He hugged me with reflexive gratitude and immediately picked up the phone. The line was dead. He said this last curtain call had not been part of their show and he was confused when it started. While they were taking their dance partners hostage and gyrating their way out of the theater, one of the pirates quietly entered the control room and bound and gagged Dominic and left him on the floor. I brought him up to speed with Stella's escape through the backstage area. He said he was afraid for her life and hoped she would escape because they had all the indications of being professional pirates who knew what they were doing and had apparently scoped out the ship and the entire stage area.

On the other hand, I said I'd hate to be the pirate that came up against Stella, and we both laughed for a moment imagining that scene.

We made our way back to the theater doors together, trying our best to calm the crowd and await Stella from the other side. Suddenly, Captain Gurtigruten's voice came through the loudspeaker. He sounded like he was reading from a script. There was no trace of jollity or even confidence in his voice. He told us to go directly back to our rooms and lock our doors. Everyone caught in the theater shouted angrily. "Let us out of here first, and then we'll go to our rooms!" "We're trapped in here!" "How the hell can we get to our rooms when no one is letting us out of here?" Dominic and I tried to shush them so we could hear more.

The captain said the officers would cooperate with the "newcomers." He did not call them pirates or Garifuna. Newcomers sounded so neutral, so inoffensive, so non-accusatory. So politically correct. He added that to his knowledge no one was hurt, and the officers and crew were doing everything they could to insure everyone's safety. He urged everyone to go to their rooms immediately and lock and bolt the doors and balcony sliders and turn out their lights until further notice. He said all announcements would be coming directly into our rooms henceforth. He said there would be no food service or room service, and all ship services and activities were suspended until further notice. As if we were thinking about a round of miniature golf at that moment!

The noise from the other side of the doors subsided. It sounded like the crowd on the outside of the theater doors was dispersing. After a while, we heard someone scratching on the other side of the door. Two staff members opened it, and the people trapped inside almost trampled each other, herding through the exit and toward the safety of their rooms. People were shouting at the air, saying things like, "How are we supposed to eat?" and "Get those damn pirates off our ship!"

Stella was not in sight.

I parted ways with Dominic and returned directly to my room. By the time I walked through my door, it was almost midnight. The Garifuna show that had started with so much promise and fanfare ended up in disaster, and we had no way of knowing how long we would be in lockdown with pirates onboard and several dozen fellow guests held hostage! I tried calling Wink, but the phone line was dead. I tried sending him an email, but there was no Wi-Fi. I was determined to find out if Stella was okay and planned to sneak down to her office sometime during the night. For right now, I had only to sit and wait. And think.

Eventually, the public address system snapped back to life. The captain said the ship was heading in another direction and we were now under the direction of the newcomers, as he euphemistically put it. He sounded very anxious. We were also heading directly into a sizable storm, and in an abundance of caution, all the onboard activities scheduled for the next day were canceled. I had to rub my temples to absorb what the captain had just uttered. Here we were, held under a pack of pirates, turning away from our original direction and heading off our course to God knows where in the middle of the night and making our way directly into a serious storm to boot. And he was telling us the ping-pong tournament was canceled the next day? This was not the Captain Gurtigruten with whom I'd just shared dinner. I could only believe he was reading from a very badly written script. The captain closed by stressing this was a very dire situation and to cooperate fully. He said to brace against some rough seas that we would start feeling very soon and would continue for the next several hours.

I went to the bathroom, and by the time I returned to my bed, I was already feeling some ominous bumps as the ship was starting to enter the storm region. It was not a good sign, and I felt very sorry for the guests sailing for the first time. I also felt very sorry for all the hostages and all the spouses who could not communicate with each other. Most of those hostages were naturists and would be needing something to wear against the cold night air. I also wondered how much expertise these pirates had with navigating a cruise ship through a storm and felt this had all the markings of a terrible outcome.

Another bump was followed by several more. They were getting harder and coming closer together. The ship shuddered when it slapped against the surface each time. It felt like we were gaining speed. One of my cabinets swung open. I went to close it and felt myself nearly fall from another sudden jerk and bump. Who was steering this thing, anyway, I wondered—certainly not our captain. Then, out of nowhere, I felt a warm puddle form in the pit of my stomach. Certainly not *my* captain, I thought.

All I could do was try to sleep and hope for the best. Maybe Captain Gurtigruten and his officers would reach an agreement and sort this out by morning. I wanted to help. I couldn't sit by and watch things spin out of control without trying something. I checked to make sure my door was locked and bolted and went to bed. Sleep didn't come. My brain wouldn't let it. I was hatching a plan.

The weather was deteriorating by the hour. By three in the morning, the ship was sailing through the roughest seas I could imagine, and I heard the people in the room next door screaming. It sounded like someone was throwing up, and I really felt badly they were going through that. I peeked outside at pitch-black nothingness. Rain pelted angrily and relentlessly at the window. Suddenly, a jerk so hard actually sent my bed skidding across the carpeted room and bumped it against the opposite wall. My heart was racing. I didn't dare leave my bed for fear of what might come next. Then an ominous announcement over the loudspeaker ordered all medics to report to a suite at the front of the ship on the ninth deck for what was no doubt a slip-and-fall incurred when someone tried getting to the bathroom from their bed right at that moment. I couldn't imagine the medics working under worse circumstances than these.

The hours wore on in nightmarish fashion as I wondered what scared me more: the pirates or the storm at sea. At least you knew a storm had to end at some point. Pirates were a loose cannon.

The next sound coming through the speaker was the hypnotic voice of Aboulef from the Garifuna show. He said we were to await a knock on the door and a dish of food would be delivered to our rooms. My watch showed about quarter past five, so I wasn't sure if the meal was going to be a snack or breakfast. He started to remind us that all activities were canceled due to an abundance of caution because of the weather, but his message was interrupted several times as he either tried to steady the microphone in the raging storm or was holding back the urge to throw up. Then he abruptly stopped in the middle of a sentence. It sounded like he may have been very seasick or else someone yanked the mic away from him.

Within an hour, there was a quick and hard rap at my door. By the time I got there, no one was there, but a paper dish covered by plastic wrap lay on the floor of the corridor. I looked right and left and watched a female figure in tights and racer t-shirt running barefoot down one end of the corridor, knocking on the doors and leaving dishes as she ran. I assumed the pirates were not using the ship's room-service staff. I also wondered who was cooking our meals.

I took the dish inside my room and removed the plastic wrap. The plate was full of fluffy scrambled eggs and a pile of warm corn tortillas. I looked for a fork. This was limited room service, so I had to scoop up the eggs with the corn tortillas. I figured it probably wouldn't kill me, and to be honest, I was hungry enough to enjoy it all down to the last bite. It could have used salt.

The weather was not improving. No more announcements out of the loudspeaker. I tried turning on the TV, but there was no reception. I tried the phone, but it was still dead, as was the Wi-Fi.

By morning, it was obvious the ship was battling for its life in a major storm. The captain's voice suddenly came back through the loudspeaker and said we were heading into worse waters and to stay in our rooms. He reminded us helpfully that all the scheduled activities were suspended.

I had a thought. It was just a glimmer of an idea, but I had to act on a hunch. Part of me wanted to shoot it all down, but I couldn't pass up our only hope. I needed to check something out because if there was anything I could do to help, I was willing to try it. I knew I would be acting directly against the captain's orders, but if the plan succeeded, it would be worth it. My captain wouldn't mind. I needed to scope out a part of the ship and see if I could catch any of these pirates doing anything at all. I needed some insight into their patterns that might help me bring them down.

When I snuck out of my room and hid in a corner near the coffee bar, there were no pirates in sight. But something curious did catch my attention. The ship always kept a table of snacks in the butler's pantry next to the coffee bar in front of the dining room. The counter was always full to the brim with a varied assortment of cookies, brownies, pastries and other appetizer-sized treats available for the staff and crew and only a few of the guests in-the-know. While I was hiding in the nearby corner, someone came out from behind the bar and replenished all the goodies. I knew these treats weren't for the guests and suspected the pirates had commandeered the ship's pastry chef to keep the cookies in supply or found them in the freezer.

As soon as the trays of brownies, tarts, cupcakes and cookies were replenished, pirates started appearing and helping themselves. I wondered how often they were replenishing these snacks. I checked my watch. It was eight-twenty. I figured the number of snacks on that table would probably last about a half hour at the rate the pirates had been swooping them up. I went back to my room and left it again at a quarter to nine and hid in the same corner as before. Almost right on schedule, a new batch of snacks was laid out about five minutes after I arrived. The pirates came by, and more hands reached out to take the goodies almost like clockwork.

It was all I needed to know, and I had no time to waste!

30

Bumps in the Dark

Day Eight: February 22, Monday
At sea with pirates on board.
Violent storm. Captain will update when possible.

I PERSEVERED, even though I could list a thousand reasons not to. It was the oldest trick in the book. Couldn't I come up with anything more imaginative? I couldn't. I went back to my room and reached under my bed to retrieve those boxes of chocolate laxatives left there from a prior occupant. I had to get a hanger from the closet to help me reach the ones that were too far back. It was a good thing I'd been too lazy to remove them earlier. Now they were going to come in very handy. I unwrapped each of the cubes and got down to work scraping them into little flakes with a plastic knife from a box of fudge I'd picked up somewhere or other. It was slow and painstaking work, but it had to be done. I was convinced lives were depending on me. After over an hour, I had a sizable pile of flaked chocolate laxative ready to do the job. I carefully transferred the pile into the same plastic bag from my molinillo purchase. I knew whatever I did from here on was blatantly disregarding the captain's orders, and I risked being thrown off the ship for real. But I also couldn't stand by and do nothing. Someone had to try something with our unwelcome newcomers, and I had a strong hunch my plan just might work.

Timing was everything, and I couldn't risk getting caught. I checked my watch and calculated that the next snack refreshment was about twelve minutes away. I also calculated that the pirates would flock to stock up on them within a few minutes of the re-stock. Slowly and stealthily, I crept along the dark corridor, watching for anyone coming through to discover me. Apparently, all hands were on deck somewhere else, and I safely made it to my secret corner unseen. The trays on the pantry counter were nearly empty, so I knew I had timed it right. The new stock of goodies should be coming in another couple minutes. I held my breath, along with the plastic bag full of laxative shavings, and waited.

Twenty minutes later, there was no sign of anything. Could I have missed my last chance? Maybe the pastry chef had replenished the trays a few minutes before I got there and was told to stop until the storm passed. Or maybe they ran out of cookie dough and weren't making any more. I felt the floor shake under me and heard what must have been a huge wave slam against the starboard side. I heard people screaming from inside their rooms nearby. The ship heaved and rose and fell again, slapping hard on the water with such force that the entire vessel shook and shuddered in nauseating motion as huge waves came one after another with no relief. I wondered if we'd smacked a whale. I was gagging and almost ready to puke. But I steadied myself, knowing I was on an important and serious mission and thinking maybe the lives of everyone on board depended on me right at that instant. Suddenly, a pirate wobbled by. At least it clearly wasn't a guest or crew member. She had a handful of cookies. Could it be they were now putting the snacks in another place? I held my breath as she passed me. Then I heard a rustle and, sure enough, the pastry chef was replenishing the snack service. I was in luck!

As soon as all the old trays were replaced with new ones, the luscious snacks piled high in tempting assortments, I moved right in and sprinkled my pixie dust over everything, heaping it up in mouthwatering mounds like chocolatey deliciousness added to all the sweets. I had more than enough, so I was able to give everything another pass with more flaky, fluffy dustings. I was careful to isolate one piece of brownie in the corner for myself. Done! With a metaphoric pat on the back, I scooted back to my hidden corner and waited. It wasn't a minute later that the hands started to appear, grabbing the cookies and brownies by the twos and threes. They didn't even bother taking the napkins that had been provided. They just scooped up the snacks and scuttled on. I knew the rest was up to nature and carefully made my way back to my room as the ship heaved and rose and slapped again over and over. I was so excited about my plan that the thought of being seasick never even entered my mind.

I closed my door behind me as the captain's voice boomed through the loudspeaker and nearly shouted orders for everyone to get back to their rooms, saying the ship was heading into the worst part of the storm. He sounded worried. Apparently, I was not the only guest creeping around the ship defying his orders. His voice was so urgent you could almost picture him shaking his finger at us. He said all the bars were going to close for the next few hours. I had not realized anything was even open and figured it was part of the script he was being forced to read. Either that, or the bars had been left open to serve the pirates, and this was a warning to them too. I started to wonder if we were in a hurricane when, suddenly, the sound of something that could have been a bomb detonating was followed by a frightening quake that I could feel in my bones. I grabbed my life jacket, just in case.

The next few hours were terrifying. With every loud crash followed by an equally humongous tremor, I swore I would never, ever set foot on another ship, sailboat, motorboat, pleasure craft or even a raft for the remainder of my life. All I could do was lie on my bed and welcome death. The ship was banging, shaking and heaving all at once in a hideous cacophony that portended a disastrous end to our cruise—and maybe our lives.

I turned on the TV and tuned in to Channel 11 for a view from the bridge. Nothing but black. Another bang and shudder. I was imagining this was what it felt like to be in an earthquake. Now the drawers were banging open and shut. The bathroom door was swinging and slamming but not latching. I didn't even have the energy to get up and close it, and speaking of the bathroom, I gauged that I could "hold it" for at least another hour. I tried to sleep away the time, but the noises were ominous, creepy and not subsiding. In fact, they were louder and coming more frequently. At one point, it sounded like the entire ship had launched into the air and then dropped smack back on the water's surface. I was stunned and braced for another big smackdown which came before I could count to ten. It set off a strange sound like a little tick that went for a few seconds, paused and started up again. T-t-t-t-t-t-t-pause-t-t-t-t-t-t-pause. It drove me crazy for the rest of the storm until much later I discovered it was a pencil rolling back and forth on my desk.

I felt very sorry for people on their first-ever cruise. This would not have been the ideal first cruise for anyone by any measure. I could imagine them drawing the conclusion that this was a "normal" cruise. It was anything but. I closed my eyes and tried to let the bouncing ship rock me. It was pitching to the left and right and yawing forward and backward, the worst combination of motion for seasickness. Between all the movement and the noise, I felt like I was getting a real workout and wondered if anyone had ever bothered calculating how many calories per hour a person can burn just from worrying. I must have worried away a pound.

Morning morphed into afternoon. I pretended to sleep, but sleep didn't come to me. Yet, I must have drifted off at one point because something startled me awake. I opened my eyes and stayed still. Something was wrong. I couldn't pinpoint what the problem was, but something wasn't normal. I held my breath and listened. Nothing. Not a sound. Not a squeak, not a creak, no grunting or groaning from the ship. Eerie. No sound at all. Not even the engine. No power. I stayed still and waited. I must have been like that for nearly an hour. The battery clock ticked. I craned my neck in the dark and tried my best to see the time—1:37. But was it the afternoon or the next morning? I honestly couldn't tell. The storm had seemed to subside, but now the ship had no power. Without power, our mighty city at sea was a helpless cork bobbing around at the whims of the winds and the tides.

The silence was ghoulish. No engine. No hum of the air conditioner. No sound from the room fridge. It was dark, too. No lights. Nothing. I stepped out of my bed and walked on the balcony. I looked right and left alongside the rest of the ship. No lights at all. I thought how vulnerable we were. A huge ship is a speck when it is powerless at the mercy of the infinite sea. I went back into the room and sat on the sofa. No TV. No refrigerator or air conditioner humming. Nothing. I waited in the dark. I wondered how many of the guests realized we were bobbing in the sea without power. Hopefully, they were oblivious.

Suddenly, the world sprang back to life again. The light on the balcony was on, as I had inadvertently flipped the switch when I walked out there. The TV turned on to Channel 11 with a click, and a shadowy view emerged from the front of the ship. The refrigerator and air conditioner purred to life. It was still raining heavily in a relentless wind, but hopefully the worst was over. I noticed the phone light was blinking and picked it up to retrieve my message. It was Wink! He said he was looking forward to meeting up at Grand Cayman. I thought that would be great if we ever got there.

I was wondering if anyone was able to get word out to the world at large that our ship was overrun by pirates. I hoped the captain had had time to send an SOS to someone. It almost seemed too ironic, with Roatan's history so immersed in piracy, that our own pirates boarded there. I also wondered if people were starting to sneak out of their rooms now that the storm had subsided. It was a very large ship to be kept in lockdown by just a couple dozen people, I thought. Then again, one or two of them hiding out on every deck with a machete or a javelin could go a very long way in keeping order.

Nearly two hours later, the captain's voice was once again ringing over the loudspeaker with another announcement. The officers were back in control of the ship, and the newcomers were confined to the infirmary. I could almost detect a snicker in his voice. Maybe the laxative trick worked and the pirates were answering nature's call with a vengeance. The timing seemed consistent in any case. I hoped there were enough bathrooms in the infirmary and was certain there were additional ones in the brig next door. The captain also said all the guests that had been taken by the newcomers had been safely returned to their rooms. The captain said he was getting us back on course to Jamaica the next day, though we should expect to arrive late.

He went on to say that, during the storm, a guest had incurred an injury so serious that it required a medevac operation, meaning that a helicopter would be rendezvousing with the ship to collect the patient. He warned guests to stay off the outside decks when it arrived, to prevent additional injuries.

"Good luck," I thought. This was the kind of gawker's moment some cruisers lived for. Imagine sending live feed back to your friends as a helicopter landed on your cruise ship in the middle of a driving storm! The captain went on to say the front of the ship was always in view on Channel 11 and to watch from our rooms. No matter what he said, I could predict guests were already sneaking up to the outside pool and jogging decks for a ringside view of the action. This was almost more exciting than being taken captive by the pirates!

I didn't want to defy the captain's orders any more than I already had, but gosh! I had to see what was going on.

31

Up and Away

I MADE MY WAY upstairs to Full of Beans, the little coffee bar that overlooked the pool deck where the captain and officers liked to start their day sipping on expresso and swapping stories with the earliest risers during an ordinary cruise. The early birds were usually the most frequent cruisers, and their observations and insights served as unofficial intel for the officers. By the time I arrived, it was already crowded with others who had the same thought—a ringside view of the show, behind the protection of the floor-to-ceiling windows. I squeezed through the crowd, pressing against the glass for a peek outside and, sure enough, guests were scattered, traipsing past the yellow caution tape that had been put in place to keep everyone off the deck in the storm. They were heading out to the pool deck where the water was sloshing back and forth so fiercely they had to cover the pool with a net to prevent anyone crazy enough from trying to swim. Guests were hugging posts to keep from sliding back and forth on the wet deck as the ship groaned and squeaked ominously, heaving from side to side. The sky was thick with dark clouds, and visibility was almost zero from the rain.

About forty-five minutes into the vigil, we heard the flapping of the chopper blades approaching as they fought against the raging storm. I was beginning to appreciate how dangerous this operation was going to be. Everything was in tumultuous motion. Rain was pelting from every direction. The waves shot up so high I could see the spray flinging over the pool deck. And someone's life was on the line. They don't medevac a patient casually. It must have been dire.

Officers were appearing from every direction to escort guests off the outer decks and back to safety inside the ship with certain risk to themselves, even as more gawkers emerged on the outer decks. Overhead, the noise of the chopper's blades grew louder as it closed in on the ship. It did not attempt to land, however, but hovered above the helipad on the ship's bow. It was difficult to see a great deal of detail because searchlights focused on the helicopter kept strobing and shifting fitfully. Eventually, a medic descended on a cable, or hi-line, lowered from the chopper. Once he steadied his footing and removed the hook from his brace, the hi-line ascended and came down once more with another medic. Following them, a big metal basket was lowered which the medics received and stabilized. Meanwhile, the chopper blades were stirring up the water below, adding even more commotion to the roiling tempest.

A ship, bouncing on rough waters in the dark during a storm; and a helicopter, fighting to stay aloft while dropping a cumbersome basket that the wind kept pulling to one side–both required superhuman skill and focus, a level of accuracy simply not negotiable.

I was breathless with anticipation—and, frankly, afraid—watching this tricky procedure. The two medics quickly loaded a passenger, still on a gurney, and what looked like several pieces of luggage inside the basket. The first few attempts to send the basket aloft failed as the strong wind kept jerking it away, twisting and tossing it. After a few minutes, the medics coaxed it upward until it finally rendezvoused with the helicopter's opening, and someone reached out and pulled it inside. I expected to see the two medics follow the basket up to rejoin the helicopter as well, but the hi-line did not descend to collect them. I guessed the weather made any more ascents too dangerous and assumed they'd leave the ship at the next port instead. Everyone cheered as the helicopter flapped away, gradually dissolving back into the rain and clouds whence it came. People around me were estimating how much that operation must have cost, and the conversations reverted to sobering realities of travel like getting sick or injured and the importance of travel insurance.

Nothing could beat all that excitement, and everyone retreated to their rooms satisfied after seeing something so remarkable. We were grateful for the temporary lull in the weather but were mindful of the captain's warnings that more severe conditions were still ahead. However, as the hours wore on, the sea calmed down by degrees, and by late afternoon, people were up and around the ship again. Stella announced that activities would resume as scheduled in the *Tides*, and life pretty much reverted to normal, except that now everyone was abuzz with opinions, reflections and conjectures about what had transpired.

❧❧❧

As soon as Stella made her announcement, I stopped in her office to see how she was. I arrived as an enormous bouquet of flowers was being delivered and placed on her desk in a gorgeous vase. There was no doubt in my mind who sent them, but the card attached was out of my view.

She said the last twenty-four hours had been draining for the officers because of the negotiations in securing the freedom of the hostages with the transfer of cash funds. That cash transfer was never needed in the end, however, because all the pirates were abruptly attacked by a violent gastro-intestinal blowout at the same time. She said they were complaining of excruciating stomach cramps and uncontrollable bouts of diarrhea. They were so debilitated that they relinquished all their demands, begging only for access to the bathrooms. The sudden hijack of the pirates' digestive systems by unknown forces probably saved the cruise line a half a million dollars, she said. "Those pirates were writhing with pain from something, and it happened to all of them at the same time. We took advantage of it and didn't let the pirates use the bathrooms unless they capitulated, which they did very quickly. Those were tense moments."

I said it was too bad the Garifuna dancers turned out to be pirates. But what Stella told me next, caught me by total surprise.

"When I went backstage, the entire Garifuna dance troupe was bound and gagged, including the musicians," she said. "I immediately knew that was why it took so long for the final curtain call. The pirates were not part of the "Garifuna Goes Bare-ifuna" show at all. They were honest-to-goodness pirates that somehow managed to piggyback onboard along with our legitimate local entertainers. We still don't know how they got past security, but the head of corporate security is on his way right now and will join the ship in Grand Cayman to investigate what happened."

I knew that would have to be Wink.

Stella said the pirates had taken Aboulef hostage, knowing that the Garifuna leader's voice would be familiar to the guests who would automatically assume the Garifuna were the pirates. Stella confirmed that Aboulef and the captain had been reading from scripts, just as I'd suspected. She said Aboulef was safely reunited with the Garifuna dancers, and they would all be escorted to an awaiting plane for their return to

Roatan. On the other hand, the two dozen or so pirates had a date with the officials in Jamaica. She remarked she'd still like to know what those pirates ate to give them all the same gastrointestinal reaction at the same time and added that it saved the day.

"What happened to the patient we evacuated?" I asked.

Stella replied, "We haven't heard from the hospital in Grand Cayman yet but assume he made it all right. I think his report said he was injured on one of your excursions – Dr. Elmer Spin."

ৡৡৡ

That night, Stella performed her second comedy act, and it was just what everyone needed after the events of the previous twenty-four hours. Nobody could have anticipated the frenzy of excitement that swirled around her second appearance. The theater filled up fast, and she came firing right out of the box, even commenting with obvious approval on the state of the audience—clothed. She congratulated them on coming around and made several funny jabs at the nudist lifestyle, which no one seemed to mind since she was equally self-deprecating. She took a serious minute to explain that the Garifuna troupe who performed for us the other night was totally innocent and was so popular they would be booked on future stops in Roatan. Everyone cheered. Then she launched into a no-holds-barred litany against piracy in general in a way that exposed the serious nature of the attacks, but with a masterful stroke of humor. We were simultaneously stunned by the facts she exposed while appreciating her levity after the intense situation we'd just experienced. She could do this because everyone was safe now, and she credited Captain Gurtigruten and his officers more than once for guiding us through that perilous scenario. She also revealed the "miracle" of Montezuma's Revenge that mysteriously struck all the pirates at the same time, pausing to let the audience speculate who exactly may have struck up that little act of genius, as she put it.

Sometime in the last few minutes of her show, I snuck down to the office because I knew she wouldn't be there. I wanted to see the card on those flowers, and I hoped she had not taken them to her room yet. When I ducked into the empty office, the vase and flowers were still there—but not on the desk. They had been dumped upside down into the waste can. The attached card hung limply from an orchid stem. It said, "Think about what I asked you. See you on the MS *Cleopatra* and hoping you'll say yes. Love, P.C."

I knew it! Perry Cardis had proposed to Stella—and she was either in denial or playing hard to get!

I raced back upstairs for the end of the show and arrived just in time for Stella's final punchline. The audience was madly in love with her and stormed up to the Paris Lounge to join her for the dance party, where she led sizzling Latin salsas until nearly two in the morning. I know because I was there the whole time.

32

Of Ghosts and Poets

Day Nine: February 23, Tuesday
Montego Bay, Jamaica
Partly Sunny: High: 79°F/26°C. Low: 77°F/25°C.

THE MORNING BROKE over calm turquoise waters. All was peaceful, a tropical idyll.

The morning announcement came, but it was from the captain, not Stella. He cleared his throat and told us we were stopping in Jamaica for the day as scheduled but calling at Montego Bay instead of Ocho Rios. He said we would arrive two hours late because the storm set us back, even though everyone knew the delay was really because of the pirates. Stella took over and explained that most excursions would still take place because Montego Bay and Ocho Rios weren't too far apart. She cheerfully reported that if we were on one of the canceled excursions, we were free to explore Montego Bay on our own.

By the time we docked, the pirates were already

being led down the crew gangway and into three awaiting police vans. They were in handcuffs and not smiling.
Once those vehicles left, a much happier group fairly
danced their way down the ramp. The Garifuna dance
troupe and their band were all smiles, walking toward
an awaiting bus to the airport for their flight home. Other guests started waving, whistling and gesturing with
a thumbs-up as the Garifuna troupe looked back and
returned our waves with thumbs-ups and big smiles. If
not for the unexpected intervention of the pirates, their
show would have been a runaway success.

My excursion was canceled, so I approached the
freelance taxi stand. Those of us who were on our own
were met by a couple dozen independent tour guides
holding up colorful laminated placards showing maps
of where the various tour options could take us. Our
hosts were very friendly and greeted us graciously to
their island. I wasn't too picky because Jamaica was
all new to me. I selected a tour that included a visit
to Rose Hall Great House, an old plantation estate
with a notorious resident ghost. When our guide had
assembled eleven of us, we boarded his van and started
our adventure. He introduced himself as Rodney.

We entered the property through an imposing
gate, which opened into a gracious, wide drive no
doubt intended to impress visitors with the view of the
sprawling plantation house. Rodney explained that the
sugar barons of the Colonial Era wielded incredible
influence and had the money to back it up. They

weren't shy about flaunting their wealth and material accomplishments. We approached the enormous Italianate villa with its spectacular view of the Caribbean Sea beyond.

The estate dated back to 1746 and eventually fell to a descendant, John Rose Palmer, who moved to Jamaica from England to claim it. In March of 1820, he married Annie Mary Patterson from a nearby plantation.

Annie was rumored to have been adept at voodoo and witchcraft, having been raised by a Haitian nanny after her parents died from yellow fever. When her first, second and third husbands died, she was suspected of causing their demise with her craft. Rumors circulated that she took on slaves as lovers, murdering each in turn, until Takoo, a slave even more accomplished in witchcraft than she, murdered her out of revenge. Over time, Annie Palmer came to be called the White Witch of Rose Hall. In the intervening years, people claimed that her spirit still wandered the grounds and reports of ghost sightings helped perpetuate the legend of the White Witch.

Rodney led us through the elaborate rooms of the infamous great house, reminding us that it was typical of the palatial residences of the Colonial Era throughout the West Indies. We asked if the story of Annie Palmer was true.

"Who's to know what parts are true, when fact and legend have become so tightly interwoven over the years," he offered. He told us that in all the times he had visited Rose Hall, he never once saw a ghost, but promised he would keep an eye out and let us know if he ever encountered one.

Rodney held up his cellphone and played a snippet from a song. When it was not immediately familiar to any of us, he said it was "The Ballad of Annie Palmer" by country singer Johnny Cash. He said Cash owned the great house directly next door to Rose Hall—called Cinnamon Hill—from the 1970s until 2012, and in Rodney's opinion its history was even more interesting than that of Rose Hall, but less known. He went on to tell us about Cinnamon Hill.

Cinnamon Hill Great House was built in 1761 by sugar baron Edward Barrett, whose great-grandparents settled in Jamaica from England in 1655. That was the same year Jamaica went from being a Spanish colony to a British colony. If it had not been for the Penn-Venables expedition that wrested Jamaica from Spain, Rodney explained, Jamaicans would still be talking Spanish. The Barrett family settled in Jamaica that year. The family grew and prospered, gaining more land and growing more sugar. A subsequent generation produced Edward, who in his adulthood was known as Edward the Builder because he had built Cinnamon Hill Great House where he and his wife, Judith, raised their five children. He also built an aqueduct. What remains of the aqueduct is now part of the Wyndham Rose Hall Golf Course and provides a popular backdrop for wedding photos.

When someone asked why Edward Barrett would have needed an aqueduct, Rodney said sugar was challenging to cultivate in parts of Jamaica where there were frequent and sustained droughts. Since sugar required ample steady rain to grow, Edward built the Roman-looking aqueduct to insure uninterrupted sugar harvests. In time, the prosperous Barrett family spread out far beyond Cinnamon Hill until they possessed a sizable patch of the island. Besides sugar and rum, they also exported pimientos, cocoa and indigo. Of course, all the labor to create that wealth rested on the shoulders of legions of African slaves.

When Edward and Judith's daughter, Elizabeth, was abandoned by her husband, she moved to London with her three young children. Eventually, her second son, Edward, became the father of the first Barrett child born in England instead of Jamaica in one hundred forty years. Edward's baby girl was born on March 6, 1806. To her doting parents, she was known as Ba. To the rest of the world, she would be famous for penning those immortal lines: "How do I love thee, let me count the ways." She was the Victorian poet Elizabeth Barrett Browning, and her worldview would be shaped broadly by her Jamaican ancestry.

Rodney said we couldn't tour Cinnamon Hill, the ancestral home of Elizabeth Barrett Browning's clan, but instead he took us to another Barrett-owned estate he described as "almost as good." It was Greenwood Estate which had been the property of Elizabeth's

"Uncle Richard" Barrett. Richard Barrett had been a prosperous sugar planter and eminent member of Jamaican society who came to an untimely and suspicious end in 1839, probably poisoned. It happened at the nearby Dewar's Estate when during a business meeting he was suddenly taken so ill he had to be rushed to a bedroom, where he died shortly after. He was buried before the coroner could arrive, and his death remains a mystery. He left behind Greenwood Estate, now a historic landmark.

While we toured Greenwood Estate, Rodney showed us the material wealth that Richard Barrett had accumulated over his lifetime, reminding us that this was typical of the riches made possible with sugar. A massive dining table accommodating two dozen place settings stretched across the enormous dining room. This was not unusual, Rodney explained, because when relatives visited from England, they usually stayed with family for months on end. It was also common practice for cousins to switch families—moving across the Atlantic in either direction—to apprentice themselves to their uncles and pay their dues while learning the ropes of different livelihoods. During their long stays, these relatives were taken in and embraced as part of the family, which in those days included the far-flung relatives.

An upright piano stood against the dining-room wall. Rodney gathered us around it and said it had been manufactured by the John Broadwood Company, an English company with interests in Jamaican mahogany. He said John Broadwood Company was the oldest continuously running piano manufacturer in the world and had been the sole licensed piano provider for England's royal family since King George II. Rodney said the connection between Jamaica and the other British Caribbean colonies could not be overemphasized because so much wealth in England during the Colonial Era had its source directly in the Caribbean. And he didn't have to remind us that the labor creating that wealth sat firmly on the burly shoulders of African slaves.

On the way back, Rodney explained that Elizabeth Barrett Browning grew up on a five-hundred-acre estate in England called Hope End. Her family enjoyed a privileged lifestyle with income from their Jamaican plantations. In 1832, a slave revolt in Jamaica reduced the family's wealth back in England forcing them to give up Hope End and the countryside, and relocate to London. Before leaving Hope End, Elizabeth's father removed the stately clock from the estate's gate and shipped it to his brother in Jamaica where Rodney said it was still ticking over the courthouse at St Anne's Bay near Ocho Rios.

While the ship drew into sight and Rodney started to wrap up his narration, he asked if anyone knew what the town of Falmouth had been called before it came into its present name. No one knew. He said its original name was Barrett Town. I wondered how much more fascinating material he could have told us about Elizabeth Barrett Browning's ancestral connection with Jamaica. As if reading my mind, Rodney said, "I've only scratched the surface!"

ee⊷

That night, I went to help Perry Cardis set up for his game show after sitting alone in the Solo Travelers' corner for the entire happy hour. Perry Cardis was not in a good mood. He asked if I wouldn't mind hosting the game by myself, saying an issue had come up and he had to check something out. It was something about some magic supplies he had ordered coming late to his room. He briefed me quickly on the rules of Peel of Fortune. He wasn't wearing his underwear and that flashing bow tie that night, and before he left, I complimented him on his beautiful Mayan shirt with its colorful embroidered button placket. He said it was from Guatemala, and he was only wearing it because Stella was forcing him to start putting on clothes.

Everyone from our original group except Dr. Turnkey was back at the table for dinner that night, and all fully clothed. The dining room was very chilly so it was no surprise to see almost everyone in clothes or coverups. The nudist theme had fallen by the wayside in the last thirty-six hours and seemed to have run out of steam. Guests were more interested and preoccupied with other things since the pirate takeover.

Our table was obsessed with the grave robberies

that had happened in the same places and on the same days we had visited. No one could stop talking about how the internet was on fire with updates and speculations over how such precious artifacts could have been secreted from their host nations so mysteriously. The air was rife with theories about who had taken them and where they had gone. I kept quiet for most of the conversation and listened. I was clinging to anything that would absolve me or convince me that I was not involved. From what my table mates were saying, the operation was carried out by a highly sophisticated plot that also may have included the trafficking of illegal drugs. The mere mention sent red alarms shooting up and down my spine. Dr. Messy had told me there were meds and supplies in those packages, and I believed her. Now, it seems that in addition to priceless Mayan artifacts, there was the possibility of illicit drugs. I was slipping deeper and deeper into my seat. I barely touched my meal.

"You look like you've seen a ghost, Marianne," Annie said as she bit into a buttery scallop.

"I might have," I said. I visited Rose Hall today and learned about the gruesome legend of the White Witch of Rose Hall. Her name was Annie Palmer."

Everyone stopped and stared at me. They were probably wondering how I could have been so out of sync to be thinking about that when they were all engrossed in the Mayan robberies.

"It's another form of piracy when you think of it,"

Butch said, returning to the subject at hand. "Pirates that take history hostage instead of living people."

Our coffees and desserts arrived as we segued to lighter conversation, conjecturing about what Stella had in store for our show that night.

Stella was in high spirits when I met her at the theater doors. She had already given two comedy acts and was not going to give a third one as long as there was another entertainer on board the ship. It was only fair, she said. She told me there were two entertainers still on the ship waiting to transfer to their next contract in Grand Cayman the following day. "Sylvia Splash and CeCe Cameleon are consummate pros and were more than happy to split tonight's headline show, each taking about twenty-five minutes," she told me privately. We turned to greet the guests into the theater, most of whom were fully clothed. I couldn't blame them, either, as the theater was not just chilly, but downright cold.

All of a sudden, Pearl appeared. I thought there might be fireworks between the two women, but there was no such thing. They greeted each other warmly with hugs. Pearl said she'd rejoined the ship shortly before it sailed and was busily catching up on reports. She asked if Stella wanted to introduce the show or if she should do the honors now that she was back in the saddle. Stella said she didn't care either way, as long as Perry Cardis didn't take the mic and both women laughed heartily sharing high-fives.

In the end, Stella proudly took the stage to

introduce Sylvia Splash. Sylvia wowed the audience with a fast-moving musical panorama through American history with varieties spanning from the Roaring Twenties through standards from the Jazz Age and on to the Rock and Rollers of the sixties with the Beatles. The audience chimed in and sang along with many of the familiar tunes. When Sylvia's show ended, Pearl took the mic and invited CeCe Cameleon to the stage. Everyone saw that Pearl was back and gave her a warm reception. CeCe mesmerized the audience with a genuine hypnosis act, inviting six willing participants onstage and hypnotizing them to do crazy things like pull their ears and howl like wolves. It seemed very real but when it was over, one of the "victims" wasn't snapping out of the trance. Everyone assumed she was faking it until CeCe had to escort her backstage to coax her back to reality. Guests left the theater completely satisfied and stuffed the elevators to join Stella's dance upstairs, a poodle-skirt sock-hop complete with a buffet of red hots, chili dogs and milk shakes at midnight.

I entered my room a few minutes before two in the morning. All I wanted was to drop on my bed and sleep solid for two weeks. But the thought of those missing Mayan mummies wouldn't let me go and kept swirling around in my head. I tried to push it out of my mind, reasoning that I could not have played a part in a sophisticated international robbery. And yet...

I plopped on the bed but couldn't sleep a wink.

33

And Then There's Sven

Day Ten: February 24, Wednesday
George Town, Grand Cayman
Sunny: High: 91ºF/32º. Low: 79ºF/26ºC.

THE NEXT DAY we sailed into beautiful Grand Cayman Island, famous for its glorious Seven Mile Beach. As I emerged from the shower, the phone rang.

"You really know how to step up to a challenge, girl." It was Wink in high spirits. At first, I didn't understand what he meant, but when he said the pirate takeover was all he needed to justify a change in his plans and join the MS *Minerva* in Grand Cayman that day, I got it. As if I'd personally planned the pirate takeover just to get him on the ship with me—really! He sounded very happy about joining our ship. I hadn't realized he'd missed me that much. He said he had meetings scheduled from the minute he came on board, but to plan on dinner together that evening.

Outside my door a crisp white envelope stood

in the mail slot. I thought it was strange because the jewelry show invitations usually came later in the day. I wasn't prepared for the message inside. I was to appear for a face-to-face meeting with immigration authorities in Grand Cayman before disembarking the ship. I suspected it had to do with that Mayan theft ring! I was to report to the library in exactly twenty minutes. I ran upstairs for a quick bite, especially needing a jolt of strong coffee.

I arrived seven minutes early. A table was set up with coffee and tea service, a couple glass pitchers of orange juice and two trays with an assortment of pastries. I didn't have to rush upstairs for my coffee after all, but who knew? Some nautical prints hung on the walls. Stella was already there and about to leave the ship, having gone through her own customs formalities. The local immigration officers, Jay and Barton, knew her and were laughing from her stories. No doubt she'd accumulated more than the usual number of things to tell them since joining this particular cruise. She had everyone in a good mood before the sun was fully up. We said a quick goodbye as an agent escorted her down the metal staircase to the awaiting tender. I wondered if I would ever see Stella again and sincerely hoped I would. Sylvia Splash and CeCe Cameleon were standing with the group of crew members ready to depart. Some might have been leaving for family emergencies back home or because their contracts had ended or they were transferring to another ship or for any number of other reasons. There were fourteen in all, so it was taking a little time to process them. One young woman was sobbing; the young man next to her looked at me, mouthing "very seasick," and made an anguished face, so I figured she was not meant for life at sea and was going home for good. When that group had disembarked, I was the last to be grilled.

I waited for Jay and Barton to call me up for my interrogation, but instead they started stacking their files and collecting their folders. They were looking forward to a lavish ship breakfast, compliments of the cruise line—a welcome perk of the job.

Maybe they forgot about me, I thought. I went over and introduced myself. "Sorry, but we don't know anything about this," Jay said, still smiling from his conversation with Stella. They turned and walked through the door.

I stood there confused for just a few minutes before someone dressed in a black leather bomber jacket with stripes on the sleeves walked in. I thought his uniform was highly irregular, but who was I to judge why people dressed the way they did on a ship? I took it the sleeve stripes lent him authority, even though they were not quite evenly separated. I chalked it up to the fact that they were stuck to leather instead of fabric. His name badge said he was Sven from Norway, but his hair and eyes were so dark he could have been Bruno from Sicily. I handed over my passport before he asked for it. He acted surprised at first, then scrutinized the picture while taking two or three good long looks at my face as if trying to think of something to say.

"I need to ask you what you know about the theft of archaeological treasures from several Central American nations and your involvement."

Well, it wasn't as though I hadn't seen that one coming.

He went on saying, "I have your signature on documents that would implicate you in the removal of said artifacts from their places of origin and evidence of your personal delivery of them to the MS *Minerva*." I tried to detect a Norwegian accent but could hear no trace of one. Norwegian, my arse.

"I did in fact sign some purchase orders on Dr. Carver's request," I admitted. "I was just picking up some medical supplies because she couldn't leave the ship," I said, wondering why I'd offered to sign anything at all—and in all of those dang foreign ports.

"Dr. Carver left no record of ever meeting you or of having any conversations with you at all," Sven countered as he shuffled through some papers.

"Then who was sitting with her at dinner in the Taipei Room on Thursday night after we left Costa Maya?" I asked.

He stopped shuffling the papers and looked up at me. "There is no record of Dr. Carver dining at all in the Taipei Room on Thursday or any night during this cruise," he said with finality.

Probably because it was a charter cruise and

nothing was done the usual way, I figured. Apparently, records were not being kept either. I was screwed... but at least I would go down fighting.

"Well," I said, putting on the best poker face I had, "that's all I know. I simply collected and brought back to the ship some meds and supplies. I was doing a favor for Dr. Messy. You should consult her for anything more specific than that."

Sven thrust a ream of papers at me and said I needed to sign them. I refused, pushing them back at him. I asked reasonably why I should sign more papers when I was already in trouble for signing papers I never should have signed in the first place. He pushed them back to me and waited, but I didn't budge. Finally, he collected the papers without a word, returned my passport to me and said this conversation would be continued later with an additional level of security. I was hoping it would be Wink.

Then he said I could go, but I was not to say a word about it to anyone.

Here we go again, I thought, remembering the gag order on the last cruise. Out of hand, I decided to ignore it this time. I had a gut feeling something was not right with Sven but couldn't put my finger on it. I would bring it up with Wink at dinner if he didn't bring it up first.

Sandy Cares

꙳꙳꙳

Relieved to be out of there, I was free to explore the immaculate little capital of George Town on my way to the famous Seven Mile Beach. It was going to be a short day on shore because we needed extra time to get to Havana the next day. A three-thirty departure also meant leaving extra time for the tender ride back to the ship.

The tender took us over luscious turquoise water for about fifteen minutes before dropping us off at one of several platforms. An official sign welcomed us to Hog Sty Bay, an early name for George Town. A friendly agent with a proper British accent in an information kiosk gave me an island map and suggested I start at the museum just across Harbour Drive, the main drag.

Grand Cayman is the largest island in a group of three. Christopher Columbus, Sir Francis Drake and various pirates stopped by to collect turtles to feed their crews on long sea journeys. But instead of being named for all the turtles, it was named after the indigenous and prolific caimans that lived there: small saw-toothed relatives of the crocodile. The 25,000-foot-deep Cayman Trench, the Caribbean's deepest section, is offshore, a perennial draw for serious divers.

Lying in the bullseye of hurricane paths, the Cayman Islands suffered through some doozies. One blew through in November of 1932. No one saw it coming because November was thought to be past hurricane season. But storm surges of over thirty-two feet killed one hundred nine people in one of the worst hurricanes in Cayman Island history. People were swimming between rooftops and clinging to branches. In its aftermath, children found pirate pieces-of-eight in the sand, and coffins floated out of their plots while booby birds' legs were stuck in the sand.

In more recent memory, Hurricane Ivan struck in 2004, submerging a fourth of the island, leaving behind nearly three billion dollars in damage.

The tiny island nation of three little islands covers a combined land mass of a hundred square miles, with the majority of its sixty thousand people living on the big island of Grand Cayman. Yet the islands welcome up to two million visitors and cruise guests a year. And Grand Cayman had much to offer: besides some of the best diving sites in the Caribbean, high-end shopping and a standard of living on a par with Switzerland's, with up-to-the-minute infrastructure and well-educated people who speak with a proper British clip.

After perusing some museum exhibits, I crossed the street and passed a busy upscale mall with the familiar brand names seen at all the Caribbean ports of call. Perfumes, bags, shoes, clothes—and especially diamonds and jewelry—tempted shoppers in all these destinations, and Grand Cayman was in line for its share of that market. I walked a couple blocks beyond the Kirk Freeport Mall and came across a corner with more local fare sold from carefully arranged stalls by local people. Here was where I saw displays of colorful little jars of homemade jellies and marmalades, straw bags made from silver thatch—the island's national tree—island dolls, toys and jewelry. One stone I had never seen before was in virtually every jewelry display. It was called Caymanite, a semi-precious stone only found in the Cayman Islands, according to a vendor. Its distinctive orange and black bands made eye-catching pendants, rings and pins. I bought one in the shape of a turtle.

One stall offered something called coconut chop. I watched as a muscular man wielding a formidable machete lopped off the end of a coconut and slipped a straw in before handing it to a patron. It looked so refreshing, I ordered one for myself. It was here that I realized four dollars Caymanian was equal to five US dollars. The Caymanian dollar was set at a fixed rate of one Caymanian dollar to 1.25 US dollars. One sip of the pure, sweet, cold coconut water told me it was worth every penny, and the vendor assured me it was as healthy as it was delicious. He said it flushes out the kidneys, and I would see what he meant in a few hours. I thanked him and left a little tip for the delicious treat and the optimistic medical advice. Across the street, some people wearing masks and fins were pointing at the water. I crossed over and saw the school of enormous tarpon swimming directly beneath them. One at a time, the bathers clambered down the steps from the platform and dropped into the warm water to snorkel among the tarpons. It was a dreamy, watercolor vista with that luscious water stretching all the way out to the cruise ships floating in a halo of hazy light a mile or two away.

I turned to head in the direction of the Seven Mile Beach and soon came across a quaint island church along the main street. It was very white and very small. The sign that said Elmslie Memorial United Church invited me inside where I saw some beautiful stained-glass windows behind the altar. A man nearby was telling his wife that the church was built in the maritime architectural style, common in seafaring societies like the Cayman Islands. He told her to look at the ceiling, which I did along with her, to see the exposed beams that looked like the hull of an upturned ship. A pamphlet about the church's history credited its origins to a shipwreck in 1846 that brought the Reverend Hope Waddell to the island's shores when his ship veered off course on its way to Nigeria. Reverend Waddell had been assessing the spiritual progress of former slaves on Jamaican plantations in the aftermath of general emancipation in the British West Indies. In fact, some of those Jamaican plantations he saw belonged to the Barrett family.

But as soon as he realized that Grand Cayman lacked a proper church, he decided to stay long enough to establish this congregation in George Town. I stepped out of the dark church into painfully bright sunlight without realizing I was standing directly in the middle of a tiny parking lot. When a car came through and just narrowly missed me, I whirled around to step back on the curb. I stood there, half-whiplashed and very relieved that it had come to nothing and decided it was time to hit the beach.

34

I'll See You in C-U-B-A

By THE TIME I settled into a beach chair, my mind was a million miles away from the lost Mayan mummies. My eyes wandered over the ultra-blue water that tickled its way from the fringes of the sand and off into infinity where it melted into the sky. The sugar sand swept across the beach in both directions forever. I fell into a deep and relaxing slumber that took me by degrees through dreams of places and people I hadn't seen in decades.

I was rustled awake by a couple fussing in their lounge chairs under an umbrella a little distance away. Every so often, it sounded like the breeze was wafting their voices over to me. I shut my eyes and allowed myself to drift off, but the man's voice kept rising over the sound of the surf. It was strikingly familiar. I knew I'd heard it before but didn't place it until I heard him say, "Dovey!" Could it be Mr. Mooney from the last cruise, I wondered? I listened more closely. Nothing could compare to that distinctive voice that reminded me of

Mr. Magoo or Thurston Howell the Third. Could it be Mr. Mooney? I didn't know how that could be possible but, all the same, my thoughts went directly back to the goofy characters I'd come to love at our assigned table, which I'd privately called Gilligan's Table during that cruise. I couldn't hear the woman's voice, so I decided to walk over and do a little investigating.

I left my things on my chair because they weren't too far away and approached the couple from the side. There, in all their pomp and glory, were Mr. and Mrs. Mooney from the prior cruise! Far from being in jail, as I'd supposed they would be by now for trying to bilk the casino, they were sitting in the lap of luxury on one of the world's most coveted beaches. Just as I recognized them, Mr. Mooney looked up from under his flat-topped sun hat and said, "Hiho! Marianne! What are you doing here?" He chuckled merrily as Mrs. Mooney fluttered around, waving and smiling and adjusting the silk scarf on her fashionably expensive straw hat.

"Mr. and Mrs. Mooney!" I said, more surprised than they were. "It's so good to see you here! Are you on one of the ships?"

"Of course we are, Marianne," Mr. Mooney said, moving his feet to the side and patting his chaise lounge for me to come and sit. Mrs. Mooney pulled her big bag away to make more room for me. I sat down. "But what are you doing here? Is there another missing musician?" Mr. Mooney laughed at his own joke.

"No," I joined the laughter. "It's nothing like that

this time. They asked me to return to the MS *Minerva* and take over as social hostess for one cruise," I said. "I'm afraid I'm already in over my head and am starting to count the days to when I can go home again."

"Well, we almost got into a little trouble at the end of the other cruise," Mr. Mooney said. "You'd never believe it, but they actually tried to accuse us of rigging our bets in the casino. But good thing I have a very sharp lawyer. He's in Miami, and he came right over and took care of everything for us. We missed our original ship that day, but we got on the MS *Athena* instead. In fact, Wink just joined our ship a couple days ago. He came from another ship that was in the Panama Canal, I think. Wink looked mighty surprised to see us, although I can't say why." I knew exactly why but didn't want to spoil their day. "So, what's new with you, Marianne?"

I certainly didn't want to bring up the accusations going on against me for robbing ancient Mayan graves. I kept it light and said I was back on the MS *Minerva* with a charter cruise and was happy to see them. Mrs. Mooney perked up and started saying something excitedly. "We talked with Ginny and Ralph while we were in St. Thomas the other day," she said. She was referring to the divorcee and widower who met on that cruise and got engaged. "They sent us an email with their phone number in Bermuda. Ginny and Ralph are getting married next month! Guess where? Marianne."

I guessed Bermuda, where Ralph lived.

"Nooo! Right on the MS *Cleopatra*! We're invited, and we already booked the cruise and RSVP'd the wedding. It's going to the Dutch islands in the southern Caribbean! They will get married in Aruba! Imagine that! Isn't it just thrilling! Your invitation is probably waiting for you at home in Michigan, and you should come for sure!" She was all giggly and happy, entertaining sugarplum thoughts of a glitzy wedding in a dreamy tropical port. "Maybe the captain will even perform their ceremony," she fantasized, looking skyward, imagining a storybook wedding.

❧❧❧

Back onboard, I heard some lively music coming from the theater and went to check it out. The snappy song that sounded like something from the Roaring Twenties was "I'll See You in C-U-B-A" by Irving Berlin, as indicated on the opening slide of the afternoon lecture about Havana just about to start. The venue was stuffed to suffocation with every seat taken as latecomers slipped in and filled any available wall space. I noticed a lineup of the officers against the back wall of the theater joined by whatever crew members had been relieved of their duties for a while. Cuba had only just opened to American cruise ships and promised a totally new experience for most Americans. We were all very curious to learn what was in store.

The speaker started right in. She said Cuba was

the largest island in the Caribbean, with a complicated history, especially since Fidel's Castro's revolution in 1959. She wanted to orient us first, and then show us some of the high points of Havana. You could hear a pin drop. Cuba is different, she stressed several times, making it clear to stay with our excursion groups and keep our Cuban visas with us at all times.

The money exchange took a little explaining because of Cuba's curious dual-currency system. One currency was meant solely for the Cuban nationals and only accepted in their local stores, or bodegas, where ration cards were also honored. The other currency was the tourist money and the only money that would be issued to us in the exchange. She said Cuba did not recognize United States banks, and there were no ATMs that took credit cards issued from US banks. She paused and waited a moment as a murmur buzzed through the audience. It was evident that she expected such a response. It came as a blow to some people who had been planning on using ATMs in Havana. She said they wouldn't accept US credit cards anywhere either. Then she was sorry to have to break it to us but advised us to bring along our own tissue because that was rarely supplied in public restrooms. Another murmur and some sporadic guffaws swept over the rows of seats.

A hand shot up with a question about buying cigars and rum. A new slide appeared on the screen with a bottle of Havana Club rum and a box of Cuban

Cohiba brand cigars, which the speaker said was Cuba's best-selling brand.

She continued, saying that both the Cuban cigars and rum were produced according to meticulous standards and sold in very closely regulated state-run tourist stores. Someone asked where to find those stores, and she assured us that no matter where our excursion went, the local guide was sure to lead us into an approved cigar and rum shop somewhere along the way. Everyone chuckled as we realized the same rule of tourism applied to Cuba as everywhere else. A guided stop to spend some money during our tour was all but obligatory. She added, with an audible wink in her voice, if any tour guide did not lead an excursion to a store for a shopping opportunity somewhere along the way, she would eat her shoe. General laughter followed, but it was evident her confidence was borne from experience.

From there she went on to show us some beautiful photographs of the highlights in Old Havana. I decided to pull myself away and headed to the excursion office before the lecture ended when, guaranteed, there would be a deluge of people converging to book their excursions.

Oscar was busy at his computer when I stepped into the office. He looked up and asked if I had a preference for a shore excursion in Havana. He said he needed me to escort groups both days in Havana, and he had automatically assigned me to one of the buses to the Tropicana on our overnight. He said to be ready for two very long days in Havana.

Since I had no preference, he assigned me to one of the rum and cigar tours, but said to be prepared to take the hit from the guests if the local guide skipped the cigar factory tour that day. He said it happened often enough but was beyond anyone's control. Even so, it was the most popular tour offered.

I asked, "They just stop the tour in the middle of things?"

He smiled. "Sometimes the powers-that-be decide to close the factories to the tours for the day. The guests will be disappointed and might blame you as the ship's liaison, so don't take it personally," he advised.

"Then what do they do with the extra time in that case?" I asked. "Return to the ship early or give guests free time to wander around?"

"Free time is forbidden to all passengers sailing to Cuba on American ships, according to our travel restrictions," he said. "Guests must stay with a tour led by an approved local guide at all times. If any part of the excursion is canceled, the guides typically take guests to an alternate venue which may be a local bar. After a few Cuba libres and the serenade of a live Cuban band and some impromptu dance lessons or a pop-up tango performance by a lovely local couple, the guests settle down and have a wonderful time. By the time they return to the ship, they are all smiles, laughing and saying it was the best time of their lives.

Not much a little Cuban rum and salsa music can't cure," he said, smiling.

I went back to my room to prepare for dinner with Wink. We were planning to meet in the main dining room at seven o'clock. On my way inside, I grabbed the white envelope waiting on the door and cast it aside while I changed. Once again, I assumed it was an invitation to one of the endless jewelry shows in the ship's boutiques and certainly not another security summons. When I came out of the bathroom, I opened the card. It was neither from the boutiques nor security, but a handwritten dinner invitation ... from the captain! He apologized for the short notice but trusted I could join him for dinner at seven.

Shoot! I had to make a split-second decision as the clock was ticking down on me. Dinner with Wink... or the captain?

I called Wink. He didn't answer, so I left a message, postponing our dinner plans until the next night in Havana.

Then I left a message at the captain's number. I said I'd just returned to my room and found his invitation. I was ready for dinner any time.

35

Some Enchanted Evening

AT PRECISELY FIVE MINUTES before seven o'clock, the same security guard who ushered me to the captain the first time was at my door again. Once more, we retraced the way back up to the captain's quarters, and he led me through the security doors, departing as soon as the captain greeted me in his suite. He was all smiles. The room was lovely as before, only there was a big bouquet of tropical flowers in the center of the table. Montalban was nowhere in sight. The captain himself poured us each a glass of sparkling water over ice. He offered me wine but, frankly, I was saving the calories for more of those macaroons.

We walked around the room, and this time he brought out a collection of music CDs. He invited me to go through them and select what I would like to hear for background music. He had a truly thoughtful collection of international music from ports he had visited all over the planet. I was intrigued by the eclectic variety of music, judging from the CD covers alone. They seemed to come from every corner of the planet. I asked him to select one he really liked because I was not familiar with any of the bands or singers, and he chose something he said he had picked up from a group he once heard playing on the boardwalk in Oslo. The music was modern and urban and smooth, and I liked it very much. I said I didn't understand how something so fresh and catchy wasn't an international hit. I also knew I would not be able to get it out of my mind after hearing it and hoped it would linger as long as possible.

While the music filled the air, we strolled out onto the balcony. He pointed above us at the bridge, where all the navigation of the ship happened. He called it his "office" and waved at a couple officers looking down at us from above. He laughed and said they were shameless about ogling pretty girls, even when they were with the captain. I glanced down at the chaise lounge where a book was left open face-down. The title was *Jaime Bunda,* and I wondered what it was about, happy to note that the captain liked to read books.

He took my hand and guided me back into his suite. He walked slowly, taking me the long way around to the table, slowing down noticeably as we passed the bedroom: the door wide open and an enormous bed between two matching vases with fresh flowers on the nightstands. The cover had been pulled down enticingly from one of the pillows, exposing snow-white cotton sheets snapping with such crispness they could have been sun-dried on a clothesline. I figured probably five thousand thread count. Two wrapped chocolates were poised coquettishly on top of the pillows. I felt him squeeze my hand ever so slightly at that point. Then we rounded out the walk to the table, where he held out my chair and dropped a napkin on my lap.

He rang a little bell, and Montalban appeared with hot serving dishes that he placed on the table, uncovering them and placing serving ware nearby. Then he silently slipped out, leaving the captain to serve our meals himself; I reminded myself that I would be serving seconds. It all seemed very dreamy and elegant and right out of a fairy tale. I couldn't believe I was here alone with this very handsome captain who had an inconsolable crush on someone else he'd never met. I brought it up first.

"Well, Captain, have you heard from Esmeralda?" I asked as I dug into a fresh and crisp Caesar salad with extra anchovies.

"Oh, Marianna," he started whining. "Not yet, but she is busy. Yes, she is very busy. She will answer, I know."

I wasn't as convinced.

"Tell me, Captain," I asked, dropping one of the anchovies from my Caesar salad on the table and trying to pick it up as discreetly as I could after it already left an oil splotch on the tablecloth. "When is the last time she wrote to you?"

He thought for a while. He looked up and said she

just hadn't had time to write yet. "She's very shy as well," he said. He scooped up a mouthful of salad.

"How did you meet Esmeralda?" I asked, putting down my fork and looking directly at him.

"The ship was in Cartagena that day," he said. "I went to lunch with the staff captain, Eduardo. He was fun and funny. He was always playing tricks on me and making me laugh," he said, a nostalgic smile spreading across his face. "I miss those times with Eduardo." He shook his head as if remembering something. Then he looked up.

"Eduardo said he knew all the best places to eat in Cartagena. He took me to Casa de Esmeralda where he pointed at a beautiful girl sitting at a table with her family. He told me she was Esmeralda and the whole restaurant was named for her."

"But, Captain," I interjected, "Colombia is famous for emeralds, so don't you think a lot of places are named Esmeralda in Cartagena? Do you really think the restaurant was named for that girl . . . or was Eduardo playing another trick on you?" It was more than I'd wanted to say, but I couldn't stop it from tumbling out.

We finished our salads, and he stood up to serve the next course of spaghetti carbonara. I was surprised it was so smooth and hot, not a bit gloppy after sitting for so long. I offered him some grated cheese, which he declined, so I heaped twice as much on my spaghetti. He commented that I seemed to really like spaghetti carbonara, and I told him it was my all-time favorite in the world. I could eat three plates of it, I said, as I savored every strand of spaghetti covered with the creamy egg sauce flecked with tiny bits of bacon. Sobering fact is, I probably could.

He circled back to answer my question with one of his own. "You think Eduardo tricked me? You don't think that was Esmeralda?"

"I'm not sure who she was, Captain. I wasn't there. When did this happen, anyway?"

"Three, maybe four years ago," he answered simply.

I dropped my fork.

"Captain, how many times have you talked with Esmeralda since then?"

"Talk? We never talked. We just write."

I was starting to wonder how an educated, skilled, man-of-the-world cruise-ship captain, responsible for the lives of thousands of cruisers and jillion-dollar vessels, could be so emotionally hijacked by the vagaries of his own misguided heart. I was beginning to conclude that this man needed some intervention, and from someone more qualified to handle this sort of situation than I was.

"Captain, what did you say to each other that day Eduardo introduced you in the Casa de Esmeralda in Cartagena?"

The captain laughed, twisting strands of spaghetti around his fork. "No, Eduardo didn't introduce us," he said. "She was too shy. Eduardo said she would write to me instead."

"And did she ever write to you?" I asked.

"Once. It was the letter you saw."

I was doing all I could to restrain from shaking my head in disbelief.

"So, you saw a woman in Cartagena about three or four years ago. Eduardo told you her name was Esmeralda and the restaurant was named for her. You didn't meet her then, and you only received one email from her in all this time. You have been sending her emails for this long, and she has never answered any of them, Captain, is that right?"

He said nothing.

"Where is Eduardo now?" I asked. "I have a question or two for him. Is he here on the ship? Or do you have his email?" I was starting to feel very defensive about the captain.

"Eduardo died," he said, pausing as for a brief prayer.

"I'm sorry," I said. But something was fishy. I twirled more spaghetti around my fork as I thought.

"Please, Marianna, just one more letter. Please help me write one more letter to Esmie," he implored. "I want her so much. My life has been nothing but trouble with other women."

The thought of Miss Fantina Monaire popped up, and I saw what he meant. I could only imagine what havoc other women had caused in his life. Now I understood he was in love with the safest one out there because she didn't really exist.

"I'll be happy to help you, Captain, but I'm afraid this may have been yet another practical joke that Eduardo played on you." I wasn't convinced it was his last. "Let's write Esmeralda a letter and see if she answers us this time. But, honestly, Captain, if she doesn't, there's really nothing you or I or any number of letters can do to change her mind." I tried to be as gentle as I could without revealing my exasperation.

"But please consider this," I pushed. "Right now there are dozens of very beautiful and talented women working on this ship that I'm sure would love to get to know you. Would you like me to introduce some to you? I think I already have one in mind right now." I was thinking about Angela, who was probably chomping at the bit to have her chance with the captain.

"No!" He held up his hands emphatically. "I never date the staff or crew or anyone working on the ships," he said.

"I suppose that's a pretty good plan," I said, wondering who he thought I was. He could read my mind.

"You are different, Marianna, just friends!" he said, smiling.

"This carbonara is exceptional," I said again. "I'm not going to be shy about serving our seconds right now. The chef really outdid himself making so much of it." I had to stand up to serve the long noodles from the tureen to our plates. I had no idea there was yet another course to follow, and equally sublime–tender lamb chops with a creamy spinach side. Heck, I thought, I'd be the captain's girlfriend just to eat like this.

We languished over dinner, chatting and laughing a lot. "Just friends" made this so easy and pleasant, I thought. No pressure, no expectations, but just conversation and simple companionship. I asked myself whose company I preferred between the captain and Wink. I knew the honest answer wasn't the "right" one. Eventually, he rang the little bell, and Montalban appeared and cleared the table. He expertly refreshed the tablecloth when he saw the mosaic of crumbs, spots, particles and that anchovy oil splotch at my place. Then he served coffee and set before us each a gooey, chocolatey, creamy profiterole. I joked with the captain that the dessert was the size of Tortola. Before Montalban left, he placed a tray heaped with a generous pile of those luscious macaroons between us. There shouldn't be any room for those after the profiterole, but I knew I'd find a way to squeeze them in.

"Captain," I asked suddenly, "I don't mean to stick my nose where it doesn't belong, but I am curious about something concerning those pirates. Did you ever learn who or what was responsible for the pirates' sudden eruption of Montezuma's Revenge that day?"

The captain tossed his head back and laughed. "You know, it was a miracle and saved us all. Thank you, Marianna," he added, looking me straight in the eyes. "We saw you in the cameras, and yes, I forgive you for countermanding my orders. I should have disembarked you from the ship the next day, but the officers and I are grateful for what you did. We are the only ones who know about it, too. It must remain our secret, yes?" The captain started laughing anew at the memory.

"You have a lovely smile, Marianna," he said suddenly. Then, taking my hand once again, he leaned in as if to kiss me and whispered, "Do you want to go to bed now?"

Oh, God, I thought. Not again!

"No, but I wouldn't mind having a couple macaroons."

Even though, to be totally honest, the thought had crossed my mind.

36

And Now There's Grau

THE PHONE STARTLED ME awake the next morning. It was barely six o'clock. I'd set my alarm to ring fifteen minutes later, so I turned it off. Sven, from the day before, was ordering me to report to the library again. He said to get there as quickly as I could before general disembarkation started in Havana. I hurried upstairs to the library, passing numerous happy couples and small groups chatting and laughing as they gravitated toward the outer decks to catch the first glimpses of Havana's skyline before sailing into the harbor. I went out for a quick look and caught the pilot boat as it was dropping off the local pilot at our ship to navigate us into Havana harbor. I knew we would be there soon.

When I arrived, Sven motioned to the chair facing him, and I sat down. This morning there was another agent sitting next to him. His name badge read Grau from Honduras. He was wearing a uniform that looked more like a royal-blue sports coat with yellow shoulder chevrons and sleeve stripes Velcroed on. I'd never seen officers wear royal-blue uniforms but, then again, he was from Honduras, and I remembered from our time in Roatan that their flag was the same color. His blond hair was shaved down to his pinkish skull, and he peered at me through steely gray eyes centered in round, ultra-modern, Scandinavian-style glasses. He looked more Norwegian than Honduran. In fact, more Norwegian than Sven. His expression was as grim as his name was ominous. It was feeling like an inquisition.

"I'll start right in, Ms. Milliner," Sven said gravely. "We are in possession of some classified information that would implicate you as prime suspect in several recent robberies of national treasures out of Cozumel, Mexico; Costa Maya, Mexico; Belize City, Belize; and Puerto Barrios, Guatemala. He looked at me and held up a copy of a document that I could vaguely recall as something I might have signed when I thought I was signing a purchase order for medical supplies.

Here it comes, I thought.

"As I already explained to you yesterday," I said, "I was just doing a favor for Dr. Messy who asked me to pick up medical supplies for her. In all those places," I added, clearing my throat.

"Certainly, you read what you signed," he said reasonably.

Of course I had not read what I'd signed. Was he crazy? I had been given orders to get the stuff back to the ship and told I might have to sign a stupid purchase order. Was I expected to go through all that fine print and scrutinize all those meds and make sure they were all there when I didn't even know what they were? I told Sven that what I was doing had been explained simply as "business as usual" in these dang foreign ports. Of course I didn't say the "dang " part. I had taken Dr. Messy on her word that this was a legitimate collection of badly needed ship supplies, and she'd confirmed it in our last conversation.

I started to defend myself, but Grau broke in.

"This is a most grievous offense," he said. "I don't have to tell you it is punishable by heavy fines and certain imprisonment. I know you may have an interest in these historic objects, or even in the very act of collecting them, as your line of work is directly involved with committing crimes and then resolving them," he said. If he was referring to my detective-writing line of work, he was way off. I would never aspire to such high-stakes—let alone such blatant illegality—to gather fodder for my books, which weren't this sophisticated anyway. They were aimed at preteens, for creep's sake. I countered that I would have no interest at all in collecting those relics or in committing crimes.

"Nevertheless," Sven moved in again, "the fact remains that precious national treasures are missing, and the only one we have to hold accountable is you."

"Missing?" I asked. "They came back to the ship with me. You said so yesterday, and I saw the crates go on board. If they are now missing, that's beyond my control." I immediately regretted opening my mouth.

"Well, rest assured that they have since come up missing, and the value attached to them is in the millions of dollars, not to mention the historical value which potentially may be lost forever," Grau said. "Now, on pain of very serious punishment, please tell us where they are. I'll have to inform you that, at this very moment, an intensive search is being done inside your room."

Oh, bring it on, I thought. They'd find my slippers, a bag full of laundry, junk jewelry from the previous cruise, some half-eaten candy bars and . . . suddenly, I remembered something I had not thrown away. All the laxative wrappers were still in a big scrunched-up ball that I'd tossed under my bed. In any event, the secret about who poisoned the pirates would be out of the bag once they came across all those laxative wrappers.

"You are welcome to anything you find in my room and to come to your conclusions about anything you see there. But I'm really sorry to say you will not find any Mayan mummies, and you certainly are not looking at the person who masterminded this major archaeological heist. If I had anything to do with it, I was only an innocent and unwitting accomplice, at the wrong place at the wrong time under a totally different assumption. You really need to find Dr. Messy and interrogate her. If she was involved, then it was very clever of her to implicate me this way and then conveniently leave the ship as she did. I know nothing about all these archaeological relics and, frankly, why would I risk this level of entanglement just to see what it might be like to steal a Mayan mummy?" I asked, "when I could concoct it all right out of my imagination..."

Sven cut me off. "All we know is that you signed for them. You just now admitted you brought them back to the ship and actually saw them loaded on board." Grau was scribbling away on his notepad as Sven talked.

Sven continued, "And they have disappeared from the ship, so you are the logical one who must know about their whereabouts. You alone hold the chain of accountability." He placed before me a sheaf of at least four dozen papers, all in minuscule print.

"Proof incontrovertible. Your signatures are everywhere," Grau said.

This was fast going from ludicrous to ridiculous. "Shouldn't you be questioning Dr. Messy? I would never even have thought to go to those places she sent me without her request."

"You would not have thought to go to the Cozumel Island Museum on your own, Miss Milliner? Or to the boardwalk in Costa Maya? Oh, come now. I have abundant proof that these are the very places you like to visit when you are knocking around on your own."

He had me there.

"But I totally expected to be going to the local hospitals to collect medical supplies," I said. "You can ask Dr. Messy. She will tell you how surprised I was when she said I'd be going to those other places to get her stuff."

"Nevertheless," Grau said.

I sat there in thunderacious silence. My heart was thumping right through my shirt. My head was about to split open from the pounding inside. I was hoping this was some kind of macabre "gotcha." Maybe Wink had set me up for a colossal practical joke, planning to rush in and rescue me in the nick of time. If this was his idea of funny, I could have cracked him over the head with a mummified Mayan femur right then. This was serious, and I was in the deepest doo-doo of my life. Part of me wanted to break down and cry. Suddenly, I had a thought.

"I don't know if it is of any importance," I said. "When I was in the Cozumel Museum, then again in the farmacia in Costa Maya and once again in a taxicab in Guatemala, I saw a man that very much resembled Dr. Percival Turnkey. He is a guest on our ship right now and joins our table almost every night. It might be a stretch but is probably worth it if you could research into his whereabouts at those stops after the excursions. If he was masquerading behind a moustache, then bushy sideburns and a beard, he might have been involved." I added, "I wish I'd taken a picture at the time, but my sightings were fleeting at best. I don't often connect dots like this," I added, "but the resemblance was uncanny. I think it needs at least to be considered."

"Dr. Turnkey left the ship in Jamaica," Sven said. "I know because I was following him down the gangway. I do not know him, but he left the ship with a simple carry-on, hardly big enough to contain a Mayan mummy."

I nearly shot up from my seat. I tried to process that. I remembered Dr. Turnkey was not at dinner with our group the night we left Jamaica. It was appearing that the two people I would have held in highest suspicion were both safely off the ship along with the missing contraband, leaving me there to hold the bag.

Sven looked at me long and hard but said nothing. From his expression, I knew that was a dead end. Either that, or I caught him off guard with an avenue he had not considered or was trying to hide. I waited, but he didn't break. Nothing changed the fact that I had signed those documents in four different ports and had accompanied priceless archaeological relics—those same relics that were now gone, as was Dr. Turnkey. I was the most convenient scapegoat with all the proof they needed to close this case and send me to prison, leaving the real thieves to run wild and do as they pleased with the Mayan treasures. I was more convinced than ever that they were all in collusion.

"I am wondering, did you see the security staff actually examine the contents of his carry-on when he left?"

"There would have been no reason for that," Grau said defensively. "It was obviously a small carry-on, not big enough for anything we are looking for."

"Well, what now?" I asked, expecting to be hauled away in handcuffs to the brig.

"We will ask that you simply comply with our interrogations over the rest of the cruise," Sven said quietly. "We will contact you after we conduct some further research."

"Meanwhile," Grau cleared his throat, "you may proceed with your plans in Havana. But stay with your group at all times. And, let me repeat, you are not to breathe a word of this with anyone at any time, on the ship or off. Or we cannot be responsible for your safety in Cuba. This is a matter of the highest sensitivity and completely classified. In other words, Ms. Milliner, this is quite frankly a gag order with serious consequences attached. Am I clear?"

I realized right then that Wink was not part of this intel and probably had no knowledge of it. Grau continued before I could answer.

"Also, if the Cuban authorities suspect anything and apprehend you at immigration in Havana, we will have no recourse or power to intercede whatsoever. You are up to your own devices in Cuba. Cuba is uncharted territory."

I had the distinct feeling they did not want someone in Cuba to know something that I knew. I looked at Sven and thanked him. I honestly didn't know why. I nodded at Grau and quietly left.

My instincts told me that something was stinking in the State of Denmark.

Sandy Cares

❧❧❧

My first stop after leaving Doom and Gloom was Pauline's office. I asked her for a bio and dossier of Dr. Messy. I knew it was a brash request, but right then I felt as if my life depended on it. I made up a story that she'd left the ship so suddenly I hadn't received any contact information, and I wanted to correspond.

Pauline balked. "No, that information is not allowed to leave our files, Marianne," she said sternly, suddenly turning very severe. "If you have any questions about Dr. Messy, go and ask her yourself. She rejoined our ship yesterday in Grand Cayman!" I was stunned. I was starting to feel like Dorothy in Oz with everyone coming and going so quickly.

Pauline was telling me this just as Perry Cardis announced the ship's arrival into Havana.

37

Exploring Old Havana

Day Eleven: February 25, Thursday
Havana, Cuba
Sunny: High: 87ºF/30ºC. Low: 77ºF/25ºC.

OSCAR SAW ME in the flood of people trying to board the tour buses and approached. His expression was both hopeful and resigned. He told me the cigar factory was closed that day, so they canceled the rum and cigars tour before it even started. He asked me to escort the walking tour of Old Havana instead.

When about two dozen of us had convened, our local guide took over, introducing herself as Celia. She spoke flawless English, and it was evident from her confidence and polished presentation that she had a great deal of experience leading excursions. She guided us out of the terminal building and we crossed the street directly out front. We stopped in a big open plaza surrounded by old buildings. Commanding attention from one side was a marble fountain whose four stately lions spewed water from their mouths.

Celia was an English teacher and loved the opportunity to practice her English while sharing her love of her country, so she gave local tours of Old Havana on the days the ships came to call. What she wasn't telling us was that legions of overly qualified professionals were streaming out of the workplace and onto tour buses to make more money from tips than they could from their jobs. By day's end, guests were talking about tour guides that were educated as engineers, university professors and medical doctors.

Celia never stopped smiling. She was enjoying our reactions to the stories she shared about her island-nation as we walked through the stunningly beautiful plazas of Old Havana, taking in the ornate facades and elegant balconies. The variety of architectural styles was dizzying, including military, Baroque, Neoclassical, Art Nouveau and Art Deco, Post Revolution and Moroccan. The Moors' influence from their eight-hundred-year occupation of Spain was clearly reflected, even extending to architecture in Spain's New World colonies. The fading pastel facades of most buildings conveyed signs of dilapidation and neglect, yet it still did not diminish their beauty from an earlier era.

Celia explained that Spanish Colonial plazas, or squares, in the New World were typically anchored on one side by a church, fronting a large open space or plaza. The plazas usually had fountains, statues, benches, green spaces or all of the above. The plaza we were standing in fit that model with a very old church and lion-festooned fountain, called appropriately the Four Lions Fountain. She said this was the Plaza San Francisco, named for the adjacent church, and the first of four main plazas in Old Havana that we would be visiting. She pointed to a building across from the fountain on top of which was a weathervane representing Mercury, the ancient Roman god of speed and commerce. She said that building once served as the mercantile exchange. She turned our attention to a bronze statue of a man sitting on a bench at the far end of the plaza saying he was the Polish composer, Frederic Chopin. People were aiming their cameras and cellphones and zooming for a closer view. Celia said she could not overemphasize the importance of education and culture, including art, music, dance and sports in Cuba.

We passed through a narrow cobblestone street where tourists were lining up to take selfies in front of a bronze statue of a bearded man caught in a mid-stride stance that Celia said immortalized a notorious twentieth-century vagabond. She said the Caballero de Paris was sometimes called the Chevalier as well, and he had been a well-known cult figure during the 1940s and '50s when he was a familiar sight walking the streets of Havana. He was often seen stopping to greet and kiss the hands of female passers-by and had the reputation of a harmless lothario. Celia said it was good luck to touch the statue's finger, beard and toe at the same time. A street clown stood nearby with his dog, all dressed up for the occasion of posing for tips. Celia said people like this clown were street entertainers, and we were certain to see more.

We took a turn down another narrow street where the remains of an underground aqueduct dating from Havana's earliest days was exposed right there in the passageway. I was quickly getting the feeling that Havana was one big living museum. The end of that street spilled into our next plaza which Celia called Old Square.

Celia said that unlike Plaza San Francisco, there never had been a church in Old Square. Its function from the start was a public marketplace, providing vendors a place to sell their fruits, vegetables, fish and wares. As she was telling us this, a rattle of music started up from one end, and before we could turn around, a phalanx of graceful stilt dancers in exotic and colorful costumes made their way across the plaza's cobblestones, waving and dancing to the seductive rhythm of an accompanying band of music-makers. We looked around at the old buildings surrounding the cobbled square where children in school uniforms emerged from their classrooms on one end of the plaza to enjoy their physical education class outdoors. They could run freely and safely here as the entire plaza was cordoned off by cannonballs strategically placed around the perimeter to block vehicular traffic. Many of the buildings in this square had distinctive and colorful windows made from stained-glass, which Celia explained was a necessity to filter out the merciless tropical sunlight.

A fountain took up the center, but she guided us to a curious sculpture in one corner of the square. It depicted a naked woman holding a big fork over her shoulder and sitting astride a gigantic rooster. Without missing a beat, someone in our group said that statue would have been right at home on our cruise, and everyone chuckled.

Celia explained that its name, Viaje Fantastico, meant Fantastic Voyage, but no one was really sure what the statue meant after it appeared there in 2012. She said some locals called it We Must Eat. Looking around, we saw several little paladars, or homestyle luncheon restaurants, on the ground floor and spilling out of balconies on the upper floors. She said there was a time in the 1990s and for years after, when food was not so available and times were very hard for the Cuban people. The Soviet economy had collapsed, ending decades of support and aid for Cuba. It left the Cuban people in the dire crosshairs of basic needs, especially for fuel and food. She said that era was known as the Special Period, and the statue we were looking at was a somber reminder of a time when food was so scarce people fried grapefruit rinds as a meat substitute. Women, especially, were impacted by poverty as divorce was common, and many were reduced to working the streets just to feed themselves. Suddenly, this image of a naked woman astride an oversized rooster had a whole new meaning. No one joked about it after that.

Someone said they'd heard about a parking lot that once occupied this space, and Celia confirmed there had been a big underground parking lot in an earlier day. By 1957, there were two hundred thousand cars in Havana! The parking lot was dismantled, and the original look of the plaza, with its stall spaces demarcated by the inlaid brickwork, was installed as part of a massive renovation project to restore the original look of Old Plaza. She gave us time to walk around or sit a while. I noticed a planetarium on one side and a curious sign for something called a camera obscura on one corner of the plaza. Celia said there was a contraption at the top of that building that had been invented by Leonardo da Vinci. Through a series of mirrors and lenses, it projected the view of Havana onto a screen in real time. She said there were fewer than eighty of them in the world, and the one in Havana was a gift from Cadiz, Spain.

We took a longer stroll down another street, passing statues, museums and street musicians serenading us along the way. A woman was chanting something that sounded like "Money! Money!" in a contralto voice as she walked by with heaps of white cones in an enormous basket. Celia told us she was calling out "Máne! Máne!" for the roasted peanuts she was selling in white paper cones. I wanted to keep hearing that voice longer and bought a couple of her peanut cones just to let her linger and hear her haunting voice a bit longer.

As I wrapped up my purchase, an elderly couple from our group approached me and said they needed to take a little rest, expressing that Celia was a fast walker. I did not know where Celia was going next and was already losing sight of the last person in our group as this lovely—but speed-challenged—couple talked on about needing some time to sit, catch their breath a bit and find something to drink. As they talked on and on, the bustle of the city crowded between us and our excursion group. I had no way of knowing where Celia was going or how to accommodate this couple's needs without being completely lost in Havana.

I invited them to sit on a bench in a small green space where a lone musician was playing his guitar. They seemed to be enjoying the respite, without understanding that by now we were completely separated from the group and on our own and I was not in communication with Celia. The couple went on, chatting happily and contentedly with each other as though the excursion were circling around their whim. I asked why they didn't take a sitting break in Old Square where we had so much free time, but they laughed and said they had no idea we would be leaving there so quickly.

Tourist groups were coming and going from all directions. At one point, the same stilt dancers we had seen in Old Square came through the street in a procession. My thought was that they might be heading toward Celia's next stop. I had to urge this couple to consider getting up and walking again, or we stood to miss the rest of our tour. My pleas fell on deaf ears. They were ignoring me, chit-chatting and laughing, pointing at the various storefronts and having fun pronouncing the Spanish signs on the streets and buildings.

The hardest part about this impasse was knowing that we were all missing out on Celia's fascinating information about Old Havana. I told the couple they were welcome to stay but would have to find their own way back to the ship because I was responsible for escorting the entire group. They looked up in surprise and the woman asked, "You don't know where they went?"

"No. Like most Americans, I have never been in Cuba before, and I have no idea where we are, where Celia and our group have gone, or where the ship is from here. My orders were to stay with the group and keep everyone together."

They looked at each other. Suddenly, the man turned on me. "You're supposed to know your way around. For what we paid for this blasted cruise, you should be our personal chaperone. Now you are telling us that we're missing the tour and you don't even know where we are? What is your name, young lady? I am going to report you."

"You are welcome to do so. My name is Marianne Milliner, and my function here is to escort the entire group. You asked for a moment to sit and catch your breath, which I trust you have enjoyed, but we have been here for a full twenty-five minutes, and I honestly do not know where our guide has taken our group. I am going to follow the stilt walkers, hoping they will lead me to the next stop on the tour. You are welcome to report me or not, you may come with me or not, but you need to make a decision right now.

They took more time to deliberate. She wanted to go back to the ship and have lunch, but he wanted to "get his money's worth" and eventually convinced her to come along. We had lost sight of the dancers by now, so I strained my ears and followed their music.

38

Havana Gems

WE ENTERED an enormous plaza, where I eventually spotted Celia and our group in a distant corner. I caught up with Celia and explained where I'd been. She smiled calmly and said it happens all the time. She said her narration in the Plaza de Armas ended with the group, but she would tell me about it in private because this was the same stop where she would give everyone time to buy cigars and rum in an official store. She turned to everyone and announced that it was time to do some shopping. Then she led the way into a little store where we could safely purchase legitimate Cuban rum and cigars with the approved seals of authenticity. Everyone followed her into the clean little store packed with crisply labeled rum bottles lined up in neat rows on the shelves and boxes of cigars in the glass showcases. Helpful clerks offered advice and recommendations and pointed out there was even a special promotion on one of the brands that day. As soon as the guests were nestled in the store and absorbed with their purchases, she took me back outside, saying they would need at least fifteen minutes.

I accompanied her into the plaza where she explained it was the Plaza de Armas, dating back to 1519 and once used for military exercises. I remembered a plaza with the same name in San Juan just as she added that it was a common name for big plazas in the Spanish Colonial world. She said the church that at one time had been on one end of the plaza had tumbled over from a hurricane. In 1792, it was replaced by a palatial estate, the Palace of the Governor General. People were milling around inside the courtyard directly behind the enormous columns because it currently housed the City Museum of Havana. She assured me the numerous rooms contained incredible treasures from Cuba's long history.

She pointed out the street that fronted the building. It was constructed of wooden bricks, meant to soften the sound of horses' hooves and carriages that disturbed one governor general's wife during her naps. The experiment didn't work to its intended purpose and she thought it remained the only wood-paved street in Latin America.

Celia took me to the gracious central green space where the statue of a man commanded the highest point. She said he was Carlos Manuel de Cespedes, one of Cuba's most revered national heroes and an influential catalyst for Cuba's independence from Spain during the nineteenth century.

Across from the de Cespedes statue, she pointed out a little temple that looked like it could have been in Athens or Rome. She said it commemorated the founding of five-hundred-year-old La Habana. Inside, treasures included original murals by Jean Baptiste Vermay and an urn containing his ashes. When she saw my expression of disbelief, she said to go on inside. I ran up the stairs, where inside were the three paintings right out in the open. I gave the matron a tip, and she invited me to take some photos without flash.

From there, Celia pointed out the moat and drawbridge of Havana's oldest Spanish fortress, La Fuerza. She said it housed a fantastic museum with exhibits containing treasure chests of real gold and silver coins and jewelry from the days of the conquest. She said it commanded spectacular views of the harbor and the city.

She pointed to the very top of the fortress where the statue of a woman dressed in Roman garb, was hoisting the bottom of her skirt up with one hand and holding a cross with the other. Celia explained that she was called La Girardilla, and meant to immortalize Isabel de Bobadilla, the wife of Hernando de Soto who went to conquer Florida and never returned to Cuba. While he was gone, she took the reins as *pro temp* governor. Celia said the image of La Girardilla was the iconic symbol of Havana. She told me to keep an eye out for her image on all the public transportation buses as well as on the label of Havana Club rum.

We backtracked to the little rum and cigar store where the last purchases were being made and the clerks were busily tallying the bills by hand. Those who made their purchases earlier were gathering outside the store, waiting patiently for everyone else while taking in the sights of the Plaza de Armas. I glanced over and saw my elderly couple engaged in a conversation with another couple. They seemed to be enjoying themselves.

Celia led us away from the Plaza de Armas and we headed to the last of our plazas, down a street where a lively band was entertaining a lunch crowd at an outdoor paladar. Everyone wanted to stop for photos and videos of the colorful and musical scene. A few started dancing to the irrepressible rhythm.

Before turning down another street, Celia told us to look to our left at a big, pink building a couple blocks away. That, she told us, was the Hotel Ambos Mundos, built in 1924. Its claim to fame was that Ernest Hemingway used it as his Havana retreat. It was his special place to write and enjoy the view of the city for seven years in the 1930s before he purchased a villa outside of Havana. She said his room, Number 511, was preserved just as he had kept it. Sadly, she had to tell us that Hotel Ambos Mundos was off limits to Americans at the time we were visiting Havana. She assured us that Hemingway enjoyed many a mojito at the Ambos Mundos, but she would take us to another Hemingway watering hole near our next stop. I remembered happily that Oscar had booked me on the tour to the Hemingway house the following day.

The next stop was a tiny plaza dominated by an enormous old church. The Cathedral of St. Christopher, locally known as the Havana Cathedral, was completed in 1777 over an earlier Jesuit church in a very small plaza that was at one time a swamp. The baroque structure with its two asymmetrical bell towers contained the possible remains of Christopher Columbus from 1795 until 1898 when they were sent to Seville. Treasures inside included a sculpture of St. Christopher, the patron saint of Havana, made in 1632 in Seville and more paintings by Jean Baptiste Vermay. Two bells peeked out from the top of one of the bell-towers. Celia said the larger one was named San Pedro and weighed seven tons. She said in 1762 the original bell was stolen so a new one was smelted back in Spain the next year. King Charles III visited the foundry and threw a gold ring in the molten metal for good luck, saying the gold would add a rich luster to the tone of the bell when it rang.

A woman dressed completely in a white gown and turban came by with an enormous cigar in her mouth. When guests started to snap photos, Celia intervened to explain that this woman was a Santeria practitioner. She explained that Santeria was a syncretic or blended religion that encompassed both the Christian saints and African idols. It emerged when African slaves were discouraged from worshiping their native gods and encouraged to adopt the Christian saints instead. She said the slaves cleverly kept their own gods by masquerading them as Christian saints, many of whom shared similar attributes. For example, St. Lazarus was the equivalent of Santeria's Babaluaye because they both protected the sick and lame.

We turned into a little alley and stopped in front of a place called Bodeguita del Medio, which Celia said was the Hemingway bar she had promised us. Music from a live band inside poured into the streets as a waiter came out with a tray full of minty mojitos that he passed around. Everyone was smiling and chattering happily in the warm Havana air, swaying to the Cuban beats wafting from inside the little pub, and sipping their mojitos. I thought of Oscar's prediction as the guests said, over and over, they were having the time of their lives!

We walked up another street where a lineup of classic American cars was parked along the curb, their owners polishing and buffing them as they waited for fares. Everyone wanted to pose near one or the other of the candy-colored cars that, Celia said, were kept running by Cuban mechanics who were more like magicians. She said under the hoods you might find parts from Russia, Korea, France, Italy... anywhere except the United States. The men in our group were nearly drooling for want of any one of those old classic beauties left behind by Americans and Cubans fleeing Havana in the 1960s.

An awaiting bus swept us off to Revolution Square, one of the must-see sites in Havana. We were surprised how new and well-appointed the bus was. Celia explained that when new buses arrived from China, they went directly to use as tour buses. After a couple of years of use, they were redeployed to the public transportation system.

We stopped in a wide-open concrete space that Celia said could accommodate up to a million spectators during the time Fidel Castro was in power. Celia added that he was famous for delivering very long and passionate political speeches, and attendance was all but forced. She giggled, adding that even in that setting, young Cubans found ways to mingle, meet and flirt quietly in the crowd. Nearby, public building fronts displayed enormous images of Che Guevara and Camillo Cienfuegos, two of Castro's lieutenants. Across the busy street, a marble statue of Cuba's most revered national hero, Jose Marti, sat beneath a tall, imposing obelisk that Celia said was the highest point in Havana's skyline and invited us to watch for its silhouette when the ship sailed out of Havana the following day.

Back on the bus, the driver took us past the capitol building. It was closed for renovations and surrounded by scaffolding at that time, but remarkably similar to the US capitol building and modeled after it ... except its dome was a few feet higher, Celia noted, adding that fact was a point of pride for the Cubans. She explained that the building was erected in 1929 during an era of prominent American presence ... and strong Mafia influence. The next year, the sensational Hotel Naçional opened its doors at a time when Havana was a popular tourist destination for Americans.

Celia said we would pass the Hotel Naçional very soon, but first to look on our left to see the memorial monument to the USS *Maine* that exploded in Havana Harbor in 1898. The explosion kicked off the Spanish-American War that finally brought Cuba's release from Spain. She said in Cuba, it is called the Cuban-Spanish-American War by law. She added that the Battle of San Juan Hill, made famous to Americans by Theodore Roosevelt's Rough Riders, was played out in Santiago de Cuba in the south of Cuba. Not far beyond the USS *Maine* memorial, she directed our gaze to the Hotel Naçional high up on a hill to our right, adding that in 1946 it was the site of a historic Mafia summit run by mobsters, Lucky Luciano and Meyer Lansky, an event later captured in the movie, "Godfather II." The list of Hotel Naçional's distinguished guests and visitors over the decades included luminaries like Nat King Cole, Winston Churchill, Mickey Mantle, John Wayne, Errol Flynn, Rita Hayworth and legions more. Even Johnny Weissmuller, aka Tarzan, swung by. She said a famous wall by the restaurant inside the Hotel Naçional featured celebrity patrons with their favorite dish from the menu. Walt Disney's? Black beans with hot chili peppers! As we neared the end of our tour the massive fortress at the harbor entrance, El Morro, with its lighthouse came into view. It had been designed by the same Italian engineer who built its counterpart in Old San Juan, Puerto Rico, at about the same time. Celia said a boom chain once stretched across the channel to keep unwanted ships out of the harbor. I remembered a similar story about the El Morro in San Juan.

As soon as the ship was in clear view, Celia reminded us to gather our personal belongings and thanked us for joining her, hoping we'd enjoyed our visit to Havana. Everyone applauded. Then, in a soft but emotional whisper, she asked if anyone would be willing to adopt her and take her back to the United States. We all stopped short of a group gasp as she promised she would eat all her meals, keep her room tidy, help with household chores and never complain. A woman broke our collective stunned silence asking, "What about your husband?" Celia answered, "He'll understand!"

We alighted from the bus directly in front of the terminal building. I longed to join the others to stretch out the afternoon with some leisurely strolling around the enchanting streets of Old Havana. It was not allowed, but after a long excursion, it was the unspoken "understanding" that visitors might want to go back to purchase mementos from the local vendors and return immediately to the ship. Still, as I entered the terminal building, I looked over the door where a tiny camera aimed down on everyone's comings and goings.

Something was tugging at me: that other matter of business that I could put off no longer. I boarded the ship and headed directly to the infirmary. I was on a mission to confront Dr. Messy!

39

Table Talk

WHEN I ARRIVED at the infirmary, a long row of patients sat in the waiting area. The nurse said there had been several minor accidents on the excursions, mostly from people tripping on the cobblestone streets while they were taking photographs or suffering from dehydration because they had not taken along a bottle of water. She said she would tell Dr. Messy I called. But before I was halfway down the corridor, the nurse ran after me and ushered me directly into Dr. Messy's office.

"I need a break," Dr. Messy said as she poured some Diet Coca-Cola over ice in a tall glass. She offered me some, but I declined. She said she was sorry to leave the ship so suddenly, but an important issue came up with some tenants in one of her rental condos back in Dayton, and she had to deal with it personally.

"So, how have you been, Marianne?"

"I could be better," I said. "I have been interrogated and am now being accused of stealing ancient

Mayan artifacts from Cozumel, Costa Maya, Belize and Guatemala," I said. "Apparently, the days we were in port when I brought the medical supplies back to the ship were the very same days some national treasures were smuggled out of those countries. Somehow, I have ended up in the crosshairs of all this and am apparently the prime suspect."

Long pause. "That's absurd!" Dr. Messy scowled. "Who said so?"

I knew I was about to break the gag order. I hesitated and then let it spill out. "Two security agents who have met me twice in the library. They thrust papers in front of me that they said had my signatures proving I am involved in some sort of Mayan grave robbery ring."

She took it in and thought for a moment. Then she walked over to a file cabinet and riffled through some folders. When she did not find what she was looking for, she went over to a lopsided pile of papers heaped sloppily over stacks of folders, balancing precariously on top of the file cabinet. She selected a folder and placed it on her desk.

She opened the folder and spread out a document, pressing it out with her hands. "This is the purchase order from the first set of supplies you brought back from Cozumel. She took a pencil and checked off the order item by item, half talking out loud and half talking to herself. "Syringes, sutures, needles, alcohol, aspirin, Bonine pills for seasickness... yes, all there," she said. She went on to the next purchase order from Costa Maya and through the other two from Belize and Guatemala. "All there. Everything is in place," she concluded and looked up at me.

"Then why did I go through those two inquisitions, and why are they saying I should have read what I signed when I believed I was only signing the purchase orders as per your instructions?"

She looked at the purchase order documents. "No signatures at all," she said. "Did they ask you to sign any of these?"

"They asked me to sign something in every case. You told me they might require a signature, so I expected it. I just signed what they put in front of me," I said. "Name, address, email, passport number and nation of origin. I signed everything, thinking it was what you meant about doing business in these dang foreign ports. I didn't think I needed to inventory everything in addition. It was all in Spanish, anyway." I reached across the desk and picked up one of the medical purchase orders. No signature. I had signed something at each stop, but apparently not these.

"Three of the packages were very big," I said. "Trunks, in fact. They looked like coffins from where I was standing farther down on the pier. I was told to leave the limo or truck each time we approached the ship by each driver. They said I could not come any closer to the cargo area. From where I stood, I honestly thought I saw you, or at least your silhouette, standing at the entrance. In any event, the only package small enough for me to carry back in my hands was the package in Belize at the National Bank of Belize."

"How big was it exactly, Marianne?" she asked with interest.

"About the size of an apple crate. "I was relieved it wasn't another one of those coffin-sized crates because my ride back to the ship was on a horse buggy with a Mennonite."

She paused for a moment, then shook her head and laughed. "Only you, Marianne," she said, wiping a tear from her eye with a tissue.

"That box you picked up in Belize should have been about the size of a... well, I can show it to you exactly," she said. She walked over to a closet and came back with a small carton containing a dozen boxes of eye drops. It couldn't have weighed half a pound. She said all the orders were about the same size, give or take. I told her the box I brought back in Belize must have weighed about ten or fifteen pounds. I remembered how relieved I was to hand it to the man who had whistled at me and took it away as I was transferring to the ship from the tender. She said the other orders were small cartons, and I should have come running to her as soon as I'd noticed they'd delivered big crates. She agreed they must have contained more than just the infirmary orders.

"Of course, I heard about the robbery of those Mayan artifacts on the news, but that had absolutely nothing to do with the delivery of supplies for the infirmary. I never gave it a thought until now. I can see how it all seems to connect, but there's something else going on here. I'm sorry it got you into trouble. Now I am wondering exactly what you did sign."

I told her how Sven and Grau had shown me the documents I signed, and they looked like lists of relics from archaeological sites of some kind or other. Again, it was all in Spanish and in minuscule print, so I didn't really know. She said they probably were fakes. I told her I suspected Sven and Grau were fakes too. She said she knew someone on board who might have an idea about what was going on and immediately dialed Wink. Wink answered on the first ring, and she told him I was in her office. I could tell by the way she was bringing him up to speed he had not been aware of anything involved in the case, including my wake-up inquisitions with Sven and Grau. Wink had transferred to our ship to investigate how the pirates got on board. This was a whole different matter no one anticipated. She handed the phone to me, and Wink said not to fret; I could fill him in at dinner. We agreed to meet in the Lido for the Cuban buffet at five-thirty. I knew I risked serious trouble breaking the gag order, not once but now twice.

I left the infirmary and headed straight upstairs to my room to change for the evening. I'd sent my three trusty black dresses to the ship's cleaners and found a blue, long-sleeved dress among the clothes I'd left in my suitcase. I cinched the matching tie-belt around my waist and grabbed my evening handbag. The usual onboard activities were suspended because we were in port overnight, and most people were dining on the ship before joining the buses to the nightclub shows at the Tropicana or the Parisién Cabaret at the Hotel Naçional. I was not in a particularly gracious mood as I passed by happy cruise guests and thought back to how surly Angela had been during the prior cruise. Now that I had a taste for how things happened behind the scenes, I honestly didn't know how these social hosts and hostesses could smile and maintain such a gracious demeanor day after day after day, and elevated them to a whole new level of admiration and respect.

అలా అలా అలా

I was at the Lido entrance five minutes early, and Wink walked out of the elevator and saw me a minute later. We hugged, but strangely I found it awkward. I was expecting a bigger hug after being separated for so long. But it wasn't forthcoming, and even though I wanted it, a small part of me was relieved. Had things already changed between us? Or was it just going to take some time to get the old feelings back?

The entire Lido restaurant had been completely transformed to resemble a Cuban paladar, or home-style restaurant, with palm trees in planter pots between tables covered with colorful tablecloths, a roving band playing and singing Cuban songs and the entire waitstaff costumed in Cuban hats and orange guayabera shirts. The offerings in the serpentine cases and along the counters included one mouthwatering selection after another from everything anyone could ever cook up in a Cuban cocina.

The menu consisted of all the favorite standbys like rice and beans in no end of variations and options. Ropa vieja is a course of pulled meat that must have been named for how it looks; like old clothes. Plantains served at least three different ways; roast suckling pig; fish; and several assorted green, fruit and vegetable salads all tempted us to try a bit of nearly everything. I eyed the dessert tray that included an assortment of different flavored flans; cheesecake; trés leches or "three milks" sponge cake; and churros, donut-like sticks coated with sugar that were both chewy and crispy at the same time, staying warm under the heat lamp.

Wink and I filled our dishes and found a small table on the outskirts of the busy dining area. We looked at each other without a word. So much time had elapsed and so many events that it was taking me time to reset back to the day we parted on the pier at the end of the prior cruise. It had been little more than a week but felt like ages.

He looked different to me this time. He seemed older than I remembered him. A little shabby and weary. Slightly unkempt. Distracted. Was something on his mind? I wondered. I chalked it up to the pressure of the job. After what amounted to sizing each other up following a long separation, he started. "Can't take you anywhere, Marianne," he said, cutting into a succulent piece of roast suckling pig. He moved the crispy skin to the side and absentmindedly wiped the grease from his fingers directly onto the tablecloth. "I didn't know you were in this much trouble already, so start from the beginning and leave no stone unturned."

I filled him in on everything that had taken place, starting with the guest injured at the Mayan ballgame reenactment that led me to my first meeting with Dr. Messy and how things evolved from there. I told him about the strange circumstances of collecting the meds and supplies in "these dang foreign ports" and how I swore I saw Dr. Percival Turnkey in disguise a few times, only to learn he'd left the ship in Jamaica. I told him about finding out that Mayan treasure robberies had taken place on the days we were in the various ports. I told him what Dr. Messy had said about the size of the medical orders compared to the coffin-sized crates that came back to the ship with me. I also mentioned seeing Dr. Messy's profile in the ship's cargo entrance. Finally, I told him about the two wake-up inquisitions I had faced with Sven and Grau and the gag order they'd imposed on me.

"Sven and Grau?" Wink looked up. "Who are they?"

"Security agents, I guess. At least they implied

they were. But their uniforms were strange. I figured you'd know them."

"Never heard of them. They must have been from the local port authority. What day did you see them?"

"I saw Sven twice. Yesterday morning when we arrived at Grand Cayman and this morning before we came into Havana. Grau joined him this morning, but I'm not sure when he boarded."

Wink was quiet.

"Well, you were innocent enough." He took a bite of black beans and rice, then looked up and called over one of the waiters. He asked him to bring some hot sauce to the table. "Someone clearly took advantage of you, but I'm fairly confident it wasn't Dr. Messy. I don't think she could have anything to do with stolen Mayan relics," he said. "I've known her for a long time. She is definitely unconventional, but she's not a grave robber."

"So, who would it be, and was it someone on the ship?" I asked. "And where did they go, because according to Sven and Grau, the loot is no longer on the ship."

Wink looked terribly worried and distracted at that moment. I noticed when he talked his eyebrows twitched in a way that was downright distracting. I couldn't imagine how I'd missed that annoyance before. A tiny blue vein on his forehead twitched like a pulse. While he chewed, the corners of his mouth opened just enough to show some of the food inside his mouth. I kept wiping the corners of my own mouth in a reflexive response. Was this the Wink I'd been head over heels with not two weeks earlier?

"That's the weird part. Also, the fact that you say you saw Dr. Messy in the cargo hold. But she does not have clearance to be there, and there would be no reason for her to go there—so it had to be someone else."

"Someone else with her profile?" I wondered out loud. "She's a bit portly, and there aren't too many officers that share her stature, at least that I've seen."

"You saw her from a distance, don't forget. What was she wearing?" he asked.

"From where I was, it looked like her lab coat. It was mostly white, anyway, but I did a notice a splash of color down the front that struck me like a Hawaiian lei from that distance.

The strolling musicians approached our table and struck up a tune I had heard all over Cuba that day. "Guantanamera," or "The Girl from Guantanamo," should be the national song of Cuba. It seems that everyone knew it, and you couldn't escape it walking around the four plazas for all the pop-up bands and soloists that were playing and singing it. It was the same song that Celia had told us was composed by Cuban's greatest national hero, Jose Martí. Fortunately, it was very pretty, and I didn't mind hearing it over and over again.

"Next time you hear from Sven or Grau, be sure to tell me when and where they want to meet with you, and I will show up. I want to know who these clowns are because I doubt they are ours. In fact, I honestly don't even think they truly suspect you had anything to do with those heists. It's sounding like they are making you the sacrificial lamb. I just wish I knew more about how all these incidents are related."

"You mean, how Mayan relics in all these different places were scuttled out of four ports in three countries on the exact days our ships called in those places?"

"You haven't lost your edge, Marianne." He grinned. For a fleeting moment, the Wink I'd known was back with me.

40

Kidnapped!

WE FINISHED DINNER and exited the ship to join the buses bound for the Tropicana. Our bus was packed with everyone carrying on in a festive mood. The ladies had not only dressed but dressed way up for the occasion in stepping-out gowns and retro dresses. Everyone chatted excitedly, and laughter filled the bus as people climbed in and took their seats. The driver, Pablo, said to prepare for a very short bus ride but a very long and fun-filled evening at the Tropicana. He said we would leave the Tropicana and return to the ship when the show paused for an intermission at one o'clock, when the local Cubans were just arriving and would continue to party until sunrise. Then he started the engine, and we chugged off.

Opened on December 30, 1959, in a transformed six-acre tropical garden, the Tropicana claimed to be "the largest and most beautiful night club in the world" at that time. When we arrived, tuxe-do-clad ushers handed each gentleman a cigar and every lady a rose. A few ladies asked if they could trade their rose for a cigar. The tables and dance floor were surrounded by a tropical setting of tall palm trees.

We sat in groups on long tables where bottles of Havana Club rum had been set with cans of TuKola, the Cuban version of Coca-Cola. We were on our own to mix our Cuba libres any way we desired. The proprietors knew we'd figure it out just fine. The music started from one direction where female dancers in colorful and revealing costumes emerged from a copse of trees while balancing huge headpieces with birds, tropical fruit and feathers on their heads. As that act ended, more young and beautiful dancers festooned in fifties-style, feathers-and-fruit-laden costumes shimmied, shook and shimmered to rousing music starting up from another direction. Rich gemstone-tinted spotlights glimmered and shone over their sculpted bodies as the combination of colored stage lights, strobes and nonstop motion created a kaleidoscopic effect.

The music was hypnotizing with its incessant and irresistible drumbeats. In no time, these engaging and talented young Cuban dancers won our hearts and we were swaying and smiling and clapping to the rhythm, completely engrossed in the experience. As the music and lights from one direction faded, another area lit up in the trees, and a new set of dancers with a different band came to life from another direction. It went on like this all evening, the troupe working their hearts out to keep the standards up to the Tropicana's reputation as Cuba's iconic night spot. Nothing stayed the same for more than a few minutes, and it was as though the performers were competing amongst themselves for our attention, becoming more daring, more colorful, faster and louder than the group that had just finished.

I looked around at the audience and it was evident everyone was enjoying the experience. But watching the show and the talented young dancers, I felt they were somehow frozen in an earlier age. The entire production, from the music to the costumes, seemed strangely like something captured in time, a fossil from the 1950s. I couldn't quite determine if that was the intentional effect, or if the Tropicana was trapped in a bygone era.

We consumed several rounds of Cuba libres as formal-clad waiters replenished the empty bottles of Havana Club and cans of TuKola. By the time the last dance was played out and the music crescendoed to its grand finale, everyone was on their feet clapping and stomping for more. We streamed out of the Tropicana and boarded our awaiting buses for the speedy return to the ship through the unlit and narrow back streets of Havana until we arrived at the familiar Maleçon, our ship looming in sight. When the bus brought us back to the ship, it was after one in the morning. The night was irresistible, with a full moon smiling overhead, its reflection glinting off the water. A delicious ocean breeze and the call of street musicians along the Maleçon promised to keep the night alive. The Maleçon was Havana's famous seawall that stretched five miles along the water's edge, paralleled by a busy boulevard. At that hour it was feeling like an outdoor disco with all the dancing and singing along the lively boardwalk.

We were about to head back into the terminal building with everyone else when Wink asked if I'd like to extend the evening a bit and take a short walk along the Maleçon. I recalled he had suggested something like that a few days earlier. We set off in the direction of El Morro and the open ocean when three figures approached us from the other direction. As they neared us, I could make them out with more clarity. Captain Gurtigruten and two of his officers were returning from a midnight stroll. We greeted each other cordially and passed. I noticed Captain Gurtigruten's eyes lasered directly to my hand, held firmly in Wink's grasp.

We passed the enormous Christ of Havana statue on the opposite side of the channel. Commissioned by the dictator Fulgencio Batista's wife, it had been unveiled at the end of 1959, only days before the Batista family fled Cuba for the last time, leaving a power vacuum that Fidel Castro filled soon after. The three-hundred-twenty-ton statue made of Carrara marble appeared as though the figure was holding a bottle of rum in one hand and a cigar in the other and we wondered if that effect had been intentional by the female sculptor who created it. As we approached El Morro, its gleaming light reflecting on the water below, Wink drew me close to him and, pulling me in, nestled his mouth over mine. All my prior reservations melted with that lingering kiss. I was feeling the same excitement and longing for Wink that I'd known just a couple weeks earlier. We hugged each other for a long time under the yellow moon that was casting so many sparkles on the dappled water beneath us.

Hand-in-hand, we turned to head back toward the ship without a word. Suddenly, some brakes squealed behind us, and as I heard a car door open, a strong set of arms wrenched me away from Wink. In that split second, I heard Wink shout, "What th–" but lost whatever followed. A smelly bag dropped over me before I was lifted in the air and someone pulled off my shoes. I felt a drawstring tightening under my bare feet while realizing the bag was so confining I had to curl myself up to fit inside. I was dumped roughly into the trunk and heard the lid slam shut over my head while underneath me the axle rumbled loudly as the car revved up and sped off!

41

Bare Trap

IT WAS DARK, hot, sticky and smelled of decaying burlap along with a cloying mixture of gasoline and rotting fish. God only knew where that bag had been! Burlap bags exactly like it had been used to smuggle bottles of bootleg during Prohibition and I wondered how old this one was. I was growing intensely hot inside the bag, with no way of escaping. I tried stripping down inside, peeling off layers of my clothes one agonizing inch at a time. I rued my earlier decision to wear the long-sleeved dress with its belt. I felt like Houdini trying to squeeze out of everything, pulling it over my head and then slowly rolling it with my feet out of the way. At one point, I was certain I was seriously overheated and expected to suffocate as I tried wrenching the dress over my head and it stuck under my chin. It was an arduous task that required patience and focus on the tiniest movements. Finally, down to my skivvies after what felt like an hour, I was only slightly relieved from the torrid heat inside the bag. I couldn't imagine where the car was taking me and why it was taking so long but could only conclude it had something to do with my breaching the gag order and had visions of spending the rest of my life in a Cuban gulag.

I was scared for my life. My heart was thumping so loudly I thought blood would spurt out of my ears. But I dared not breathe fast for fear of using up the tiny bit of available oxygen, imagining it was dwindling by the minute. I breathed at a turtle-slow pace, sipping the precious air as if through a narrow straw. I had to make whatever was in there last if I was going to survive this ride.

After what seemed the entire night, the car stopped. The trunk opened, and someone yanked me out roughly and tossed me over his back like a sack of onions. I could hear another voice shouting as it approached. It sounded like the new voice was yelling at the person holding me, and suddenly I was transferred to a new set of arms—strong, calm and gentle. The trunk slammed shut as I was carried away, cradled safely like a baby. The person holding me walked swiftly across what felt like an open field, and his footsteps changed when he entered a building. I could hear them go from muffling on the ground to slapping against a hard floor. I heard crickets chirping from every direction, and concluded I must have been brought into the countryside and the doors were open inside the building. I could feel fresh air seeping through the tiny holes of the sack and breathed it in hungrily, in spite of the inescapable foul odors of gasoline and fish that were embedded in the burlap.

Whoever was holding me slowed down and then suddenly stopped walking. I heard male and female voices all around me chattering and laughing calmly and dishes clattering softly. As the arms held me tightly, someone else took the bottom of the bag and pierced it with a pair of scissors, careful to push my bare feet out of the way inside. I was fairly certain whoever was cutting the bottom of that bag open was also cutting up my clothes, scrunched in the bottom. Sure enough, I heard an exclamation of surprise from a new voice and watched the shreds of my blue dress fall to the floor as I was freed from the bag. The strong arms put me down, and I found myself standing with nary a stitch on in a room full of strangers. Strangely, I was not embarrassed or self-conscious, as I'd become so accustomed to bare bodies on the nudist charter. I didn't know why I was brought to this place and expected the worst. Were there instruments of torture? I looked around but saw nothing of the kind. Most people there barely noticed me.

I turned to the person who had carried me to safety, still standing next to me. He was young, very good-looking and dressed in a white suit with impeccable drape, suggesting a very high-quality linen. His white Panama hat sat jauntily on his head. He could have walked out of a *Great Gatsby* poster. Meanwhile, I was still standing there nearly naked and very chilly when a woman I judged to be a few years younger than I brought me a dress. It was soft and mauve and sleeveless. I pulled it over my head, and it fell to my ankles. Then I started rubbing my exposed arms from the breeze coming through the open windows and doors. She walked away and returned a minute later, handing me a long gray sweater without saying a word. I thanked her in Spanish. Hearing my voice for the first time since my abduction, I was surprised at how calm I sounded. I listened for any clues about who these people around me were or where I was, but I came up at a total loss. My fledgling Spanish couldn't keep up with the fast banter coming from every direction. The gentle chatter, interrupted by occasional bursts of quiet laughter, continued as swirls of fragrant cigar smoke wafted across the room, mingling with the smell of fresh coffee and something yeasty and sweet. I did not know why I was brought to this place, where I was or who these people were, but strangely, I felt safe.

As the conversation rolled on, I tried to make mental notes about everything around me. There was about an equal number of men as women, all sitting congenially on the couches and around little tables in what looked like a combination living room and kitchen. In any other setting, I would think they were the older relatives gathering after a family wedding or good neighbors convening to enjoy the night air and catch up on neighborhood gossip. Outside on a cement patio, I noticed two elderly men playing dominoes.

It was like a scene from a painting of the old days in Cuba. Guitar music strummed softly from a very old-fashioned radio.

"Great Gatsby" guided me to a faded upholstered couch that came out of the 1930s or earlier and sat down next to me. He introduced himself as Hector and offered me some rum. When I declined, he called out for tea and the nice woman brought a tray with a china teapot, the pink and yellow design faded almost to invisibility, an equally faded teacup and sandwiches. She poured me a cup. While I was sipping on the hot tea, Hector assured me I was safe and promised that no one would hurt me. He apologized for the rough transfer from the ship and said the driver had been "handled" for that. Hector said if all went well, I would be returned to the ship by daybreak.

"Can you please tell me what this is about?" I asked, starting in Spanish baby talk but slipping back into English.

"We have reason to believe that you were complicit in expediting the smuggling of Cuban treasures out of several Latin American countries and back to your ship. The Cubans want to have our treasures back in our country."

I was confused. "I thought I smuggled Mayan mummies back to the ship," I said, immediately wishing I'd not worded it so carelessly, but it was too late to retract.

Hector said he knew nothing about Mayan mummies and wasn't concerned with them. But he was about to give me a little lesson in history. "In 1519, Hernan Cortes, a Spanish conquistador, embarked on an expedition from Cuba to establish trade relations with indigenous chieftains on the mainland. Recruiting hundreds of soldiers and slaves, he set off from Cuba and arrived at Cozumel where he likely realized for the first time that the indigenous people he was meant to trade with were technologically sophisticated and culturally advanced, not barbarian heathens as the Europeans had believed. Knowing this, he went from Cozumel to the mainland and worked his way into the heart of Mexico, transforming his trade expedition into one of conquest. Cortes brought uncounted valuables of Spanish origin to Mexico from Cuba. From there, the Cuban treasures were dispersed far and wide throughout Latin America by the conquistadors and their descendants over the many intervening centuries. The Cuban people feel those historical treasures belong in Cuba because they were and remain part of this island's earliest history."

"In other words," I tried to reconstruct what he was telling me, "Spanish artifacts that had been transferred to Cuba as the necessary trappings of a New World Spanish colony were in turn taken from Cuba by Cortes and his conquistadors and were eventually scattered across Mexico."

"Not just across Mexico but over other parts of Central America as well," Hector corrected me. "Remember, these conquistadors were young men on the go, eager to explore new vistas and settle new places. And now it appears these Cuban treasures were secretly stowed in the crates that made it to your ship at three Latin American ports. According to our informants, someone is attempting to smuggle them off the ship again and transfer them illegally to a private collection in Europe, possibly in Seville."

"So, the Spanish consider them to be their treasures and want them back too," I said.

"Precisely," Hector replied, lighting up a cigar. "But history will show that they were legitimately brought to Santiago de Cuba by the island's first Spanish governor, Don Diego de Velazquez, to help him establish the first European towns or "villas" in various places around the island.

"And here I am, caught in the crosshairs of this treasure theft because I signed some documents that I thought were routine purchase orders for some medical orders," I said in disbelief.

Hector nodded as he took another puff on his cigar.

"I still don't understand why I am being held in suspicion of everything going on around me like this," I said. "Yes, I may have unwittingly accompanied some things back to the ship, but I had reason to believe they were medical supplies. At worst, I am an unwitting player in this odd web of deception."

"You were no more than someone's pawn and a convenient scapegoat," Hector said.

"So, why am I here with you?" I asked again. "Why did you kidnap me, and what is my presence here supposed to accomplish?"

"As our cooperative hostage, you are our bargaining chip, Marianna. To put it quite frankly, we know that ship will never leave Havana until they have you safely back on board. We could have taken anyone else from the ship who happened to be strolling along the Malecon tonight. However, your involvement in the other matters underscores that we have intelligence in different aspects of this case, so they must take us more seriously. We need to make them understand how important this is to us. Now we are going to communicate with your ship. While you are in our custody, they will be much more likely to cooperate with our simple demands because they want you back."

He said Mariel, the nice young woman who had been helping me, would show me to my room so I could at least lie down and rest a while. "Grau and Sven are on the ship right now trying to locate the missing treasures to remove them right here in Havana. You no doubt have figured out they are working on our behalf."

I had missed that one and was inwardly kicking myself.

"They are not Cuban, but mercenaries of undisclosed origin—useful idiots—who will do almost anything for almost anyone—for a price. They are ruthless and could have done you harm. They placed you under a gag order that you disregarded, and they found out. Your telling people has created complications for everyone and put you in more peril. It is one more reason we brought you here. If anything happened to you, we would have lost our best bargaining chip. But we are most interested in obtaining those treasures, or at least learning exactly where they are or how we can get them back. And until either of those conditions is met, you stay here with us. Besides, we know you are of especial interest, perhaps even an object of romance, to the cruise line's head of security."

"You mean Wink," I said without thinking.

42

To Trap and Trap Not

A SMILE SPREAD across Hector's face. He said
everything was planned to the last "t" and that his years
of experience as an official in the Cuban government
taught him to watch over details and plan for every
contingency. He said when I had been kidnapped, all
traffic was intentionally stopped along the Maleçon,
where a temporary barricade had been placed. "In his
panic to rescue you, Wink commandeered a car that
came by just then, never suspecting it was a plant."
Hector looked at me and added, "You be sure to tell
Wink that if he'd seen that car in the light of day, he
would have realized it was a bright-red 1953 Chevrolet
Bel Air convertible with white interior, mint condition.
Grown men would shed tears of joy for a ride in that!"

He said Wink tried getting the driver to follow the
kidnap car, just as they expected he would, but instead
the driver was instructed to take Wink around parts of
Cuba that would frighten him out of his wits. "Those
old Russian high-rise buildings will scare most any

American in the daylight, let alone the deep of night," Hector said, clucking quietly and shaking his head. "The driver was instructed to stall and go down back roads and take long detours—anything to agitate and frighten Wink into imagining the worst was happening to you while he was helpless to do anything. It was all part of a plan for the greater good," he said. "By the time you were brought here, Wink was returned to the ship and focused totally on getting you back to the ship as well, just as we knew he would do."

Hector assured me once more that I was safe and encouraged me to get some rest. He said they would keep me comfortable and pointed to the people sitting around the room, saying they were all very nice family folks who worked on the estate. He anticipated the impasse would resolve in a few hours, especially now that Wink was in full control and painfully aware of the dire situation. Wink would give Sven and Grau full clearance to search every nook and cranny of the ship and would no doubt add some of his own staff to the project.

Mariel stood up and escorted me to a bedroom. She smiled and said they would come for me when they were ready to take me back to the ship.

Mayan Mania

Day Twelve: February 26, Friday
Havana, Cuba
Mostly sunny: High: 86ºF/30ºC. Low: 75ºF/27ºC.

Progress took longer than they'd hoped because I woke up the next morning to the sun glowing high up in the azure sky. For the first time, I could see my surroundings and noticed everything about my room was screaming mid-twentieth-century with old issues of *Life* magazines piled on tables and bookshelves crammed with old books. The furniture looked very minimal and retro, and for all I knew I had been brought to a mid-century-themed hotel.

Then I looked up and saw the stuffed heads of exotic animals that could have been trophies from African safaris mounted on the walls. I ducked into the bathroom, where no end of magazines was piled on every possible countertop, and a curious ledger of what looked like a weight chart was penciled in a wall above the toilet. The windows were thrown open, and the fresh morning air blew through, already trying to keep up with the fast-heating air of the sunny day shaping up outside.

Still in the mauve dress and gray sweater from the night before, I emerged from my room looking for Hector. I didn't see him, so I asked a woman mopping the floor. The strong smell coming from her steaming mop bucket was astringent and acidic and smelled nothing like the Pine-Sol or Spic and Span fragrances of the cleansers I used. She told me in Spanish that Hector was on his computer and pointed to a little room with open French doors set off the main living room where he was sitting at a table with his laptop. Two other women were cleaning the house, too preoccupied with their gossip to notice me. Mariel came out of the kitchen and welcomed me to a lovely breakfast she had spread out on the cracked and faded linoleum table. I looked around and couldn't help feeling that I was in a very old but special place. I would have expected to see more guests if it had been a bed and breakfast, so I ruled it out and had to assume the house belonged to Hector and that these were his relatives. When I finished breakfast, Mariel invited me to walk around the property with her, and I eagerly accepted. The grounds outside were lush with green trees and abundant colorful flowers and had a vantage that afforded a distant view of what must have been Havana.

We came to a spot on the ground marked by wooden borders she said was once used for cockfights. She explained it was a favorite pastime of Spanish people who brought the sport to the New World. Then she pointed to an expansive green space protected by shrubs and a fence where she said the neighborhood children came to play baseball. She told me baseball is so popular in Cuba that every little boy dreams of owning his own bat and mitt, and every province in

Cuba has its own baseball team, park and mascot. We continued down a path with a raised wooden walkway that brought us to a wooden boat. It was a fishing trawler and in mint condition. The name PILAR was stenciled artfully on the back. Pilar! I thought, with a sudden rush of chills rolling up and down my spine. This was Ernest Hemingway's famous fishing boat!

Could this house be the famous Ernest Hemingway house? Could I have slept in Hemingway's house?

Mariel confirmed the house was called Finca Vigia and told me Hemingway had written *The Old Man and the Sea* while living there. She said the housekeeping staff was cleaning it for the arrival of the daily busloads of visitors that came from the cruise ships. She said visitors were not allowed inside but could see everything from the open windows and doors.

I was still glowing with the realization that I had slept in Ernest Hemingway's house—and possibly his very room!

Just as we approached the house, we heard Hector calling Mariel. His voice came from above, and when I looked up, I saw a tower of sorts that I had not noticed earlier but which stood out prominently now with the sun's full rays bouncing off it. Mariel told me to follow her up the steps quickly, and when we ascended to what at one time served as Hemingway's writing nook, Hector told me to stay there and promise not to make a sound. Three busloads of tourists were approaching the grounds, and it was imperative that no one should see me. I opened my mouth to ask him a question right then. I wanted to know exactly who he was and by whose authority he was conducting this mission and how he came to occupy the Hemingway house, but he turned abruptly. As he descended the stairs, he looked up once and said the tower was cordoned off so the tourists would not be able to ascend the stairs that day. I felt a little like Rapunzel, minus her seventy feet of blond tresses.

I watched, feeling more detached and isolated than ever, as Hector and Mariel entered the house while the local guides started leading groups from the buses across the grounds. I saw people I knew in the excursion groups: my friends and colleagues from the MS *Minerva*! I could hear the guides talking about the history and what they could see from the outside through the open windows. Against my better judgment, I looked out from my perch, and there in the crowd I saw Butch and Sally Albert, Ted and Annie Clarkson, Max and Cathy Ringler, Baron and Baroness Proulx, the Simlingtons, the Triminghams, the Smothers and the Cooks. I even recognized Burt and Lily Smothers, the couple with the long story about how they became nudists and met at a volleyball game. Judging from all the buses that kept pulling in, it certainly was a popular excursion. I wanted to wave and shout in the worst way and assure them I was absolutely safe and sound. But the reality was that they probably didn't have a clue that I was a hostage in the Hemingway house at the same time they were touring it or that negotiations were being worked out about the fate of some Cuban treasures...and me.

Progress must have been slow or stopped completely. The crowds had long since gone away, with the buses rumbling and tumbling back down the dirt driveway and returning to the ship. Departure was scheduled for four o'clock, but it was already well past two. I had not heard from Hector or seen Mariel since morning. I was still wearing the same mauve dress and gray sweater from the night before and starting to rub my elbows from the chill of impending evening. I had a premonition that I might be spending more nights than I'd bargained for in Hemingway's house.

By sundown, I was still in the tower.

43

Farewell to Harms

Finally, I heard steps ascending the staircase to the tower. Mariel said it was time to return to the house. The tourists were gone for the day. She motioned for me to go first and followed me down the narrow staircase. Inside the house, Hector was still sitting at the table with his laptop. He was talking with someone simultaneously on his cellphone. I recognized Wink's voice on the other end. They seemed to be in a heated discussion. Mariel said she was sure they would be taking me back to the ship very soon.

I looked around the room in the growing dark. Only a solitary table lamp cast some pale light against the walls. A ceramic plate hanging on a wall to my right caught my attention, and Mariel saw me staring at it. She said that was the famous ceramic plate by Pablo Picasso depicting a bull. She said since tourists couldn't enter the house to take a photo of it, they often asked the housekeeping staff inside to take a picture for them; the staff was always happy to oblige and grateful for the little tip that came when they returned the camera.

I tried to make heads or tails out of the fragments of Hector's conversation, but he was talking too rapidly for me to follow and using expressions that were unfamiliar. He seemed to say "sí" quite often, and I took that to be a hopeful sign. Every so often he actually smiled and nodded.

At one point he looked over and caught me in a daydream. He came over and sat in the chair next to me. He said they were making some progress and that Wink had reported that Sven and Grau conducted a thorough search of the ship with every allowance permitted them from the officers and with help from the ship's own security staff—but came up with nothing. All sides were satisfied that the loot was no longer on the ship, so the investigation was moving on to learn when and where it left the ship in an effort to locate where it was and who had it. And how to get it back. I asked Hector why this was so important to him and by what authority he was using the Hemingway house as his lair. If he was surprised by the forthrightness of my question, he hid it very well. Leaning back, he clasped his hands behind his head, his elbows stretched apart. He said he was a direct descendant of that first Spanish governor of Cuba, Don Diego de Velazquez. Hector said his father had been a scholar of the conquest and always believed that treasures belonging to Cuba had been dispersed throughout Central America by the conquistadors. In fact, he had written a book about it. He walked over to one of the bookshelves and brought back a leatherbound book with a title in Spanish writing, of which I could easily identify the words Conquistadores, España and Cuba. The author was Don Juan Diego de Velazquez. He put it in my hands and I turned it around, impressed that this subject meant so much to this family and their nation.

"You are continuing your father's investigation," I offered.

"Sí," Hector said. "It is a matter of national pride. Also, as you can imagine, some of those treasures rightfully belong in my family, as they were taken from my ancestor. Don Diego de Velazquez was actually related to Hernan Cortes by marriage. Cortes was married to one of Velazquez's sisters. But not the sister he wanted to be married to. And Cortes was, I think you would call it, a lady killer."

"Very good-looking," I said.

"That too," Hector said. "Cortes murdered his wife when she visited him one time in Mexico after he had conquered the Aztecs. He was living with an indigenous woman with whom he'd had a son. His wife was indignant when she discovered that, and the couple had words. Everyone knew what happened when the woman didn't wake up the morning following a big fight in the bedroom the night before, her neck covered with black and blue marks. It was all brushed under the carpet, and Cortes went on with his life. But he took his wife's jewelry, which was part of the Velazquez legacy.

My family wants those treasures back to resurrect the memory of our murdered relative."

"What happened to the indigenous woman?" I asked.

"She went on to marry another one of Cortes's officers eventually. She had served Cortes as his loyal interpreter, and in many corners she garnered more respect and power than Cortes himself. Scholars argue that her influence was key in helping Cortes vanquish the Aztecs. For that reason, she is often characterized as a traitor to her people by historians."

I had never heard about this part of the Aztec conquest story and could have listened to Hector talk for hours. But I also wanted to return to the ship. I still had a couple more questions.

"So, how do you have the authority to take over the Hemingway house?" I asked. "And who are all these people?"

"They are the staff. They start early in the morning and don't go back to their homes until very late at night. There is always something to do around here, and when they're not cleaning or maintaining or repairing something, they genuinely enjoy each other's company. When Hemingway left Cuba in the summer of 1960 after living here for twenty years, Cuba was already in the early days of Castro's revolution. Remember, he took power at the beginning of 1959. Once Hemingway left, he would never again return to Cuba because of political relations and his own devolution into deep depression leading to his suicide in 1961. The property fell into the hands of the Cuban government and was opened to tourists in 2007.

As a personal friend of Ernest Hemingway and a fellow writer, my father visited here from time to time. I remember he brought me along a few times. It has become my personal refuge for reading and writing, and no one would deny me it out of respect for my father's intellectual relationship with Ernest Hemingway. So, it followed that I would stay here during these negotiations. It is safe, remote, and I have the key.

We heard Wink calling Hector from the computer, and Hector returned to his desk with me in tow. I could tell from Wink's tone that he trusted and respected Hector and was working in a cooperative spirit. The conversation between them was calm and conciliatory, a model of international diplomacy working for results. Wink urged Hector to consider arranging my return to the ship because it no longer made sense for the ship to stall in Havana, taking up valuable dock space from another ship. He promised the investigation would continue even after the ship sailed from Havana, and he would keep Hector in the loop at every point. Wink reasoned that since the loot was no longer on the ship, the investigation had to switch focus to locate it and my function as hostage had served its use.

Hector agreed and then promptly arranged for my immediate return to the ship. Before he signed off, he urged Wink to hand Sven and Grau over to the authorities in Miami. He told Wink they were mercenaries, and he had a strong hunch they should be investigated. Wink promised he would do his best, but with no evidence of anything against them stronger than a hunch, it might not be possible. Hector insisted they were up to no good. Then my driver arrived, and it was time for me to return to the ship. This time, I sat in the comfortable back seat of a roomy and luxurious old limousine. I wondered if it was a holdover from the Mafia era in Cuba.

I arrived within the hour, disheveled but safe. The gangway was still extended to receive me. Six ship officers were standing in the security area along with the security staff, watching as I started to ascend the ramp. Wink was nowhere in sight, but as I took my first step up the ramp, someone ran down to me in a flash of navy and brass, planted a big kiss on my cheek, swooped me into his arms and carried me up the gangway like a baby. It was Captain Gurtigruten. He asked if I was okay, and I assured him I'd been treated respectfully and was not hurt at all. He, on the other hand, was a mortal wreck.

"Please to have dinner with me tomorrow night, Marianna," he whispered excitedly in his "almost" English. "Just friends," he added. I said of course I would join him as he put me on my feet again, and I fished my ship card out of my tiny evening bag, which miraculously stayed with me the whole time as though it had been surgically attached. Once past security, I looked up.

Wink was standing there taking it all in. He hadn't changed his clothes since I'd been kidnapped, and he looked greasy and tired. He needed a shave. He said he wanted to hear everything that happened and that he'd come by my room in a half hour and take me to dinner.

Less than a half hour later, he was knocking at the door. I was ready, and as I came through the door, he took me in his arms and gave me a big, tight bear hug and didn't let go. We lingered there for a while and then slowly walked, hand-in-hand, toward the elevator bank. He said he'd reserved a table for two at Serenade, the quietest of all the specialty restaurants. Cleaned up and shaved, he smelled and looked good in a crisply pressed linen shirt under the same mint-green blazer he wore on the last cruise.

At the restaurant, Emil, the maître d', greeted us with a gentle smile before we were guided to our table. It was tucked back in the corner—very private with a window to view the lights of Havana as the ship slowly slipped away.

"I was never so scared in my life," Wink started, looking into my eyes. "I just thought—well, I'm not exactly sure what I was thinking," he said. "But I was frantic with the thought of something happening to you, and not seeing you again was enough to kill me. I'm just so relieved you're okay."

He wanted to know everything, starting from the split second someone pulled me away from him on the Malecón and stuffed me into the trunk. I told him how rough that ride had been and how I'd managed to strip down to almost nothing because it was so hot in that burlap bag and how every breath was precious and how I had images of ending up in a gulag. Then, I told him how respectfully Hector and Mariel had treated me when I arrived at the house. He was interested to learn that they had been headquartered in Hemingway's house, saying Hector never revealed where he was keeping me. I laughed and said I probably slept in one of the island's most historic houses and didn't even know it until morning when I saw all those mounted safari trophies and the fishing boat, Pilar, in the back yard. He was fascinated by my description of the house and Hemingway's boat and said to be sure not to leak the fact that I was there to anyone until I was off the ship in Miami.

We languished through delicious courses of appetizers, salads, entrees, desserts and espressos. After that, we relaxed even more with Sambuca and Italian biscotti.

Wink had no end of questions until I stopped and asked what had happened to him. Just as Hector had described, Wink said he had commandeered the only car on the road, not realizing it was a setup until much later. I interrupted him right then to tell him about the car that brought him back to the ship, remembering Hector's description of the 1953 red Bel Air with white interior in mint condition that Wink rode in. Wink said he would have given anything to ride in that car under calmer circumstances. But the driver took him on a hell ride through the dark until he arrived back at the ship. By then, the driver had filled Wink in on the missing Cuban treasures and told him that Hector would be in touch. He said nothing to assure Wink that I was okay or to disclose where I was, however. Wink kept saying he was never so afraid in his life, watching me disappear in an old car trunk in the dark of night, powerless to help in a place where his cellphone didn't even work. He kept taking my hand and squeezing it as if to reassure himself that I was okay. He said there had been one point where he really believed he'd never see me again, and he looked away. I sensed there was something more he wanted to tell me.

Soft music played in the background as dinner wore on. We looked around us and realized we were the only ones left in the entire restaurant. Wink glanced at his watch. Nearly ten o'clock. He looked up at Emil, who was coming over to tell us to take all the time we wanted. We finally left a half hour later.

Wink brought me back to my room and came inside. We sat out on the balcony for a good long while not saying much and mostly listening to the sound of the ocean as the ship sliced through the shiny, black water below us. It was always the same but always different.

Turning to him, I broke the silence to thank Wink sincerely for all he did to free me and get me safely back on the ship. He said he was taking over the case and that I was officially off the hook. I had done more than my part and had gone through more than my share, and it was time for me to relax and let him and the authorities handle everything from there on out. I was no longer in any danger, and even Sven and Grau couldn't harass me anymore, likely facing an interrogation of their own with the authorities in Miami.

As he rose to leave, Wink asked what I wanted to do the next day in Key West. Without a second's hesitation, I said I wanted to visit the Hemingway house there while the one in Cuba was still fresh in my mind.

He said, "It's a date!" and smiled, wrapping me in a big hug. I felt safe in his arms. But I knew it wasn't the same. And I couldn't identify why. Maybe I'd been swept up with the romance of falling in love on that first cruise. Or maybe I was still too raw from the breakup with Seth and was still on the rebound. Or maybe I'd been reading into things that were never really there to begin with. Or most likely it was all of the above. What I couldn't deny was that whatever was once between Wink and me had lost its luster. And I dreaded the inevitable conversation I had to face, but it could wait another day.

Just as he was about to leave my room, someone knocked softly at the door. A room-service waiter wearing white gloves brought a beautiful cake inside and set it on the coffee table. I could tell from the handwriting on the accompanying envelope it was sent from Captain Gurtigruten. But what struck me even more than

that was the smooth, luxuriant frosting, ornately decorated with intricate curlicues and extravagant swirls. I
had only ever seen such lavishly decorated cakes once
before—on the prior cruise. This was unmistakably the
handiwork of Sorrenta, the woman I always suspected
of having her sights set on Wink.

"She's back on board now too, isn't she?" I asked
Wink, already knowing the answer.

"There's something I have to tell you," he said.

44

To Rethink Wink

Day Thirteen: February 27, Saturday
Key West, Florida, USA
Partly cloudy: High: 81°F/27°C. Low: 74°F/23°C.

HE WAS BREATHING hot air on my face and neck and moaning hungrily as we rolled around, squeezing each other, our mouths clamped tightly together. We had been riding peaks of passion all night, and the first glimmers of morning were already streaking through the partially open curtains when he started right back in again. The blankets were all over the floor along with our discarded clothes, our naked bodies tangled in the twisted sheets and pressed together as hot desire swelled into yet another irrepressible surge of euphoria. He never stopped, and I couldn't get enough. "Yes! Yes! Yes!" I heard myself say. Again and again, we rose to rapturous heights of elation without so much as pausing to savor the moment, then started in again, barely coming up for air. I never wanted to let him go, and when he suddenly shrieked "Esmie!" I thumped him on the head but didn't stop him. "Yes! Yes! Yes!" I cried. I wouldn't have cared if he'd called me Enzo right then. My fingertips gripped his arms to the point of denting his skin. Over and over, like the unending waves in the sea, we ebbed and flowed, riding the restless crests and troughs of our mutual intoxicating cravings and embracing sublime release. The man was unstoppable! "Yes! Yes! Yes!" I cried, my hand smacking the mattress. "Yes! Yes!...."

The phone jarred me awake. Wink said he was already running behind schedule and might be a couple minutes late.

It was the last day of the cruise, and as I stretched myself awake, I was as much as already flying home in my mind. Just in the nick of time, too, I thought, smarting from my dream. I couldn't fathom any more involvements with anyone and extinguished any fantasies that the dream suggested. I welcomed the prospect of spending an entire day free from thinking about stolen Mayan mummies or smuggled Cuban treasures.

I stood over the balcony for a few moments and watched as the captain skillfully maneuvered the ship into its place alongside the dock. Say what you wanted about his unrequited love life, you had to admit Captain Gurtigruten was a seasoned and skillful captain. Tiny blue waves danced all around us as the old Key West Aquarium building and touristy Sponge Market came to life with crowing roosters heralding the new day.

I was fairly certain Oscar wouldn't need me for any group assistance in Key West when I stopped in to check, and he told me to enjoy the day on my own. He thanked me for all my help through the entire cruise and said he hoped our paths would cross again someday. Then he reminded me to return the ship's escort shirt at my earliest convenience.

I waited for Wink on the pier after the ship was cleared. He joined me a few minutes later and we set off for Mallory Square to take in all the busts of the famous people in Key West's history. Roosters scuttled busily across the streets as we went to check out the souvenirs in the Sponge Market. From there, we strolled past the Shipwreck Museum, comparing treasure finds of the past to the stolen Mayan relics. We passed the old cigar factory converted into a tourist mall and the stately red Customs House, now an art museum. Nearby was the Mel Fisher Maritime Museum and the Audubon Museum across the street. You could spend a week just taking in the history of Key West alone.

"So, what's going on," I started in, ". . . with Sorrenta?" I didn't have to add that part.

"Sorrenta?" Wink sounded genuinely surprised. "She's been on the ships with me, but she's working in the galley frosting cakes. Nothing's going on."

"I'm so confused, Wink," I said. "Angela told me you two certainly had something between you, and seeing how she clung to you on the last cruise, I couldn't deny it if I were from outer space. Now you're telling me she's back on the ships with you again, but nothing's been going on?"

"I can't make up people's work schedules, Marianne," he said. "Yes, we've been on the ships together, but there's nothing going on between us, and hasn't been for a very long time, and I mean that. Whatever Angela told you about something that happened a long time ago has been over and done with for years."

Wink took a long breath. "Well, I have to come clean about something, anyway, Marianne. May as well tell you now. And I'm really so sorry to have to dump this on you right after all you've been through. But it's not about Sorrenta at all."

He took another deep breath and kicked a little stone out of his way. "The truth is, Angela and I have been on-again, off-again for years. Sometimes I can't live with her, but I always can't live without her. You know what I'm saying?"

Wow! I didn't see that one coming. My head was about to explode.

"Oh, Marianne, I couldn't press charges against her, even after what she did to you on the last cruise." He was referring to that little catfight on an open deck that nearly landed me on a shark's menu that night. "She was reacting the whole time and projecting her frustration with me onto Roy. Roy knew what was going on, and that's why he felt free to partner with you in the dance contest. Angela and I had been through a very nasty breakup right before that cruise, and you entered the picture like a miracle balm. I honestly thought she and I were over for good, but she never gave up. All along, you were her real threat, and not over Roy but over me. Imagine!" he chuckled. "She honestly thought there was something happening between you and me."

My neck almost snapped from turning so fast. I looked at him and said, "So, what was not happening between us that I missed?"

"Oh, Marianne! I really have enjoyed our time together. You are an amazing woman, and my feelings for you are strong. But you came along at a time I thought things might be over between Angela and me. We were at an impasse during the last cruise, and I honestly thought we had moved on. Angela is temperamental and quixotic and has a low flashpoint, but... well, I'm so in love with her. I'll never forget our time together, Marianne. And, honestly, I believed in my heart things might have gone forward for a while. I never intentionally led you on, but we were having so much fun. And all along, I wasn't sure we would ever see each other again because I knew you would go back to Grand Rapids and ..."

His thoughts wafted off.

"And?" I broke the silence, genuinely curious. "What did you think would happen in Grand Rapids?" I asked.

"I saw that look between you and Seth the day he left the ship with Beth. I honestly wasn't convinced it was really over between you two."

I was so stunned, no words came to me and I flashed back to that moment remembering the look in Seth's eyes, the look that was only and ever meant for me and me alone. Had I looked at him the same way? I wondered.

"Oh, Marianne, in the end my heart is with Angela." He sighed heavily, took both of my hands and added, "I am so sorry."

I couldn't complain. After all, I was dreading having to break up with him, and here he was doing my dirty work. Still, it didn't make things feel any better.

"So, when are you proposing to her? Unless, of course, you already have?"

"I selected a ring for her during our stop in Cartagena. In fact, that was the real reason I got myself on that ship heading to the Panama Canal because I knew it would call at Cartagena, and she loves emeralds. I'd already boarded the MS *Athena* when the call came that they had room for me on the MS *Aphrodite*, and I tore off the ship to get to the airport for the next flight out. It was a close call! Would you like to see it?" he asked. "I mean the ring," he clarified. He was excited as a little boy with a jar full of fireflies.

Here we go again, I thought; another ring for another woman. I was thinking back to the last cruise where Seth proposed to someone else with the same ring he'd intended for me.

"Sure," I said, not sure of how I really felt. "I'm really happy for you two." I knew deep down this should have come as a relief, but hearing it actually happen still didn't stop that feeling of being sucker-punched.

"What do you think, Marianne?" Wink showed me a huge sparkling diamond surrounded by a setting of glimmering Colombian emeralds.

"It's stunning!" I said. "Angela should be very happy."

Wink was all smiles as he took it and dropped it in his jacket pocket. "We're going to continue together on the MS *Minerva* next cruise," he said. "I was able to finagle the schedule for both of us. Angela doesn't know yet. She thinks she is leaving for Portugal when we get to Miami tomorrow and that she'll be joining the MS *Juno* that departs out of Lisbon. Well, she'll get new marching orders to stay put right here on the MS *Minerva,* and when we arrive at Antigua in three days, I hope she will say yes when I drop to my knees in the sand and propose to her at Runaway Beach. I can't wait!"

"I can guarantee she will say yes," I said. "Congratulations!" I meant it, too.

My thoughts drifted back to the day Angela came down to my room and how she was so convinced–and convincing–that the captain would show an interest in me and made me promise I would accept his overtures and join him for dinner. Now it was evident she was trying to get me out of the way to clear her own path back to Wink. I also remembered how she'd recognized his carry-on in my room and took it back with her, promising to leave it in his office. She no doubt took it to her own room instead.

About ten minutes later, we stood in front of the Hemingway house, bought tickets and entered. It was almost slightly reminiscent of Finca Vigia in Havana but without the extensive display of mounted safari trophies. Unlike the Hemingway house in Cuba, tourists were allowed to go inside the one in Key West. The docent kept making references to Cuba and said Hemingway moved to Cuba after living in Key West. Of course, he had another wife by then, too.

Cats were sprawled around everywhere. Lying lazily on the beds, listlessly on the floors and leisurely in the gardens. Many had literary names, and they all quite obviously enjoyed a very coddled life with a full staff dedicated to their every feline need. All of Hemingway's cats and their progeny famously had at least six toes. Wrapping up his narration, the docent advised us not to pick them up or pet them. Of course, to some people that is an open invitation to do exactly that and, right on cue, one woman bent over to talk to an uninterested cat. She went to pick him up, but he took a strong swipe at her with his six or seven toes that sent her howling and a stream of blood oozing from her arm. It wasn't as if she hadn't been warned.

I said to Wink on a reflex, "Well, at least she doesn't need to be airlifted." Suddenly, the thought of

Dr. Spin being airlifted from the ship in the middle of that storm jumped to the front of my mind. I said, "I've got to run back to the ship!" I left Wink in a cloud of dust as he gathered his wits and chased after me. I didn't slow down until we were back on the ship and racing to the infirmary. When we arrived, I told the nurse I had to see Dr. Messy urgently.

45

Follow the Loot

DR. MESSY WAS IN ONE of those rare moments without a patient. "I was just contemplating going ashore for some conch fritters," she told us. "Wish you'd brought me some," she said with a mischievous smirk. She saw my breathless urgency and ushered us into her office. "Sit down, sit down!" she said. "What's going on, Marianne?"

I took a deep breath so I could get the next sentence out without stopping. "Did Dr. Spin ever make it to the hospital in Grand Cayman after they airlifted him off the ship?" I asked.

Dr. Messy thought. "I don't really know," she said. "No record of it came to my attention, and I'm embarrassed to admit that I did not follow up on it because I wasn't on the ship when it happened. I re-boarded the ship the day after he left." Then she said, "Wait a minute. I'll find out right now."

She called the hospital in George Town at Grand Cayman and learned that no one by the name of

Dr. Elmer Spin had been admitted that night or any other night.

"That tells me he wasn't really injured," I said. He had another reason for leaving the ship that night, and I have a hunch it had something to do with smuggling rare and valuable treasures off the vessel.

"While I was in Cuba, Hector told me that Hernan Cortes scooped up riches from the governor's treasury that had been transported from Spain to help the founding and settling of colonies in the New World—silver and gold religious accoutrements, coins and jewelry. They were small items but priceless in value. Cortes brought them to the mainland to trade, and the treasures were in time scattered throughout Latin America."

Dr. Messy sat back in her chair as she took it all in. Wink sat forward in his chair. They both stared at me. I went on.

I asked her one more time what Dr. Spin was a doctor of; she said art history but wasn't certain about his specialty. She Googled his Wikipedia page, and it said Spanish Colonial art in Latin America. She reminded me that he had been ambassador to the Vatican.

"Yes!" I said. "I did not forget that."

"So, what am I not getting here?" Dr. Messy asked, looking back and forth between me and Wink.

"I'm beginning to believe the Mayan relics may have been a ruse," I said. But no one would question it because all these things were collected in ports famous for their Mayan ruins. Besides, three of the boxes that came back with me looked like they could have contained mummies. If that's the case, it was a very clever case of using a decoy. But the Cubans are convinced that their treasures came onboard, and they want to take back what is rightfully theirs.

"I suspect that Dr. Spin had located the objects before booking this cruise and organized them to correspond with this itinerary. But when he found out you were making medical pickups at the same stops, he combined them to better hide the evidence," I said, looking at Dr. Messy.

"Come to think of it," Dr Messy said, "I actually told Elmer that I was going to ask you to collect those meds for me when he came in that day after he was hit by that Mayan ball. He's always volunteered to do it for me in the past. Now I'm beginning to see why he was always so eager to volunteer to make those pickups in the past and wonder how many other treasures may have made their way on and off our ships with him over the years. Obviously, he has forged some strong relationships with his shoreside contacts in these ports. It's all making sense now. It would have been nothing at all for him to switch out the paperwork so you would be signing the archaeological documents instead of doing it himself," she said, shaking her head, "and not knowing what you were actually signing."

I said, "I believe Dr. Elmer Spin may have smuggled the Cuban treasures off the ship the night of the medevac. I suspect he boarded an awaiting vessel in

George Town and headed for the Atlantic and Europe, possibly Seville or even the Vatican, with the contraband. I read somewhere in researching one of my detective books that the Vatican has some of the biggest collections of the world's art, and he was an insider there, after all," I added. "Is there any way to check if any ships or seaworthy yachts left Grand Cayman a day or two after the medevac?"

Wink said there was a way to check, so Dr. Messy and I followed him back to his office where he contacted the harbormaster at George Town. There was no record of any vessel coming or going in the three days following the airlift. Wink checked the nearest other yacht club which was in Jamaica at Montego Bay and struck gold! He learned that an ocean-worthy superyacht, *La Malinche,* departed after the storm subsided on February 23rd. That would have been the day we arrived in Jamaica. *La Malinche* had been chartered by a Dr. Elmer Spin, and the ship was headed for Civitavecchia, the port of Rome! *La Malinche* was scheduled to leave early in the morning, but they had to wait a couple hours for another member of their party to join them, and then departed at noon instead.

"That must have been Dr. Percival Turnkey!" I said, remembering that he'd disembarked in Jamaica where we arrived two hours later than scheduled.

"Can you tell me if Dr. Elmer Spin and Dr. Percival Turnkey knew each other?" I asked Dr. Messy.

"Yes!" she said. "And quite well. Dr. Turnkey was Dr. Spin's advisor for his doctoral dissertation."

"Wait a minute!" I stopped her. "Do you mean Dr. Turnkey is not a pathologist, as he claims, but an art historian instead?"

"Both!" Dr. Messy said. "He started out in pathology, then got a degree in art history. Then he went back to pathology because he said he'd go with whichever gave him a job first. But it was during the time he was a professor of art history that he acted as Dr. Spin's doctoral advisor. They are about fifteen years apart in age."

"So, now it was suddenly making sense that I saw a Dr. Turnkey look-alike in three of those pickup points. He must have been the one who made sure the documents were switched so that I signed the wrong ones," I said. "I saw him at all three pickup points except in the Bank of Belize, but he no doubt was there earlier than I was since I arrived so late with Gabriel's horse and buggy."

Wink sat up, opened his mouth as if to say something, then thought better of it.

Dr. Messy used Wink's phone to call a colleague at Vanderbilt University right then, saying she needed to confirm something. She hung up and said her informant confirmed that Dr. Turnkey had an impressive personal collection of Spanish art and treasures that was the focus of admiration among Vanderbilt staff who knew him. Dr. Messy's contact also verified that Dr. Spin's doctoral thesis was about Spanish treasures scattered throughout Latin America by the conquistadors.

"He probably knew there was an effort afoot for the Cubans to obtain them and felt they really belonged back in Spain," I said.

It was looking more and more evident that Dr. Spin and Dr. Turnkey were trying to smuggle the Cuban artifacts out of Central America and get them to a private exhibit in Rome, possibly in the Vatican itself. "If someone could intercept *La Malinche*," I said, "I would bet almost anything that they would find on board the missing Cuban treasures that the Cubans want back."

"But first," I said, "I have another question."

I knew exactly who had the answer!

46

EsmieXXX

WE ALL RETURNED to Dr. Messy's office where she dialed the bridge, and after answering a few security questions, Captain Gurtigruten picked up the line. Dr. Messy handed me the phone.

"Marianna, are you okay?" he asked. "You are still coming to dinner tonight, yes?" he asked. He didn't wait for my answer. "Esmeralda answered the email, and I have to show you what she wrote. My heart is so light! I need you to write another love letter for me," he all but sang.

"Captain Gurtigruten!" I tried to stop this operatic aria before Dr. Messy and Wink picked up on it. I wasn't sure how much of it they could hear. "Dr. Carver just determined that the night of the medical evacuation, the patient, Dr. Spin, was never admitted into the hospital in George Town. Instead, he was taken to Montego Bay where an ocean-going yacht was awaiting him.

"Would you happen to know who operated the chopper that performed that rescue?"

Captain Gurtigruten made an immediate about-face to focus on business, saying that they offered to call the emergency medical evacuation outfit the cruise line usually used, but Dr. Spin insisted on calling his own rescue service instead, saying it was included in his elaborate insurance plan. Captain Gurtigruten added that when the chopper arrived, he and the other officers did their best to identify its origins, but it was blacked out. If there had been any lettering on it, they did not see it.

I recalled two medics descending and placing the patient and his luggage into the basket, then guiding it up over the water as the hi-line pulled it toward the helicopter. But I never saw those medics ascend and figured the storm precluded that maneuver.

The captain confirmed that they departed the ship in Jamaica the next day.

I wasn't convinced that was the end of them or that they departed for good and secretly wondered if they might have come back on board.

I thanked Captain Gurtigruten.

"So, what next?" Wink asked, taking more of a spectator role as I did more of the work.

"It is pretty obvious that Dr. Spin smuggled the loot in the basket to the yacht in Jamaica," I said. "Or maybe there was too much to take in one load, and someone had to bring him the rest.

"Maybe Dr. Turnkey had to bring along the remaining treasure and that was why he disembarked in Jamaica," I theorized. "The timing would seem to corroborate it, especially knowing the MS *Minerva* was a couple hours late coming into Montego Bay, and *La Malinche* waited for a member of their party to arrive before weighing anchor. That late-arriving guest had to be Dr. Turnkey."

"And you're thinking he took more of the loot?" Wink asked.

"According to Sven, who followed him down the gangway in Jamaica that day, he left with just a carry-on. No one bothered inspecting what was in it, but it could easily have accommodated more stolen gold and silver, especially if he made room for it by leaving his own clothes behind. What do you want to bet he did just that?"

Dr. Messy called Irina, the manager of the housekeeping department, to see if Dr. Turnkey had left anything behind when he departed in Jamaica. Sure enough, he had. Irina said he'd left his entire wardrobe on the bed and personal items in the bathroom. Everything was neatly folded and in three piles, and one garment was set apart on the desk. She said they had reported it to reception, and she was still awaiting instructions for what to do with the discarded clothes. She was happy Dr. Messy called right then and asked where to send it. Dr. Messy said to put everything in a plastic bag and set it aside. She would collect it later.

I guessed that both Dr. Turnkey and Dr. Spin were sailing from Jamaica and asked Wink if he could find out where *La Malinche* was at that very moment, asking, "What would it take to identify and intercept a yacht at sea?"

"We're about to find out," Wink answered, already dialing a number on the phone.

A few minutes later, the harbormaster in Montego Bay said the yacht had blown off course for several hours and was behind schedule, battling high winds and strong currents in international waters between Haiti and Cuba. The nearest port city of any size was in the south of Cuba. He said the yacht was probably fighting its way toward the calmer and more sheltered waters between the islands in the shallow Bahamas Straits, but was clearly more than a day behind schedule.

Wink called Hector in Cuba and gave him the latest information about Dr. Spin and Dr. Turnkey and the position of *La Malinche*. Hector checked with the harbormaster at Santiago de Cuba, who said his team would watch for the yacht and be ready to intercept it if it should drift into Cuban waters. I heard Hector shouting orders to someone and could fairly imagine the bustle of activity my hunch had galvanized. I thought, with any luck the treasures would find their way back to Santiago de Cuba within the day.

❧❧❧

I headed back to my room to pack. I didn't have much, but I took my time. We would be back in Miami early the next morning, and by evening I would be inside my own cozy house at long last, leafing through about a month's worth of mail.

I was wishing the captain could write his own love letters, but a promise is a promise, and I was ready when the security agent came shortly before seven to escort me up to the captain's quarters for the last supper. Captain Gurtigruten greeted me with a bright smile. He was not wearing his uniform jacket this time, but a pressed navy polo shirt with khaki pants. He said he was off duty that evening and could leave the work on the bridge to his capable officers. He would be back on duty to bring the ship into Miami the next morning. We walked out to the balcony as usual, and he told me he had read the full report Wink sent him about Dr. Spin, Dr. Turnkey, the helicopter evacuation, the yacht *La Malinche* heading for Rome and the Cuban connection. He filled two champagne flutes, admitting he didn't do it often but would make an exception to toast me for a job well done in helping resolve a complicated mystery. He took a sip of his champagne and set it aside while I drained mine.

"Let me see Esmeralda's letter," I said, bracing myself for the worst. He took my hand and walked me over to his desktop computer and opened the screen. The letter was right there, waiting. It read: "Dear Gerty, I'll give you the terms of engagement when you are in Cartagena, so let me know next time you are here. Okay? –Esmie"

He was beaming. Was something lost in

translation? I wondered. I rubbed my eyes and read it again. How could I explain to him who Esmeralda was and her line of work when he was in such colossal denial? They say love is blind, but could the captain be this smitten? He was so happy that I didn't want to burst his bubble; but I didn't think it was right to string him along, either. He was being set up for a terrible fall, and he was really too nice for that.

"Captain Gurtigruten," I asked slowly, "do you have any idea what Esmeralda is telling you here?"

His face lit up. "Of course, Marianna! She accepts my proposal for marriage at long last! She wants to tell me next time I visit Cartagena! My heart is so full of happiness! No doubt she is giving me the answer I have been asking her for! She's waiting to tell me in person, yes? How not?"

Where to start, I asked myself. I would have liked to meet Eduardo before he went and died. I would have set him straight about a couple of things, and taking advantage of a friend's innocence was at the top of my list. Sending Captain Gurtigruten an email from an escort service and leading him to believe it was a love letter from that blushing milkmaid he saw in Cartagena was the height of cruelty. I didn't like to think ill of the dead, but Eduardo was evil!

"Well, Captain," I said. "Let's look at her words," I said, with all the patience I could muster. "What do you think she meant by 'terms of engagement'?"

Long pause. "Marianna, no doubt she wants to get engaged! How not?"

An audible groan escaped me.

"Captain, I need to tell you something, and I hope you won't take it too hard." I broke the truth to him about Esmeralda's livelihood.

"No! Marianna! No!" he protested. "That can't be true! I know my beautiful Esmie is sweet and shy, and she really loves me."

"Okay, Captain. You know her better than I do." I gave up and bit my tongue.

Together we composed a letter that I judged was kind but noncommittal. Luckily, the captain read love and valentines into it that weren't really there. I knew Esmeralda would figure it out. She had to be business-savvy if nothing else.

"Tell me something, Captain," I asked as I clicked the SEND button and got up from the chair. "When is the next time you will actually be going to Cartagena?"

He looked at me with sad eyes. "I don't know, Marianna," he said. "Not at least for another two years. After this cruise, I have a vacation before returning to sail in the South Pacific on the MS *Musa*. Then I take over the MS *Pandora* to the Black Sea. But Esmie will wait for me!" He said this resolutely while he looked into space. I half wondered why he didn't plan to visit her during his upcoming break but decided against suggesting it.

We proceeded to the table where a dinner had been

set up under covered dishes. He served me family style as before: savory chicken tajin with steaming stewed vegetables and warm, soft flatbreads – comfort food.

"You're going home tomorrow," he said, looking dejected. "Will you come back?"

"No, Captain," I said honestly. "I don't think this life is for me. I love the ship and the guests and the officers and crew, don't get me wrong. And it has been a pleasure to come to know you. I've enjoyed our dinners very much," I added.

"I know, I know. Especially the macaroons," he joked.

"It's time to go home now, back to my own life," I said. I believed it with all my heart.

47

Bottoms Up

Farewell from the MS Minerva!
February 28, Sunday
Miami, Florida, USA
Showers Clearing to Partly Sunny: High: 81°F/27°C. Low:
73°F/23°C.

THE NEXT MORNING, I was up, packed and ready
to disembark before the ship had even pulled in. I
stood on my balcony and drank in the Miami skyline
brightly lit against the dark predawn sky. A giant
Ferris wheel glowing with white lights commanded a
prominent place along the waterfront where throngs
of tourists would congregate in just a few hours.
From there my eyes were drawn to a moving image
on the Intercontinental Hotel, rising high above the
shoreline and reflecting on the water below. Composed
of a million ever-changing lights in constantly shifting
colors, the figure danced with graceful, unending
movement, even morphing between female and male,

never pausing in its lively, eternal display of dazzling youthful energy that so aptly symbolized the city of the future. Miami: *The Magic City*!

I stopped by the office to say goodbye to Pearl, Oscar and Pauline. These departures were always quick and unsentimental. The entire staff was already engrossed in the business of moving one group of people off the ship and bringing a new group onboard.

I sat on a windowsill to wait for my luggage tag color to be called to allow me to disembark. I pulled out the copy of the *Popol Vuh* I'd picked up in Cozumel and read a few paragraphs to pass the time. I stopped cold when I came across these words:

"Cortes and his men saw many books when they landed on Cozumel and there is good evidence that the loot they took away with them included the Dresden Codex."[**] The Dresden Codex was one of the early Mayan books that escaped burning and somehow turned up centuries later in Dresden, Germany. If Cortes took one, who was to say he and his conquistadors didn't take many? What if the Mayan loot was not mummies, after all, but Mayan books? I mused.

Then, a couple of paragraphs later, it said that the Maya embedded complex messages in their textile designs.

Suddenly, a thought struck me like a bolt of

[**] Dennis Tedlock, *Popol Vuh: The Definitive of the Mayan Book of The Dawn of Life and the Glory of Gods and Kings,* (Greenwich, CT: Touchstone, 1996), 23

lightning. I ran to Wink's office and blew right through his door. He looked up, startled. "What if it wasn't mummies at all, but Mayan books?" I fairly exploded, repeating, "What if the Mayan loot didn't contain mummies at all, but rather Mayan books?

"Those shirts that Dr. Turnkey was always wearing were Mayan from Guatemala," I steamrolled on without allowing Wink a word in edgewise. "The ancient Maya wove complex messages into the designs in their textiles. Dr. Turnkey's shirts might have had some sort of symbols of communication woven into them! Like wearable sticky notes!"

Wink looked at me as if I were stark raving crazy. "I thought you said the mummies were only a ruse or a decoy," he said.

"I'm reconsidering," I said, musing out loud. Maybe there was a parallel plot to rob Mayan graves and consolidate them along with the Cuban treasures." A theory was fast forming in my head. I asked him to call Irina in housekeeping and ask about the isolated garment left on Dr. Turnkey's desk the day he left in Jamaica. Could they bring it to the office? I suspected it might have been one of his Mayan shirts with some sort of message woven into it. It seemed to have more importance than the rest of the clothes piled on his bed. Irina put him on hold and then came back to the phone, saying it was gone. She said it was a white Mayan shirt with colorful embroidery down the front placket. A housekeeper had found it with a note tucked inside that instructed it to be delivered to Room #6081. Irina said the housekeeper had delivered it. Wink checked, and #6081 was Perry Cardis's room!

Wink shot out of the office like a cannon, yelling instructions into his walkie talkie as he ran. I had a hard time keeping up with him, dodging and weaving my way between clumps of people milling around with their carry-on luggage in tow. When we arrived at Perry Cardis's room, room service was just leaving a breakfast tray. Perry Cardis saw us and invited us in. He was wearing the Mayan shirt: white with some colorful embroidery on the button placket. He said he had to wait for a porter to help him take his magic crates through customs, so he was killing time with room-service breakfast.

I asked Perry Cardis if I could examine his shirt, and he willingly took it off, saying he had more because the Mayan shirts were the only ones he could wear as they were so roomy and airy.

I held up the shirt and looked for symbols embroidered into or around the colorful flowers on the button placket without knowing exactly what I was looking for. Nothing stood out. While I was examining that shirt, Perry Cardis grabbed another from one of the trunks and put it on. He turned to the side briefly, but just long enough for me to see how the boxy shirt accentuated his stomach—and I realized that from a distance he could have passed for Dr. Messy!

I handed the shirt back to him, and as he turned

his back to tuck it into the trunk, I noticed something that startled me. The back of the shirt he was wearing had subtle images of symbols woven into the cloth. Most of the symbols were in gray threads, but the few that stuck out were black. The black stitches were not the same size and seemed less uniform than the gray ones. They also seemed newer than the gray ones because some went right over the gray stitches, as though they'd been more recently added. I went over and looked closely but discerned no cryptic words or messages. But when I squinted to blur my eyes, something incredible appeared.

Along the back yoke of the shirt emerged a row of four small black boxes. Three were oblong and one was square. At the bottom of each oblong box was the image of a tiny profile that looked remarkably similar to the glyphs we had seen on our tours of the Mayan ruins. The three long boxes each had the profile of a face that could not be mistaken for anything other than a Mayan ruler. The square box contained what appeared to be a smaller square at the bottom. But most curious of all was that inside each box and directly above each glyph in every case was a faint line stitched in wispy black threads. I was trying to figure out what the symbols were telling me when that treasure hunter in Roatan who found silver ingots under a false bottom suddenly came to mind.

I opened one of Perry Cardis's crates and started to empty it above his shouts and remonstrations. "What are you doing? Are you crazy? I've got to get these off the ship, and I'm already running late! My driver is waiting for me! You're messing up my plans!"

I didn't care because there was something those symbols were telling me about the crates. I emptied the first crate right down to the bottom. I put my hand there, but it was not level with the floor. My hand was resting on the bottom of the trunk but clearly eight or ten inches above floor level. It was a false bottom! I called Wink over, and he took one look shouting, "What the hell is going on here?" He summoned security to the room immediately, ordering them to bring a crowbar. While they were on their way, I systematically emptied Perry Cardis's other two crates and dumped the contents all over his bed. He was frantic, but I didn't care.

When security arrived, they applied the crowbar to the false bottom of the first crate and peeled it completely away. Inside was a carefully wrapped mummy! He opened the bottom of the second crate which revealed another Mayan mummy. No surprise when the same thing happened with the third crate.

Perry Cardis was on the edge of his bed, crying in his hands. He looked up and said he had no idea what was going on. He said he had shipped his magic paraphernalia and charter cruise props and party favors to the ship in these crates, but they didn't arrive on time and straggled in at three different ports. All three were labeled "Perry Cardis's Magic Paraphernalia" and each had a permanently affixed decal from a magic emporium in Colon, Michigan. I'd never heard of the place, but Perry Cardis assured me it was one of the biggest magicians' suppliers in the nation. The decals looked legitimate on the surface. The crates looked like the same ones I saw from a distance being loaded onto the ship the days I picked up the medical orders.

"When did these arrive on the ship?" I asked him.

"They were all supposed to have arrived together on the first day of the cruise," he said. "But not one arrived that first day. They all came later, one day at a time, all at different ports. I don't remember which ones. Somewhere the hell in Central America. I went down to receiving, watching for them every day. I needed them for all the parties and games because I'd packed most of the charter stuff along with my magic tricks. I travel with these trunks every time I host a charter cruise."

"Did you bring them back to your room yourself as soon as they came on board?" I asked.

"No. They wouldn't let me. Once I saw them loaded into the ship, I had to wait for receiving to process them and then wait for the porters to bring them up to me. They always came a few hours later or the next day."

I watched Perry Cardis nearly melting down. I believed with all my heart he was innocent. For all his annoying personality, he was not an evil or conniving man, but just a fun-loving mischief-maker. Besides, he was so in love with Stella, and I still hoped things would work out for them. I could believe more easily that he had been framed than complicit in an international grave-robbery ring.

I asked him where he got the shirts, and he said one was delivered to his room after the ship left Jamaica. Dr. Turnkey knew that Perry Cardis liked those shirts and had left one behind for him. The other was a gift from Dr. Messy. She told him to feel free to wear it to the airport for his flight home. Then, suddenly, he said he didn't want anything to do with either one of those shirts and, taking the one off, he pulled the other one out of his suitcase and rolled them both up in a wad that he handed to me. He reached into his carry-on for a light-blue polo shirt and pulled it over his head. Holding both shirts, I noticed something in the pocket of one of them. It was a note with the words, "Yes, Perry C!" and signed "Stella."

Stella Laffer had accepted Perry Cardis's proposal! I quietly left the note on top of his desk.

I was convinced these were the same casket-sized containers I had seen from a distance in Cozumel, Costa Maya and Guatemala. That still left one box unaccounted for; the square box I had picked up from the Bank of Belize. It was time to pay Dr. Messy another visit.

Wink called security right then, and they informed him that Dr. Messy had already left the ship and was currently in the customs and immigration area collecting her baggage. We ran through the security stop and into the terminal where we saw her from a distance and watched as a porter was loading her suitcases on a trolley and heading for the customs checkpoint. He was chatting and laughing merrily with Dr. Messy. In her hand was the same box I had retrieved from the Bank of Belize!

Wink got over to them and asked her point blank what was in the box she was holding. Dr. Messy looked miffed and said her medical equipment and supplies, of course. What else would he expect? She was taking them across the pier to board the MS *Athena* and had to get right over there. Wink ordered her to open the box, and she refused, saying she took her medical supplies back and forth so often between the ships that the customs officers didn't even question her anymore. Wink persisted, and she rebuffed him, directing the porter to proceed to the checkpoint. She waved at the customs officer who hailed her over to his checkpoint, flashing a wide smile.

By the time she arrived at the checkpoint, the customs officer had all but given her the green flag to proceed to the exit, but Wink prevailed. He took the box from Dr. Messy and placed it on the table where the inspector reluctantly opened it. He removed a stethoscope and some medical devices and a few boxes of over-the-counter aspirins and eye drops and looked at Wink as if to say, I told you so. The box looked empty, and Dr. Messy, huffing with exasperation, started to repack it when Wink knocked on the bottom. Hollow! Wink's security aide stepped in and applied the crowbar to the false bottom and peeled it away. I held my breath. I was not expecting to see a mummy this time, but something else. What came to light was an ancient Mayan book made from fig-tree paper, shellacked with a lime wash to a patinated shine and containing some gloriously colorful and whimsical Mayan symbols and pictographs!

Everyone stood in stunned disbelief. I knew that what we were seeing represented something of incredible historic value, perhaps even more valuable than all three of the Mayan mummies combined. This was a rare Mayan book, or codex, that had been miraculously spared from being burned in the sixteenth century! It most likely had been taken along by a conquistador on his travels through Central America and ended up in the private home of one of his descendants. Now that it was in Dr. Messy's possession, I guessed it was illegally headed to a collection somewhere in Europe. The treasure of information it contained would change the world's understanding of the entire civilization of the Maya. This find had to be priceless.

Dr. Messy was extremely agitated, but for all her claims that she was in a rush to get to the MS *Athena* across the pier from us, we knew otherwise. There was no rush to board the MS *Athena* that day at all, as it was not calling in Miami until the following day. She was in a rush to get somewhere, all right, but it wasn't on that ship! The customs inspector opened her purse and there, lying neatly on top, was a Lufthansa ticket, final destination, Dresden, Germany!

Dresden was the name of arguably the most important Mayan book in existence up to this point. The Dresden Codex, as it was known, was in the Saxon State and University Library in Dresden, Germany. I looked at her through new eyes and for the first time realized that Dr. Messy was wearing a Mayan shirt. I walked around her to see what the back looked like and, sure enough, there were the same four symbols as on the shirt she had given Perry Cardis. That shirt was still in my hands. I compared the two, and the images were exact duplicates on both shirts: three rectangles with Mayan ruler heads on the bottom and one square with a smaller square on the bottom. All four had that superimposed line-stitch that hinted of the false bottom in each box!

Dr. Messy was in for a long day that would not include a flight to Dresden. It would eventually emerge that Dr. Messy had been involved with Mayan grave robberies since she started work as a ship medic and actually sought the position to enable her to pursue her side job.

I tried to reconstruct the scenario, proposing to Wink that Dr. Spin and Dr. Turnkey must have intercepted Perry Cardis's magic crates from the ship's shoreside agents. Those are the local companies in every port that act as the ship's liaison, receiving and holding mail and packages until the ships call in their ports.

Once Dr. Spin and Dr. Turnkey secured the crates in each port, they took each crate respectively to the Cozumel Island Museum, the beachside farmacia in

Majahual and the Chiquita warehouse in Puerto Barrios where they planted the stolen Mayan mummies inside and covered them with the false bottoms before replacing Perry Cardis's possessions on top. They had to make room for the Cuban treasures as well, which were routed to the same entrepots. Since the Cuban treasures were much smaller, they could fit easily amongst the magic paraphernalia. Then, when the crates arrived in the hold of the ship after I personally escorted them each time, the doctors Spin and Turnkey intercepted them again to remove the Cuban treasures, leaving Perry Cardis's clothes, charter supplies and magic accoutrements on top of the false bottom with the mummies still hiding safely underneath. Brilliant!

But I also knew there had to be yet another accomplice to receive and redirect the crates at the airport and get them through customs inspections. The stealth operation required an airport insider to identify the crates, unpack them, strip out the false bottoms to remove the Mayan treasures and get them on the appropriate flight to the next destination. When I exposed this angle to Wink, he asked me who I thought was the insider at the airport, logically ruling out Dr. Spin and Dr. Turnkey who were on a yacht heading for Rome.

I offered two names: Sven and Grau. I said I was convinced they were the same two medics who joined the ship from the helicopter that night in the storm and never returned to the helicopter. The captain said they disembarked in Jamaica, but they could have stayed in

Dr. Spin's vacated room. They only needed a little help from an insider. Wink called security and asked where Sven and Grau were at that moment, and he was told they had been detained in the interrogation room of the immigration office because of inconsistencies in their passports. We ran over to the office. Sven and Grau were jumping out of their seats, shouting that they were late for their jobs and had to be released to get to the airport. They were both wearing airline uniforms and each had an identification tag for Lufthansa Airlines. The names on the tags were Steven Prebe and Gary Combs.

The immigration officer told us they were first cousins who recently had moved to Dayton, Ohio. I remembered Dr. Messy mentioning that she lived in Dayton, and how she had disembarked the ship during the cruise to deal with some tenant issues there. On the very remote chance that Sven and Grau were her tenants as well, I asked the immigration staff to look up their addresses and check them against Dr. Messy's. Sure enough, their condos were in the same building, and Sven and Grau were her renters! And that would make Dr. Messy the logical insider that kept Grau and Sven on the ship.

While they were in look-up mode, I asked if they could check out one more address–Dr. Turnkey's. Sure enough, he was not a resident of Coral Gables as he had announced that first night, nor was he a widower. Turns out he lived in Dayton with a wife who was very much alive–Dr. Messy Carver!

48

Here We Go Again

As the immigration officers were connecting the dots, Wink stepped out of the room to receive a call from Hector in Havana. A few minutes later, he brought me up to speed as he escorted me through the immigration line. Hector told him the Cuban authorities had successfully intercepted *La Malinche* with the stash of Cuban treasures onboard, when it drifted into Cuban waters after running out of fuel. The Cuban military was handling Dr. Spin and Dr. Turnkey as, all the while, archivists were making a mad scramble from museums in every province in Cuba. The priceless treasures that had been snatched out of Cuba by Hernan Cortes nearly five centuries before had finally come home again through its southern port of Santiago de Cuba. Ironically, the first mayor of Santiago de Cuba was the conquistador himself— Hernan Cortes!

Wink stayed by my side as I approached the immigration officer. "I guess this is goodbye," I said. "I probably won't see you again but wish you and Angela the best. She's nice, and I wish I'd known about you two on the last cruise. She and I might have been friends. Anyway, we were getting there this time," I rambled, not quite sure where I was leading with it.

"Well, I guess there's a reason for everything," Wink said, clearing his throat nervously. "Do you think you'll hear from Seth?" he asked out of the blue. I wondered why he would be asking that question.

"No, but I assume he and Beth are on their way to nuptial bliss. Probably booking the reception hall as we speak," I joked.

"Well, just remember it's not over 'til it's over," he said mysteriously.

"Yeah, and I'll still have to get my carry-on from him," I said, remembering that Wink had sent it to Seth's address on the luggage tag.

We hugged briefly, and I turned to board the transfer bus to the airport. I missed my flight, but Delta got me on another one; two hours later I was in the air. I settled into my seat with my copy of the *Popol Vuh* and felt an extreme weight off my shoulders. I was going home! The flight was the best kind—uneventful—and a few minutes before ten that night, I walked through my heavy front door after struggling with its predictably sticky lock and was met inside by all the familiar old smells of polished wood and books and the faint potpourri of spices living in my kitchen cabinets. I stood to take in my surroundings as though seeing them for the first time, and marveled that so much had changed in my life since I'd last stood in this very spot.

やややや

A week later, I was still catching up with house-work. I went into the laundry room to start a dryer load when the doorbell rang. I knew it was Seth returning my carry-on. He'd offered to drop it off since he was in my part of town and hinted that he'd like to talk. I was curious and admittedly looking forward to seeing him again. As far as the contents of the carry-on went, I couldn't even remember what was in it and had lived without it for so long it wouldn't have mattered if he brought it back to me or not. I was happy enough just to see Seth.

But when I opened the door, there was a package lying on the welcome mat. I bent down to pick it up just as another hand swooped down and took it first. When I looked up, there was someone I knew but didn't at first recognize. He held the box out for me as a warm smile spread across his beaming face.

"Can I please to come in for coffee?" he asked. "I brought the macaroons."

CPSIA information can be obtained
at www.ICGtesting.com
Printed in the USA
BVHW030157061021
618251BV00001B/20